MAE
WEST

MAE WEST

a biography

by

George Eells and Stanley Musgrove

WILLIAM MORROW AND COMPANY, INC.
New York   1982

Library of Congress Cataloging in Publication Data

Eells, George.
  Mae West : a biography.

  Includes index.
  1. West, Mae. 2. Moving-picture actors and
actresses—United States—Biography. I. Musgrove,
Stanley. II. Title.
PN2287.W4566E3   791.43′028′0924   [B]   81-16791
ISBN 0-688-00816-X   AACR2

Printed in the United States of America

First Edition

1 2 3 4 5 6 7 8 9 10

BOOK DESIGN BY MICHAEL MAUCERI

In memory of Bess Eells Schmidt
1912–1979

—GEORGE EELLS

For Robert Wise, in gratitude

—STANLEY MUSGROVE

Acknowledgments

In addition to those mentioned in the text, grateful acknowledgment is made to the following institutions and persons:

Robert C. Peters, senior vice-president of Paramount Pictures; Ken Clark and Albert Van Schmus of the Association of Motion Picture and Television Producers; Robert Knutson and Alvista Perkins, Special Collections, Doheny Library, University of Southern California; Coleman Jennings and William H. Crane, curator, Hoblitzelle Theatre Arts Library, University of Texas at Austin; Paul Myers, the late Betty Wharton, Maxwell Silverman, Roderick Bladel, Dorothy Swerdlove, Brigitte Kneppers, Don Fowle, Monty Arnold and David Bartholomew, Theatre Collection, Lincoln Center Library for the Performing Arts; Brooks MacNamara, Shubert Collection; Caroline Schaffner, James F. Davis, Billie Turley, and Joe Mauch, Museum of Repertoire Americana, Mount Pleasant, Iowa; the late James Powers, AFI, Los Angeles; the late Arnold Weissberger, Ted Fetter, Mary Henderson, Bill Richards, Wendy Warnken, Museum of the City of New York; the staff of the Library, Academy of Motion Picture Arts and Sciences.

Allan Davis, Ms. Steve De Jonghe, Richard Lamparski, Frank Liberman, R. C. Perry, Tony Dexter, George Leigh, Liz Smith, Esther Hoff, Bennett Green, Wymar Gard, Dr. Ed Hertford, James Cresson, Richard Fisher, Jack Reed, Jack Langdon, Helen Ford, Keenan Wynn, Wynn Gibson, Maggie Maskell, Bernard Hoffman, Mr. and Mrs.

Samuel Siegel, Harold Hecht, Lloyd Bridges, Lloyd Nolan, Gilbert Roland, Leonid Kinsky, Stoddard Kirby, Cris Marx, Bill Fletcher, Derrick Thomas, Madeline Gaxton, Peter Garey, George Clemmons, Sol Jacobson, Lewis Harmon, Jill Jackson, Michael Sean O'Shea, Albert H. Lewis, Edward Risman, Eddie Jaffe and Kent Saxon.

Special thanks to David Charnay for checking the material on Frank Wallace; Tom Clapp for editorial checking and suggestions; Patrick Pacheco for turning over his research file on Miss West; and Tim Malachosky for use of his extensive photo collection.

—G. E. and S. M.
June 14, 1981

MAE WEST

Prologue:
1980

A low-slung 1965 Cadillac limousine glides to a stop. The driver, a former muscleman, wearing a blue-black suit, a navy shirt and white tie, leaps out of the left side and rushes around to open the rear right-hand door. There is a bulge low in the left side of his coat, caused by the revolver he always carries. He leans solicitously forward to help the occupant emerge. Her movie-star blond hair—or more accurately her wig—remains frozen in the style popularized by Brigitte Bardot in the early 1960's. Tonight, as usual, she wears a pastel slack suit and a long satin coat which is an uncharacteristic black.

The driver offers his arm, and together they move slowly along the bricked walk. The blonde clutches her companion's muscular arm tightly, shuffling along on eight-inch platform shoes that create the illusion of greater height. She appears bone-tired as she carefully moves her tiny feet over the uneven bricks. They reach the door, and her escort rings the bell.

The door opens, and as it does, the woman straightens her spine, throws back her blond head and flashes her famous smile. Simultaneously she performs an act of extreme will, projecting the image she has held in her mind's eye for over fifty years. Mae

West's unwavering dedication to preserving that image succeeded in creating an illusion that was a reality not only to her but to an entire public as well.

"People speak of the mystery of Garbo or Dietrich or other superstars, but to me the real mystery has always been Mae West," said Jean Howard, a celebrated Beverly Hills hostess. "Who ever really penetrated the façade?"

Many people who never met Mae thought they had. The rumors that surrounded her included the kind of preposterous stories that inevitably circulate about the celebrated. It was whispered:

. . . that "the queen of sex," "the camp vamp," far from being lustful actually was frigid.

. . . that she possessed both female and male genitals.

. . . that she had undergone the first sex-change operation.

. . . that the world's most enduring sex symbol was a virgin whose erotic adventures were confined to masturbatory fantasies.

. . . that this world-famous sex goddess was not a woman but the greatest female impersonator of all time, despite costume designer Edith Head's testimony: "I've seen Mae West without a stitch and she's all woman. No hermaphrodite could have bosoms . . . well, like two large melons."

Even though Mae did not originate these tall tales, she would have if they had suited her purpose. No claim was exaggerated if it enhanced the legend she spent a lifetime creating, that of the archetypical sex goddess, but what she concealed was as important as what she revealed. Whenever she was asked to define her celebrated sex appeal, she would evade specifics and say, "It's not what I do, but the way I do it. It's not what I say, but the way I say it."

Whatever, sex permeated her life, and she believed that "an orgasm a day keeps the doctor away."

Mae was a flamboyant, witty, larger-than-life personality who became a legend in her lifetime. During an evening she emitted a glow that made it a special pleasure to be in her company.

Legendary stars are endowed with the ability to earn the love of large numbers of people through behavior that would be judged unacceptable in ordinary company. Like W. C. Fields, Charlie Chaplin, Judy Garland, Joan Crawford, Marlene

Dietrich, Groucho Marx and scores of other superstars, Mae had more than her fair share of character blemishes. Like most legends, she had achieved her position not only through talent, hard work, dogged persistence and luck but also through a willingness to maintain her superstardom by employing fair means and foul, trickery and ruthlessness. In the rough-and-tumble world of show business, the self-enchanted Mae was willing to sacrifice any relationship to stay ahead of the pack. An idol of clay she may have been, but what a lovely work of art.

Mae candidly and unapologetically admitted that she thought and cared only about herself. "My ego is breakin' records," she said, and for six decades she carried on a public love affair with herself. "I see myself as a classic, yuh know what I mean? I'm in a class by myself. Who else can do what I'm doin' and look the way I look?"

Appropriately enough, at the inception of the 1970's, the period that Tom Wolfe labeled "The Me Decade," Mae emerged from self-imposed retirement, saying, "The important thing about me is I still look like Mae West. I lift weights to give myself muscle tone. Store 'em under the bed. I walk to keep my waist. So my measurements are still the same as Venus de Milo's, only I got arms. My teeth are my own, too. I never had a cavity.

"I never wanted motherhood because you have to think about the child and I only had time for me. Just the way I didn't want no husband because he'd of interfered with my hobby and my career.

"A great star has to think of herself. Now I'm the only one left. Oh, there used to be Garbo and Dietrich—and maybe one or two others. But they sorta wore out. To look at me, a person'd think I was twenty-six."

Despite advancing years, her almost unblemished skin and snow-blinding smile encouraged the press to overlook the fact that her figure was not quite what it once had been. Mother Nature, Mae insisted, was a bitch who had to be shown who was boss or she would make a hag of you.

Mae's narcissism pushed aside all self-doubt about either her accomplishments or her youthfulness, nor did it allow room for approval of, or enthusiasm about, other actresses. For instance, when the then-reigning First Lady of the Theater, Katharine Cornell, appeared in Mae's Broadway dressing room to say how much she had enjoyed her performance, Mae responded,

"Thanks, honey. Hope I can say the same for you sometime."

Mae dismissed all other "sex personalities." Her predecessor at Paramount Pictures, Clara Bow, struck her as "boyish." She claimed Jean Harlow just "acted sex." Hedy Lamarr was "only a face"; Rita Hayworth, "a body"; and Betty Grable, "good legs and a nice smile." Lana Turner was "a schoolgirl." Ava Gardner had "no humor," and Elizabeth Taylor was just "another face." Mae conceded Marilyn Monroe "had something. She photographed well," but then added, "Of course, she copied me." Raquel Welch ("Rachel Walsh" to Mae) and Farrah Fawcett were "synthetic." Ann-Margret? "All of 'em imitate me. But who can imitate Ann-Margret or most of the rest of 'em, know what I mean?"

Merle Oberon, a major star of the 1930's and '40's, once gushed over Mae's hands, unmarked by veins or brownish spots. "Look at them!" Merle exclaimed. "So soft, so smooth, so pink,—"

"That's me all over, honey," Mae cut in, flashing her wicked smile.

When Merle raved about Mae's performances, Mae regally accepted the praise without reciprocating. But later, as director George Cukor was escorting her to her limousine, she said, as if it had just dawned on her, "Yuh know, I always liked *her* pictures. I guess I shoulda told her."

She and Marlene Dietrich did become friends after they were assigned side-by-side dressing rooms at Paramount in the 1930's. Mae was pleased to have Dietrich prepare good German food for her. "But I had to pull back when she started wantin' to wash my hair," Mae said. "I was afraid it wasn't all on my head."

One of the rare occasions when Mae questioned her ability to fascinate occurred before a dinner in 1969 at George Cukor's to which both she and Greta Garbo had been invited. That day Mae agitatedly called a friend to ask, "What'll I talk to Garbo about?" After further fretting, Mae finally laughed and said, "Oh, she's probably just like me. Only interested in talkin' about herself."

On the appointed evening both Mae and actor Roddy McDowall, the other guest, arrived early. Mae said, "You know who else is comin', doncha? Garbo. I'm just tellin' you because it would've been terrible if yuh hadn't recognized her."

Upon Garbo's arrival Mae surprised everyone by kissing her on the cheek and saying, "Hello, dear." Mae told her host afterward, "I wanted to make her feel at home."

From the beginning it was obvious Garbo was more curious about Mae than Mae about her. At one point Garbo, inquiring about Mae's stilt-high Wedgies, got down on the floor and lifted the leg of Mae's pantsuit to inspect the shoes.

The next day Mae summed up the evening by saying, "Garbo said she loved my pictures. I told her the same and said she oughta get back in front of the cameras. She said, 'I dunno. I'll have to think about it.' But she could still work if she'd just agree to do character parts."

Mae always resented any woman who appropriated her voice or dressed in Gay Nineties clothes. When she heard that Barbra Streisand imitated her in *Hello, Dolly!*, she threatened to get an injunction against 20th Century-Fox, even though she was filming *Myra Breckenridge* at the same studio. "I'm a copyrighted character, see? But I guess it wouldn't look good to sue the company I'm workin' for.

"I got a better idea," she later announced. "You know how they have them titles at the bottom of the screen in foreign movies? Well, whenever she starts doin' my stuff, they can flash a line, 'Now she's imitatin' Mae West.'"

Several months later, at a gala party, she and Streisand met for the first time. Barbra, notorious for her aloofness and put-downs of other stars, surprised everyone by rushing to the table where Mae and several friends were sitting. Kneeling before Mae, she took her hand, kissed it and said, "Oh, Miss West, you have no idea what a thrill it is to meet you. I idolize you. In fact, sometimes in *Hello, Dolly!* I consciously imitated you. And sometimes unconsciously."

Mae sniffed and said, "Yeah, I know."

"Then you saw the picture?" said Barbra.

"Part of it once, in a drive-in."

"Do I take it you don't like it that I imitate you? After all, imitation is the sincerest form of flattery."

"Not to me, it ain't," Mae said. "For your own good, you ought to try to develop your own personality and stop imitating Fanny Brice and me."

Often underappreciated are the hard work and creativity Mae invested in molding her public legend. At five, six or eight years old (depending on which age struck her fancy the day she told the story) Mae made her debut as a child actress . . . first as a professional amateur, then as a stock-company child star . . . a strong woman in an acrobatic act . . . a singer, dancer, male impersonator in vaudeville . . . a Broadway sex personality and playwright . . . a forty-plus movie siren . . . a nightclub entertainer . . . a rock and roll singer.

Early in her adult career she set out to outrage—and succeeded so well she landed in jail. Rising to the occasion, she wrapped censorship around her voluptuous figure and emerged a national celebrity. Later she added a uniquely humorous approach to sex and won the admiration of sophisticates.

As an actress she instinctively knew that for her, personality was everything. The vein of talent she worked was neither wide nor deep. Yet the impact of her freewheeling ladies changed America's view of women as sexual beings and remained a dynamic part of our social-sexual history long after the exquisite art created by a Duse, a Barrymore or a Laurette Taylor existed only in the yellowing pages of theatrical criticism and the memories of contemporaries.

As a playwright she saw herself as an innovator. Hadn't she taken the word "sex" out of the medical books and put it into common usage when she used it for the title of her first play? Hadn't she exposed corrupt beauty contests in *The Constant Sinner*? Treated the subject of homosexuality seriously in *The Drag*? Dealt with satyriasis and castration in *Pleasure Man*? Portrayed interracial love in *The Constant Sinner*? Re-created the Gay Nineties raffish spirit in *Diamond Lil*?

At a Friends of the Libraries luncheon at the University of Southern California in honor of Tennessee Williams, actor Laurence Harvey described the honoree as the greatest figure to emerge in American drama. When Williams responded, "I always thought Mae West was the most famous figure in drama and she has the figure to prove it," Mae, after pondering it, stated, "It's true. When you think about it, what other playwrights are there besides O'Neill, Tennessee and me?" With this self-appraisal of her writing talent, she was mystified when Percy Hammond opened a review of one of her plays with "Quick the flit!" or when Joseph Wood Krutch wrote that her plays drew audiences from the "lower forms of animal life."

But it remained for motion pictures to establish her as an international star. In her forties she dimmed Dietrich's allure, outshone glossy Joan Crawford and overpowered Garbo's subtle eroticism. Everyone from grandmothers to tiny tots was issuing her invitation to "Come up 'n' see me sometime." Depression-numbed audiences were stimulated by her unapologetic exhibitionism, her cynical love-'em-and-leave-'em behavior. In her films she was the first woman to function as a leading man.

With *She Done Him Wrong* she claimed to have single-handedly saved Paramount from bankruptcy. This was not true, but she did measurably improve Paramount's fiscal condition and probably saved it from being absorbed by MGM, and her casting of Cary Grant as her leading man transformed him from a run-of-the-mill juvenile into a star.

Four decades later Grant approached Mae at a party. "Remember me?" he asked.

"Do I!" she replied. "You're still a handsome thing!" Afterward she commented, "If he'd just dye his hair, I could still use him."

There were numerous rebuffs and disappointments in Mae's life, but publicly she chose to ignore them. When she wrote her autobiography, *Goodness Had Nothing to Do with It*, one of her advisers, Larry Sloan, criticized the manuscript for failing to spell out the struggles and disappointments that are a part of any life. Mae rejected his criticism. "*Her* fans don't want Mae West to have problems 'n' have to struggle," she explained. "Mae West always triumphs."

For decades, like Narcissus kneeling by his pool lost in self-adoration, Mae reclined on her satin-sheeted bed, gazing rapturously at her misty image reflected in her mirrored ceiling. Self-hypnotized, she believed so deeply in her youthful luminosity that like the great French Impressionists, she persuaded the public to see things through her eyes—to accept the legend of the unchanged and unchangeable Mae West.

I

At six years of age Mae already was unrelentingly vain, insisting her mother bedeck her in dainty organdy dresses before she would run an errand. Then, instead of taking the shortcut across a vacant lot, she would follow the right-angled sidewalk so that she could admire her reflection in the plate glass windows that lined the route. "I was always careful how I looked. I wanted to make a good impression. When I was a kid in Brooklyn, I'd eat my dinner with a mirror by my plate. I hated seeing women chew like cows. I'd practice eating."

As her career progressed, Mae's accounts of her early life became subject to many revisions. What is certain is that she was born Mary Jane West in the bedroom of John Patrick and Matilda West in a one-family dwelling located on Bushwick Avenue on August 17. Various sources have given the year as 1887, 1888, 1892 or 1893. Dr. Jules Stein, founder of the Music Corporation of America, offered one clue. At eighteen he played hot fiddle for Mae's vaudeville act in Chicago and his advances were rejected by her on the grounds that she was twenty-six and too mature for him. Since Stein was born in 1895, by his calculations Mae's birth would have occurred in 1887 or 1888.

However, the declassified 1900 U.S. census lists three children in the John and Tillie West household—Mary Jane (Mae), six; Mildred (Beverly), three; and John Patrick West II, three months; that means she would have been born in 1893.

The births of all three children were attended by an aunt who was a midwife. "She was a strong Roman Catholic," Mae once said, "an' after she saw some of my plays 'n' movies, I think she kinda wished she'd dropped me on my head the day I was born."

To her neighbors, Matilda was a shrewd, slightly aggressive, but inoffensive businesswoman. To Mae, her mother was the dominant figure in the West household, as glamorous as Lillian Russell and a model of maternal perfection. Matilda reciprocated those feelings, always treating Mary Jane as special and, unlike Mildred and John Patrick, exempt from punishment. Much of this pampering was due to the fact that the first child born to John and Tillie had died in infancy.

When she began performing, Mae changed her name from plain Mary Jane to the more glamorous Mae, sometimes spelled May as late as 1913. She later said she preferred the *e* to the *y* because *e* was up and *y* was down.

Just as Mae went to extraordinary lengths to make the world adopt her view of Matilda, having her favorite photo of her mother retouched so extensively that its subject resembled a wax dummy, so did she refuse to be consistent about her mother's family. In 1911 Mae identified her as Matilda Dilker. In version number one Matilda was a Frenchwoman born to the Patrick Dilkers in Alsace-Lorraine. ("That's why I was given private French lessons as a girl," Mae claimed, ignoring the fact that she had had to learn the song "Fifi" phonetically for *Every Day's a Holiday.*) In version number two Matilda became a Delker and then a Delker-Doelger and her birthplace, Württemberg, Germany. ("When Grandpa Joseph Doelger—he started the New York breweries—visited, they'd talk German, the kind with English words here 'n' there. I couldn't speak it, but I understood," she said.) Whatever maiden name Mae gave her mother, she always claimed Matilda was a first-cousin-once-removed to millionaire-playboy Harry K. Thaw, who earned a footnote to history by shooting and killing architect Stanford White for compromising Thaw's ex-showgirl wife, Evelyn Nesbit.

Before marriage Matilda worked as a corset model and studied to become a modiste. "She never made clothes. Her father didn't want her to go into trade," Mae said, adding, "She was sexy, but refined, see? And spoiled! Quality, quality, quality. She didn't want nothin' but the best." Those demands caused her husband, Jack West, teasingly to nickname her Champagne Til.

Mae's father, John Patrick West, also known as Battlin' Jack, was, according to Mae, a tough Irish mick who, upon finding himself menaced by a gang of Brooklyn toughs, once seized two beer mugs, smashed them on the bar and, holding the handles and remaining shards of glass, slashed a bloody path to freedom. The cause of the fight? Battlin' Jack's determination to defend Champagne Til's honor.

In Mae's early published accounts Battlin' Jack might have been played by James Cagney in a 1930's Warner Brothers film. She said he flourished as a never-defeated light heavyweight champion of Brooklyn during the Corbett-Sullivan era. But as Mae climbed the ladder of success, her father's status also rose, first to a livery stable owner and then to a founder of a private detective agency and a chiropractor. By 1928, in the *New Yorker*,* Thyra Samter Winslow recorded Mae's claim that he was a "doctor practising medicine in Richmond Hill."

At one point he became the grandson of "the well-known Pittsburgh Copleys" and a cousin to Marie Devere, whose ankle-length hair earned her a featured spot in advertising for the Seven Sutherland Sisters hair tonic and an offer from Florenz Ziegfeld. Whether Mae's grandmother, who, according to Mae, sported three breasts, was related to Miss Devere or belonged to her mother's family is unclear.

Her parents' religion is as clouded as their lineage. She sometimes said her mother was Lutheran, at other times Catholic or Protestant. At a party given by the Jules Steins in 1971, the noted neurosurgeon Seth Weingarten asked Mae if she were Jewish. "Half 'n' half," she told him.

Screenwriter John Bright speculated that Mae changed her nationality and religion to suit whomever she was talking to. "I could easily pass for a Jew, and I think Mae assumed I was. Anyway, she told me her mother was Jewish. Then one day she asked me my real name. I told her John Bright. 'Then you're not Jewish?'

---

*The current librarian sent a note with the West profile saying the magazine's content had not been meticulously checked for accuracy in the early days.

"'No, and if I were, so what?'

"'Nothin'. Nothin'. I got no prejudice.'

"But after that she spoke of her mother as French and there was no more mention of religion."

She usually said her father was a Roman Catholic but occasionally called him a Protestant. Explaining his Catholicism, Mae said a maid had sneaked him off to church for his baptism " 'n' that's how he got to be a Catholic." About her own religious training, she was consistent only in saying that attending Sunday school had always given her a headache.

Mae conveyed the impression of solid middle-class comfort. She told of her mother's travels by carriage or sleigh provided by Battlin' Jack's livery stable. She claimed their standard of living grew opulent after he founded the first detective agency that provided night patrols. There also was talk of his burgeoning real estate holdings.

Nonetheless, something seems amiss. For example, when speaking of her teenage brother, Mae recalled, "Instead of lookin' for a job, he was just lookin' around." When John claimed he didn't know where to start his search for employment and a friend suggested the want ads in a Brooklyn daily, John replied that his family didn't subscribe to a paper. What prosperous family, one wonders, didn't buy a daily paper?

Mae's sister, Mildred, was a pale carbon of Mae. Like Mae, she discarded her dreary first name and rechristened herself Beverly. Handicapped by a clubfoot, she nevertheless became an entertainer. Late in life she frequently berated herself for placing herself in the shadows professionally in order not to interfere with Mae's career. Hearing this, Mae sniffed. "She should've changed her name like Joan Fontaine."

On the other hand, John West II was enough younger and of the right sex to win Mae's support. Although she claimed she had no maternal instincts, Mae obviously harbored motherly feelings toward him. In later years she fondly recalled his exploits and bright sayings, telling such stories as the time he once sneaked over to their father's livery stable. "Is this my papa's place?" he asked the groom. Told that it was, little John inquired, "And are these horsies my papa's?" They were. "And do these buggies belong to papa?" They did. Satisfied, he looked up and inquired, "And is all this horseshit my papa's, too?"

Mae said she had never heard her father laugh so infectiously before or after as he related the story to Matilda. It was a rare, pleasant memory of a man by whom she hated being kissed because of his ever-present evil-smelling big black cigars and whose knobby muscles repelled her. Adherents of the repulsion-attraction theory can make their own interpretations of her later well-known predilection for wrestlers, boxers and musclemen.

By the third grade Mae was too busy with life to attend school. When she was a top Hollywood star, she claimed to have been privately tutored, but she seldom read anything except her own scripts, and her difficulty with writing made descriptions of comedic actions a burden. "I don't bother to write it all down," she explained. "I got it all in my head. So when there's comic business, I abbreviate—*b-i-s.*"

Nor did she have time or patience for professional training. After a few weeks at "Professor" Watts's dance academy she entered a Sunday night amateur show at the Royal Theater on Fulton Street, Brooklyn. In her show business debut she was announced as "Baby Mae—Song and Dance."

After watching the professional vaudevillians who preceded the contest, Mae yearned for a spotlight to set off her gold-spangled pink-and-green satin dress. Backstage she nagged the stage manager and the electrician for special lighting until they promised she'd have it, but when the emcee who announced her exited on the opposite side from her entrance, the spotlight followed him. Onstage Mae planted her tiny feet, shook her fist and glared at the light man. Suddenly the spot hit her and the audience roared at the sight of the temperamental tyke. Said Mae: "I had 'em before I began."

Happily content, she sang her first song on any stage—"Movin' Day"—and followed that with a skirt dance. From that moment on she was, as far as she was concerned, "in the show business" and joined the professional amateurs who went from theater to theater. Gradually, with the help of "Professor" Watts, she worked up a tap routine and learned "Ephriam Johnson, He Don't Live Here Anymore" and a comedy dialect number, "My Mariooch-Maka-Da-Hoochy-Ma-Coocha in Coney Island," as alternatives, should another contestant sing her standards, "Movin' Day" and "Doing the Grizzly Bear."

To make herself taller, she insisted on wearing her mother's oversized hat, which forced her to keep her hand at the back of her head to hold it in place. This led to the one-hand-at-the-back-of-the-head, the other-on-her-hip stance that was to become a trademark.

Eventually Hal Clarendon, an actor-manager who headed his own stock company at the Gotham Theater in East New York, hired Mae to sing, perform eccentric dances and mimic such diverse stars as Eva Tanguay ("The I Don't Care Girl"), Eddie Foy and Bert Williams (Ziegfeld's black comedian). After she scored a great success as Little Eva in *Uncle Tom's Cabin*, Clarendon cast her in a series of children's roles in such plays as *Ten Nights in a Barroom* and *For Their Child's Sake*.

On weeks when there were no acting parts for her, Mae performed as a vaudevillian or was lent out to other troupes in Brooklyn, including the famous Spooner Stock Company and one headed by Corse Payton, an eccentric ham who wore red satin suits on the street and gloried in billing himself as "The World's Best Bad Actor." On the rare occasions when no engagement was available in Brooklyn, Mae's mother took her to another borough for amateur contests, where she sang such old songs as "That Cello Melody" and "Waiting for the Robert E. Lee." "I had a rough, husky voice that struck audiences as funny comin' from a little kid," Mae recalled. "I always won first prize— unless, of course, some out-of-work ham was there posin' as an amateur."

Mae's famed sexuality began asserting itself when she performed her skirt dance on amateur nights. The dance was, she said, "innocently brazen," but the innocence soon vanished. The gossip of older girls in the neighborhood and backstage badinage made Mae sexually curious early in life. She maintained she experienced her first erotic dream shortly after her twelfth birthday. Her partner was a bear with a reddish brown penis, about four inches in length and the diameter of her thumb. "I was modest in my demands," she said, recounting the dream. "But *why* a bear? I was never interested in them. Lions were what I found fas-cin-a-tin'."

When she heard that after a girl began menstruating, intercourse could result in pregnancy, Mae decided to experiment before the onset of puberty. "I wanted to find what all this sex stuff was about without any risk," she explained.

She described the loss of her virginity to Karl and Anne Taylor Fleming in their book *The First Time*. Her father had built a stage in the basement of their home where she lifted weights and took instruction in music and dance from a young male teacher with whom she would hug and kiss. Nothing more transpired until one night he walked her home from the theater. "It happened on the stairs in our house, in the vestibule," she told the Flemings. "It was winter and I had on my fur coat, and I was standing on the stairs one step above him. He was afraid, so I told him I had done it before. I wanted to see what it was like. I lied to him so he would do it. I felt ashamed to say I hadn't done it. He said, 'Are you sure you've done this before?' and I said, 'Sure, a couple of times.'

"My mother and father were upstairs. I would have been able to hear them.

"And they wouldn't be able to see anything because I had my fur coat wrapped around me. The underwear was that long kind with a string that tied around the waist and a slit down the front that folded over. . . .

"It hurt the first couple of times, but I wasn't frightened. What was there to be frightened of, for God's sake? I felt right doing it, and after the first couple of times it felt good."

That was for public consumption. As Mae amended the story privately, her first lover was a handome ex-actor who had no idea of her true age, only her assurance about her previous experience. He guessed the truth only when she bled profusely. "He might not have known much about me, but everybody in Brooklyn was afraid of my father, so the next day this guy left town!" she said, chuckling at the remembrance.

Mae's father tried to establish strict standards, setting a ten o'clock curfew. "That still gave me plenty of time to do what I wanted to do." Mae laughed. However, a six-year-old cousin precipitated a crisis by announcing her older sister wasn't allowed to visit Mae because she stayed out late and played with the boys. When Battlin' Jack confronted Matilda, she protected Mae by saying she was never later than ten-thirty and the boys were gentlemanly.

Matilda had her own way of dealing with Mae and sex. Whenever she saw Mae concentrating on any boy, she would praise him highly, seasoning her comments by criticizing his weak points and eventually deflating him in Mae's eyes. Mae later contended that was how the pattern of multiple men in her life developed.

Shortly after her first lover left town, Mae's brother developed pneumonia and the nurse hired to take care of little John introduced Mae to handsome blue-eyed nineteen-year-old Joseph Schenck, the leader of a ragtime band who became one of the team of Van & Schenck—not the film tycoon. As he and Mae grew closer, he would sometimes bring the six musicians in his group to the Wests' home, where Mae would sing with them.

When Matilda worried that Mae was getting too serious about Joe and urged her to see more of other men, Mae took her mother literally and began working her way through the band. One by one, she led them on conducted tours of the house and in the process learned each had something a little different to offer. By this time Mae had begun menstruating, but she guarded against pregnancy. "Joe always had plenty of protectors," she recalled. "But I learned about another way, too. You tied a piece of sponge on a silk string. Attached, see? Yuh wet the sponge in warm water before puttin' it in. Afterward you pulled it out and washed it.

"Later Fanny Brice was a close friend of mine. And she was always gettin' pregnant. I tried to tell her, but she wouldn't use either protectors or the sponge. And it really worked great. I don't know why women don't use sponges today."

Many old-timers suspected the mannerisms of the Mae West character evolved from burlesque. Her only admission to appearing in burlesque was at the Columbia, flagship of the Columbia wheel, in Sunday night concerts given by vaudevillians so that Broadway producers and big bookers could assess a performer's potential. Yet her undulating hips and shoulders invariably stirred memories of the burlesque "talking woman" whose perpetual gyrations traditionally led the comic to call out, "Hey, honey, you left your motor running." Burlesque capitalized on its bawdiness; vaudeville, on its refinement.

After Mae became too mature to play child parts, she worked briefly as an understander in an acrobatic act, helping to support three males and lifting a 500-pound weight. In the 1928 *New Yorker* profile Mae said she could still carry four men on her back and was continuing to maintain she lifted a 500-pound weight to develop her figure.

But acrobatics were only a stopgap. She soon teamed up with vaudevillian Willie Hogan, who toured in a *Huck Finn* act, playing

Huck as a typical rube or Toby character, donning Toby's traditional red wig and painted-on freckles and departing from the classic Toby only in blacking out his two front teeth. Hogan was past thirty but, with careful lighting, could pass for a twelve-year-old. Mae played what came to be known in the business as a Sis Hopkins, a country girl in a sunbonnet, gingham dress and lace-trimmed bloomers. The comedy was bucolic. Said Mae: "I screamed when he showed me his worm."

While touring with Hogan, Mae met Frank Wallace, the man she would eventually marry. Wallace, also known as Frank Szatkus, was the son of a poor Lithuanian tailor. To help support his family, the older Szatkus moonlighted by playing fiddle at banquets and celebrations. He returned home from these affairs with a pocketful of tips and a headful of funny, exciting tales of what he'd seen, inadvertently awakening a desire in his young son to follow the adventuresome career of an entertainer despite strong parental opposition. His mother and father's dream for him was to obtain a steady job, meet a sensible girl, marry and escape the squalor in which they lived so that he could provide an easier life for their grandchildren.

Frank saw show business as the means to this, although his father warned him that flashing smiles and eye-catching costumes were often mere window dressing for empty, frustrating existences. To mollify his parents, Frank accepted a job at Western Electric on Bethune Street during the day and competed in amateur contests at night.

In 1907 he caught sight of a cheeky young performer who was a star on the amateur circuit. It was Mae. Wallace, impressed by her "coon shouting" and saucy, skirt-swishing, petticoat-slipping dance numbers, thought of teaming up with her, but before he could summon the courage to suggest doing a double, he was offered a part in McIntyre and Heath's cross-country tour of *The Ham Tree*.

Upon his return, he persuaded booking agent Fatty Marcus to give him a week at the Imperial, at 116th Street and Lenox Avenue. This led to bookings in many other small-time vaudeville theaters in New York at one of which in 1909 Wallace found himself on a bill with Hogan and Mae. Their *Huckleberry Finn* preceded Wallace's song-and-dance single, and he topped them as an audience pleaser at every show.

Frank wasn't tall, dark and handsome. He was of medium

height and merely pleasant appearance, but his jazz dancing was a hit with audiences. Mae, thinking she detected a big personality—and with Mae, bigger was always better—proposed to Wallace that they do a double. Wallace admitted interest but said he wasn't ruthless enough to cut out Hogan. Mae assured him she would take care of Hogan, and Wallace promised to give her his answer the following week, when both acts were scheduled to appear at a theater in Canarsie.

Wallace later described Mae as "on the lean side, a slinky, peppy, classy little German girl, who lived with her mother," who, he said, was also "quite a looker" and who, because of her devotion to her daughter's career to the exclusion of almost all family obligations, was known as a show business widow. Matilda, he said, spoke with a German accent. After one performance she and Mae paid a visit to his dressing room, where Matilda was even more insistent than her daughter that Wallace and Mae work up an act. The women persuaded Wallace to join them at their home on Bushwick Avenue, where they wooed him with a "midnight lunch" of pigs' knuckles and sauerkraut.

Wallace was eager to team with Mae, but he still held off, worrying about Hogan. Mae again assured him she'd take care of her partner. On these terms they made a date to begin rehearsing in the Wests' basement at 11:00 A.M. next day. Mae did dispose of Hogan. How is not known.

Thereafter Wallace journeyed daily from Maspeth, Long Island, where he lived, to the West household in the Ridgewood section of Brooklyn. To his surprise Mae insisted the association be strictly business with no romance involved. Yet she dressed in pink rompers and gray oxfords, wore no stockings and would unnerve Wallace by lying on her back, throwing her shapely legs in the air and engaging in a bicycling motion. Whenever Wallace volunteered to show her a pleasanter exercise, Mae would leap up and insist they tend to business. It was agreed that he dance and fake the singing while she would do the opposite.

According to Wallace, "She never got to be much of a hoofer, but at warbling she could bounce them off the wall. I'll never forget how she could gargle 'Lovin' Honey Man' and 'When My Marie Sings Chidee Bidee Bee' . . . in which she did a comic Italian dialect." In addition, Mae sang "Jealous," Wallace did a dance and the two of them sang and danced to Harry von Tilzer's "I Love It," which they managed to infuse with a strong sexuality.

In a series of interviews with David Charnay of the New York *Daily Mirror,* Wallace revealed that Mae's bearing and wardrobe made a lasting impression on him when the two went to talk to Pat Casey of the Fox vaudeville circuit about bookings. Twenty-five years later he could still be astonished by her provocative, slightly tough approach to Casey. In response to Casey's offer of a ten-week engagement at $50 a week, Mae called Casey an old skinflint and tried to banter him into increasing their salary. Casey advised them to accept before he changed his mind. Mae and Wallace signed. When, after reaching the street, he questioned her tactics, Mae responded, "Let me be the business. You just play it straight."

While they were on the bill at Fox's City on Fourteenth Street, Mae suddenly changed her attitude toward Wallace. One evening, when he made what had become a ritual pass at her, she threw herself into his arms in the way he had always dreamed she would. It was 3:00 A.M. before, their passion drained, they groped their way out of the darkened theater. That night Wallace, who had thought himself a man of the world, learned tricks that less imaginative girl friends hadn't taught him. Spent as they were, as they walked along the empty street, every few steps he and Mae would fall into one another's arms and kiss passionately.

By the end of their ten-week tour they were in love, although Mae cautioned Wallace that her parents must not find out. At this time Mae, assuming she was born in 1893, was almost eighteen years old. Luckily they were immediately hired as the juvenile couple for producers Jacobs and Jermond's *Sporting Widow* (sometimes called *A Florida Enchantment),* which was either burlesque or small-time vaudeville, and rehearsals were to begin immediately in Philadelphia. The company included Hugh Herbert (later a popular film comedian), the Musical Gorman troupe and Etta Woods, a comedy character woman known as the Duchess of Porkschnauzer, whose popular tag line was: "I drink my sandwich and eat my beer."

By the time the troupe was ready to open in Philly, Wallace was regularly proposing and Mae was just as regularly rejecting him. Not that that kept her from some uninhibited lovemaking. "Everybody in the company, including the stagehands, thought we were engaged," said Wallace.

Mae saw it differently. According to her autobiography,

Goodness Had Nothing to Do with It, when he proposed, she told him there was only a physical thing between them and that he didn't appeal to her finer instincts. When he asked what those were, she replied she hadn't found out yet but that she must have them.

As the show moved through Pennsylvania, Ohio, Indiana and Illinois, Mae's need for more than one man in her life asserted itself. She began surreptitiously fooling around with other actors in the company and sneaking out with the stage-door johnnies who were constantly sending back invitations. Wallace, who had despaired of ever actually making her his wife, was upset but overlooked her indiscretions rather than risk losing her.

One afternoon Etta Woods took Mae aside to warn that with the hordes of men who were pursuing and too often catching her, sooner or later she would find herself pregnant. Woods, a clearheaded pragmatist, suggested Mae solve the problem by marrying Wallace, but Mae wasn't worried. As she confided to a friend in later years, "I had these protectors if the guy didn't. So for all the fooling around I did, I never needed an abortion or got the bad disease."

Still, seeing a certain logic in the Woods argument, Mae agreed to marry Wallace secretly. On April 11, 1911, the two of them slipped down to City Hall in Milwaukee, took out a license and were wed by a municipal judge with Woods and a janitor who had been emptying spittoons as witnesses. In her autobiography Mae claims she spent her wedding night in a separate hotel room, a situation similar to the one at the heart of her final movie, *Sextette.* Even the line "I don't rehearse marriages, I rehearse honeymoons" might fit.

That's Mae's version.

Wallace's memory was quite different. As he recalled, he and Mae were sitting on a moonlit park bench after the show. Mae was restless, and when Wallace asked what was on his dear Mamie's mind, she responded by saying she now was in a mood for marriage. And so, as the writers of serial stories used to say, the momentous decision was arrived at. They would marry.

That night Wallace tossed sleeplessly, thinking of the future with Mamie, their home and children. In his happiness, he arose at 5:00 A.M., left his lodgings and paced back and forth outside Mamie's rooming house, staring at the window until at last she appeared. When she did, "the sunshine seemed brighter"—in his words—and they "feasted on doughnuts and coffee." She asked whether he was happy. He wanted to know how she could ask, and she whispered, "If you feel the same way I do, then I'm sure you are."

They hurried to City Hall to obtain a license before rushing back for rehearsal of new material being added to the show. Then they sought out their friend Etta Woods to tell her their news. "Throwing her arms around Mae and myself," Wallace reported, "she hugged and kissed us. 'You lucky kids,' she cried."

Wallace's only regret was that he was poor, but Mamie comforted him by saying that if she'd married a Rockefeller or an Astor, she "wouldn't be able to play the circuit" and "make hops" with him. The manager, observing how much in love they were, gave them the evening of their marriage and the following day off as a wedding gift and, said Wallace, "We had some honeymoon!"

The show moved from Milwaukee to St. Paul, where Wallace borrowed $50 from the manager to buy Mae her first diamond. In St. Paul, Wallace began to realize something was amiss. Either connubial life in a second-rate hotel or the sanction placed upon their relationship by marriage cooled Mamie's ardor. By the time the troupe arrived in Minneapolis the situation had grown worse.

In Minneapolis a Curse Club was formed. Weekly dues were a nickel, and anyone heard uttering an obscenity was fined a penny for each dirty word. Any girl who dated a towner paid a dime fine. By the end of the week Mae owed Little Gorman, the treasurer, fifty cents for five infractions of the towner rule, but what hurt Wallace most was Mae's locking him in his room each midnight. Even though he pleaded with her not to leave, she'd laugh, lock the door and not return until 3:00 A.M. When he asked what he had done to deserve this treatment, Mamie told him that he was silly, that she wasn't doing anything wrong—just having a little fun.

The following week in Buffalo, at a party the company threw with the dues and fines from the Curse Club, Hugh Herbert took Mae aside and informed her that the entire company resented her cavalier behavior toward her husband. Mae brazened it out and insisted that she was only having a good time. Herbert later said he felt she was so absorbed in herself she lacked compassion for others.

By the end of the tour, even though Wallace knew that theirs was never going to be a conventional marriage, he was so passionately in the thrall of Mae's sexual repertoire that he was willing to do anything his Mamie might ask to preserve their relationship. For this reason, upon their return to New York, Wallace agreed that in the interest of secrecy, Mae would live at her parents' home while he continued to stay with a sister in Maspeth. The Wests had heard rumors of the marriage, but Mae held Wallace to his promise to deny it. Only Beverly, who was also breaking into show business, was let in on their secret.

Whatever rosy daydreams Wallace may have indulged in, it is clear that Mae had decided he had neither the drive nor the stamina to attain the heights for which she felt headed. Her only problem was to divest herself of him so gently that no one realized what had happened—least of all Wallace.

2

Describing her career in the years after her marriage to Wallace, Mae wrote:

> I'd be in vaudeville, then do a show for the Shuberts or Ziegfeld and then go back to vaudeville again. In the early days when I was laying off I even went into talkin' pictures—before pictures could talk. The actors sat behind the movie screen with scripts and read dialogue. I'd try anything to get ahead in show business.

The field that offered her the richest opportunity for refining her technique was vaudeville. The problem for a relatively inexperienced performer such as Mae was how to create a lasting impression on audiences in an entertainment medium made up of such stars as Annette Kellerman (sex in a single-piece bathing suit), the Three Keatons (knockabout acrobatic act), Julian Eltinge (female impersonator), the Four Marx Brothers, Mysterious Edna (mentalist), Sarah Bernhardt, Fred and Adele Astaire, Al Jolson, Willard ("The Man Who Grows—Seven and a Half Inches Before Your Eyes"), to say nothing of Barnold's Animal Actors (featuring Dan the Drunk Dog).

She tried various approaches. With Wallace she played a

Sunday afternoon fill-in date at the Palace Hall. Headliner Sophie Tucker, then called the Mary Garden of Ragtime, gave them strong encouragement and opened doors to their booking at the Bay Ridge Theater in Brooklyn. When Mae held up the performance for fifteen minutes and the outraged manager warned Wallace she would have to change her ways, she threw a temper tantrum and they walked out.

She and Wallace then split professionally, and she recruited dancers Bobby O'Neill and Harry Laughlin as support in her "nut act," which was canceled by an outraged New Haven theater manager when a "poorly constructed" strap on her gown broke. Yale students vented their frustration by tearing out the theater seats. HER WRIGGLES COST MAE WEST HER JOB was the newspaper headline.

Mae was soon back in smaller theaters. She played five-a-day at Pittsburgh's Family, under the management of Clarence W. Morganstern, a man who was to figure prominently in one of her later notorious escapades. Wherever she appeared, in Mae's mind *she* never failed. Her partners might fail, her accompanists, her writers, her songsmiths, even the audience, but as far as she was concerned, whatever she did was wonderful.

In March 1912 Frank Bohm booked a new offering of hers into the American Roof at Forty-sixth and Broadway, and persuaded Sime Silverman, founder of *Variety,* to see it. Silverman covered the turn in his "NEW ACTS" section. He found Mae "as far above the American Roof clientele as the roof is above the street." In his opinion, "The wiser the house the better Mae will go." She might be too rough for Keith's Philadephia, but Sime thought she rated "a date at Hammerstein's."

After a brief fling in a Broadway musical she reteamed with O'Neill and Laughlin but quickly decided they weren't worth the $50 plus coffee and cakes she was paying them and set out to work up a single.

Mae's act was heavily influenced by Eva Tanguay, whose wildly uninhibited antics and theme song, "I Don't Care," made her the preeminent exponent of the anything-goes type of vaudevillian. In both the big time, made up of the major houses on the larger circuits which catered to prosperous, educated audiences, and the small time, which included the modest, less prestigious theaters, mainly patronized by the working class, managers emphasized "polite" entertainment in which even such words as "heck" and "darn" were prohibited.

But Tanguay's flamboyance and spicy innuendo made her one of vaudeville's brightest and most highly paid stars, a fact not lost on Mae. In her debut as a single, her wardrobe, dialogue, songs and freakish behavior were intentionally outrageous. If she intended to shock, she succeeded, but until she developed a unique personality, she would suffer by comparison with such headliners as Ethel Green, Belle Baker and Blossom Seeley.

Mae found inspiration in the work of Thomas J. Gray, who supplied special material for such headliners as Bert Williams, Trixie Friganza, Seeley and, most significantly, Bert Savoy and Jay Brennan.

Savoy started his career in female impersonation as a "red-haired harlot" and an understudy to a cooch dancer before teaming with Jay Brennan of the aristocratic profile. Together they did a man-woman comedy act that many considered the precursor to Burns and Allen, Block and Sully, Fred Allen and Portland Hoffa and numerous other two acts.

A bejeweled comedian who worked in slit skirts, fancy garters and a red wig, Savoy was unlike Julian Eltinge, of whom one reporter wrote: "Many a feminine heart was stirred with envy of the achievements of this man in the very sacred realms of feminine charms," or Barbette, whose patrician features and chic gowns Cocteau immortalized in a series of line drawings. Savoy played a cheeky dame who had a kooky, mischief-making roommate named Margie about whose shocking behavior she was always gossiping. Example: Margie played hot piano at choir practice and the minister remonstrated, "Don't you know the Ten Commandments?" To which Margie replied, "No, Preacher, but if you'll hum a bit for me, I think I can play the tune," a line Mae could have adopted as her own.

Watching the pair work, Mae sensed that there was something in Savoy's approach she could adapt for her purposes. When Savoy, dangling his hotel keys, would let his glance survey Brennan from the tip of his toes to the top of his head and *all* points in between and remark, "Oh, you're lonesome, huh? Well, it's your own fault!" Mae wouldn't forget it any more than she would forget another female impersonator's entrance as Cleopatra on a litter borne by husky six-foot six-inch blacks. Years later in her nightclub act she'd make *her* entrance on a chaise borne by nine musclemen. And at the finish she would pass out a key to her hotel suite to each of the body builders.

With the help of Savoy's writer, Thomas Gray, she highlighted the impersonator's characteristics, combining them with the egotism of Eva Tanguay. She believed her act now incorporated those elements which had made Savoy and Tanguay the preeminent headliners in that era.

In later years she recalled Savoy's death: "He was as big a camp offstage as on. He didn't care what anyone thought. Everybody was sad when he died, but even then he handed them a laugh. He and some friends were walkin' on the beach 'n' this storm come up. There was a big clap of thunder. He stopped in his track 'n' put his hand on his hip 'n' said, 'That'll be enough out of you, Miss God!' Just then the lightning hit a piece of metal jewelry around his neck, killin' him on the spot."

In September 1912 Mae opened at Hammerstein's, expecting enormous success with her new act. She sensed from audience response that she had taken an important step in her development. The point of view of the act can be gathered from the titles of Gray's songs: "Isn't She a Brazen Thing?," "It's an Awful Easy Way to Make a Living," "International Rag Song" and "Good Night, Nurse," which was singled out for show-stopping applause.

When Mae made her debut as a single comedienne on the Keith Circuit of theaters in 1913, she finally had made the big time. She now was billing herself as "The Original Brinkley Girl"—Nell Brinkley's dimpled, fluffy-haired creation who had succeeded the Gibson Girl and preceded the John Held, Jr., flappers. With her increasingly flip dialogue and exaggeratedly sexy, comedic approach, Mae enlarged and refined the character until one critic after another began labeling her "America's leading female impersonator."

By 1913 her salary had become large enough so that she could afford not only the necessary songs and jokes but also a flashy new wardrobe. Leading columnists praised the look of her act, citing especially a purple velvet evening gown set off by a cerise chiffon coat and hat to match. Added flash was given by the proverbial red carpet which was rolled out before she slithered to the center of the stage. By ordinary show business standards Mae would seem to have made it. But she allowed a torrid love affair with a man she referred to only as Mr. D to deflect her from her course in 1914. She recovered with a highly praised act in 1915 and, astonishingly, at her mother's urging, suddenly teamed up with her sister, Beverly, in 1916. During those years the acts she presented were sometimes ecstatically received, sometimes totally rejected by audiences and critics. Still, by trial and error, she gradually found her way.

In reminiscence, Mae's memories of her vaudeville experiences were happy except for occasional setbacks, especially one involving Beverly. The sisters shared an intense love-hate relationship. Beverly resented being overshadowed and dependent on Mae, and Mae was impatient with her sister's weaknesses. It was incredible to Mae that she consistently would jeopardize her career. "I think the only things she ever really cared about were men and drinking," Mae once said. "When she'd find a guy she liked, I'd sit back and watch. Sure enough, he'd turn out to be a boozin' partner.

"It started way back when she got to running around with the fast crowd in high school. I wouldn't have considered workin' with her if my mother hadn't begged me. We had this act where she'd come out as the old-fashioned girl and sing about how it was in them days; then I'd come out as the modern girl who was having all the fun. Then, while she did a song, I'd get into a tux and top hat, and with me as the man we'd finish the act with this dance that really got a hand.

"The act went over with a bang. But right away Beverly started drinkin'. I'd talk to her and she'd promise to stop, but she'd meet some guy 'n' stay out half the night. She thought she was putting something over on me. So I spread newspapers on the floor. And even though she took off her shoes 'n' tried to tiptoe in, when she stepped down, the papers'd rattle and I'd say, 'I hear you, Beverly!'

"It got worse. She'd stay out boozin' with these guys before shows until she'd hardly make the performance. She'd come runnin' through the stage door tearin' off her coat, put on the costume 'n' just barely make her entrance. It was somethin' terrible on my nerves. But we had a solid twelve-week bookin' and I didn't want to give that up, know what I mean? Finally, it got so bad I told my mother, 'You're tryin' to make me Beverly's stepmother. I'm not ready to be responsible like that. You take her home.'

"After Beverly left, what I came up with was first I'd enter in a breakaway dress and a picture hat as the old-fashioned girl. During the applause I'd tear off the dress 'n' hat in the wings, and underneath I had on a modern dress with a lot of fringe. I'd frizz my hair 'n' come back 'n' do a shake dance. Then after that I'd have the lights dimmed and I'd appear with this male dummy. I had clamps attached to my legs so his feet moved with mine, see?

"It went over good. There was a guy, Owen McGivney, a quick-change artist. He made maybe a dozen lightning changes. I figured if he could do twelve, I ought be able to do three. After all, I considered myself twice as talented as he was."

Mae's recollections were greeted with skepticism. But John Wharton, the distinguished theatrical attorney, recalled seeing the girls at the time they were breaking in the act. (If indeed Mae actually fired Beverly, she did so after *Variety* reviewed them at the Fifth Avenue Theater in New York.) "I lived in East Orange, New Jersey, in 1916 and was sick," Wharton said. "The doctor wouldn't permit me to go to New York, but he would allow me to go to Newark, and Newark had Proctor's Vaudeville. Two different shows a week. I saw every one of them. And for years afterward I rarely saw a vaudeville act that had not been at Proctor's.

"One of the acts was Mae West and another girl who was billed as her sister. As I recall it, Sister was a sweet-looking girl and put on quite a shy act.

"At the time there was a joke that if a man took a girl out in an automobile and she didn't submit to his lascivious advances, he made her walk home. And the sister was involved in such an experience.

"Then Mae West came on as the tough sister, and I recall to this day, she had a recurrent line in the song to the effect that *she* never walked home.

"I imagined these two girls were on their way up. This was a first-rank house where vaudeville people tried out their material and if it didn't go, they changed it. They were probably shooting for New York. I remember Mae did a kind of cooch dance. I don't remember the male impersonation, though. Of course, that was sixty or sixty-one years ago. But when Mae West began to emerge as a personality in the 1920's, I remembered that stand in Newark, and I realized she was going to play very tough parts.

"When I saw her again after that first time I don't remember, but I never forgot her from this vaudeville act—and I never heard of Sister again until now."

On July 10, 1916, *Variety's Sime* reviewed the act, which shared the bill with a Fatty Arbuckle film short and playlet called *Finders Keepers* written by and starring George Kelly, who later would win a Pulitzer Prize for his *Craig's Wife. Sime* gave the sister act a surprisingly harsh review:

> Mae West in big time vaudeville may only be admired for her persistency in believing she is a big time act and trying to make vaudeville accept her as such. After trying several brands of turns, Miss West is with us again, this time with a "sister" tacked onto the billing and the stage. "Sister's" hair looks very much like Mae's, and there the resemblance ceases in looks as well as work, for "sister" isn't quite as rough as Mae can't help being. Unless Miss West can tone down her stage presence in every way she might just as well hop right out of vaudeville and into burlesque. . . .

Alluding to the dance Mae, wearing a dinner jacket and silk topper, performed with Beverly, *Sime* closed his review:

> Perhaps if Miss West would wear men's dress altogether while upon the stage and stop talking, she would appear to better advantage. With "sister" they could do a boy and girl "sister" act.

There was no further mention of Mae in *Variety* until November 17, 1916, when this tiny story appeared:

> An act written by Blanche Merrill will return Mae West to vaudeville under another name and as a male impersonator.

Charlie Abbott, who worked on several bills with Mae, maintained in 1978 that until 1920 she was never truly accepted by vaudeville performers, who were clannish and inclined to take a prudish view of any suggestive material. "She was a draw, but she wasn't a draw like Nora Bayes or Lillian Shaw ('The Blue Streak of Vaudeville')," he said. "It wasn't that she did anything dirty the way they do now when they take off their clothes as they walk onstage and anything goes after that. But she got a reputation, and she was smart enough to keep developing that slant and eventually to cash in on it.

"She kept to herself, but she gloried in the stir she caused wherever she went. Sometimes she played next to closing, the best spot on the bill, but even so, traditional vaudevillians made her feel like an outsider."

Theater of all kinds was class-conscious in those days. On the legitimate stage no supporting member of the cast dared address Ethel Barrymore as anything except Miss Barrymore, and when one presumptuous youngster called her by her given name, she slapped his face. In the *Ziegfeld Follies* Bert Williams was recognized as the peer of any comedian Ziegfeld ever hired, including Will Rogers, but because Williams was black, he was never on intimate terms with his costars. And in vaudeville the more conventional singers and dancers would no more have had "midnight lunch" with Mae than a minister's wife would have invited a gang moll to tea.

Late in the summer of 1919 Mae returned from a Broadway show to vaudeville with another act created by Gray—"*I Want a Caveman*," "*I'm a Night School Teacher*," "*The Mannekin*" and "*Any Kind of Man*."

Opening night was hot and humid, and the audience was restless until Mae, wearing a spectacular jet and silver gown, a sequined cape and plumed hat, turned up in the fourth spot. Her improved technique and air of confidence brought the onlookers out of their torpor and onto their feet at the end of the act.

She seemed set for an auspicious tour, but during the week she became ill and canceled. When she reopened for a swing around the New England circuit, reviews were indifferent. The vitality was gone.

In her official biography Mae claims that in 1921 she began writing her own material and looking around for a versatile accompanist. "I needed a piano player who could deliver some straight lines," she recalled. "Somebody came up with Jimmy Durante. I wasn't too crazy about the idea. Then I thought of Harry Richman. He wasn't as funny as Durante, but he sure was better in other ways."

The way Mae told it the act she wrote for herself and Richman—of the straw hat, cane and lisp—gave him his first opportunity to speak lines or sing on any stage. They were a vaudeville sensation. (They segued into the *Ginger Box Revue* in the Greenwich Village Theater for eighteen months, during which time Richman became a "three-way performer"—singing, dancing, acting.)

E. F. Albee, the vaudeville magnate, proposed a three-year contract, but Mae would commit only on a month-to-month basis. She and Richman also received an offer of 50 percent interest in a club if they would headline a show. She turned it down since J. J. Shubert already was looking for a play in which to star her, but she urged Richman to accept. He became so popular the club eventually was named after him.

Richman in his autobiography says he was nervous about auditioning for Mae's act, but she put him at ease as her glance traveled appreciatively up his six-foot-plus frame and she said, "You'll do." He became anxious again when he learned he had to speak and sing. Mae, reassuring him about his lisp, said, "Don't worry about it, big boy. That lisp could be the makin' of you. It's distinctive."

Through Mae, Richman began a career that was to make him the idol of Broadway. He developed a provocative Don Juan image, publicly and privately. Jerry Hoffman, an editor of the *Clipper,* a theatrical newspaper, and later a Hollywood press agent, recalled a visit to Richman's apartment. "He had a bachelor pad and was at stud," Hoffman said. "Really at stud. I went up there more than once and I'd find four or five dames sitting around in their underwear, waiting to get back into the bedroom with him."

Richman filled time in the act while Mae changed costumes. One of his songs was "She's Waiting for You to Love Her All the Time." As he sang another, "The Gladiator," he was required to do a kind of refined male striptease. When Mae appeared, she performed several numbers, finishing with "Frankie and John-ny." Richman recalled that in this song she interpolated the line "If you don't like my peaches, don't shake my tree," which set males in the audience wild. After a theater manager warned that Mae's suggestiveness might bring police action, Albee asked to see the act again. When Mae came to the most controversial line, she delivered it to Albee with hands clasped innocently at her temple and cheek, her eyes cast heavenward and her delivery childlike. Albee's reaction was that the line wouldn't offend a priest.

At the next performance she reverted to the sexy interpretation. Shortly after, the act broke up. Years later Richman explained why to director-choreographer Charlie O'Curran. "In those days Harry was black-haired, tall, handsome—just beautiful," O'Curran said. "He knew Mae wanted to make it with him. But he'd been warned by friends that once he had an affair with her, he'd be fired just like that. So he kept thinking, 'No, I've got to listen to what those guys told me or I'll lose this job.' He stalled her and stalled her. Every night she was getting more furious. The show deteriorated, and she stopped being charming and funny. Everything was like an argument because she took out her frustration on him while they were onstage. So finally Harry decided he didn't give a shit and would go up and bang her.

"That night he did, and the next day the performance was fantastic. It had never gone so well. But right after that he was given his notice. They say she used to do that in the old days. Once you'd swing with her, you were finished. She'd had you. You were old-hat. You might say Harry traded one kind of job for another."

Before the split Mae and Richman played the Palace Theater, though it is not mentioned by either in their autobiographies. Yet the reviews of the engagement exist. *Sime,* who five years earlier had suggested Mae hop right out of vaudeville and into burlesque, was bowled over: "How the showmakers have let that blonde baby get away from them so long . . . is inexplicable."

Although Mae claimed this was an act she wrote herself, credit is given in *Variety* to Neville Fleeson:

> If he wrote it, the boy wrote something, and had he scoured the world he would scarcely have equalled the performance Miss West contributes to it. She warmed up the house, held it, tied up the show and made a graceful little speech. Where has she been so long if she has possessed for any length of time what she revealed at the Palace?

Fleeson, who subsequently wrote lyrics for *The Gingham Girl* (1922) and *Bye Bye Bonnie* (1927), played the Palace frequently between 1927 and 1931, performing his own material. He undoubtedly provided the witty act *Sime* raves about while Richman gave the balance Mae needed to make the most of her overpowering personality. If it is difficult to understand why she never cited the Palace review, one cannot overlook her desire to grab all the glory, and possibly she wanted to forget the credit given Richman and especially Fleeson.

3

Between vaudeville bookings Mae began appearing in Broadway musicals. One of the things that she and Wallace tried shortly after their marriage was attending a "cattle call" or open audition for William Le Baron's sketch *A la Broadway*, which was being added to the program at the Folies Bergere Theatre Restaurant. Mae was chosen; Wallace, passed over.

The Folies Bergere, which *Variety* called "that little hatbox of a pretty reception room," was the forerunner of smart supper clubs. Dining tables were on the orchestra floor and in the boxes, and only the balcony had conventional theater seats. Because the small seating capacity of this novelty house made it profitable only if it was sold out for all performances, the producers added Le Baron's skit, a satirical treatment of sentimental musicals, in hopes of beefing up attendance.

Mae played Maggie O'Hara, a part she altered from a conventional Irish maid into a saucy wench. She persuaded the show's lyricist to write three extra choruses in various dialects and then created two more herself for encores of her "They Are Irish" number. She never doubted she would need them.

She also stood out in "The Philadelphia Drag," which started at a zippy pace and slowed down until, at the end of the number, the dancers sank slowly to the floor only to be awakened and revived at a cock's crow.

The New York Times reported, "A girl named Mae West, hitherto unknown, pleased by her grotesquerie and a snappy way of singing and dancing."

In spite of Mae's personal success, *A la Broadway* fared badly with audiences and critics alike. The show opened on September 11, 1911, and closed on October 1. Yet in recalling this, her first Broadway production, Mae used a technique she often employed: accentuating the positive and overlooking the negative. She told of being moved from the chorus girls' dressing room to share quarters with the star of *Hello, Paris,* the other sketch. Without actually saying so, she conveys the impression that she reigned over an enormous hit. However short the run, it did represent a step up for her. In 1935 Le Baron, then an executive at Paramount Studios, where Mae was the top star, told an interviewer, "Her hoydenish routine and her remarkable delivery of the songs stopped the show. . . . She was a riot. I predicted stardom for her—and she won it."

A month later she opened in New Haven at the Hyperion Theater in *Vera Violetta,* starring Gaby Deslys and Al Jolson, for the Shubert Brothers. A concrete example of how casually shows were assembled in those pre-Equity days was Mae's surprising freedom to dress and make herself up so flamboyantly that upon her first appearance the audience mistook her for Gaby, thereby killing the star's entrance. "My big mistake was timing," she said. "They changed my entrance to after Gaby and made me tone down my makeup. I shoulda waited and pulled that at the New York opening."

On the Saturday after the New Haven premiere Yale's football team was at home against Princeton. Because the provocative material in the production was thought suited to the sporting mood of the town, the management raised ticket prices to $3. What the audience did not know was that having received complaints about "the objectionable aspects of the show," the New Haven chief of police had taken it upon himself to cut parts of Gaby's and Mae's performances. Angry at having lost to Princeton in the afternoon and to the chief of police at night, the Yale students expressed their displeasure at this "largest, most elaborate production in North America" by running amok and tearing out the seats. Mae was reported "in the middle of the fray, if, indeed, she did not start it."

Vera Violetta, based on a German play, turned out to be "a fifty-minute sketch padded out to two hours." Al Jolson made a hit with "Rum-Tum-Tiddle" and Gaby Deslys with "The Gaby Glide." Mae was nowhere to be seen at the opening at the Winter Garden in New York. *Variety* reported she had been "stricken with pneumonia."

In her late eighties, looking back at her decades of self-involvement, Mae claimed that Ziegfeld wanted to star her but that she inspected the stage, didn't like its proportions and turned him down. "Imagine a fresh kid talkin' to him like that," she marveled. "But I knew how I got my effects. So I hadda push people around, no matter how big. Otherwise, there wouldn't have been no Mae West. I was an original. There'd never been anybody like me before."

Eventually she did appear for Ziegfeld in *A Winsome Widow,* but she was by no means the star. In fact, on April 12, 1912, it must have galled Mae that Harry Conroy, Frank Tinney, the Dolly Sisters and half a dozen other cast members rated attention from reviewers while her "La Petite Daffy" was ignored.

She stayed with the show for 172 performances and, according to her recollections, didn't appear in musical comedy again until October 1918, when she was cast in *Sometime.* However, Hugh Fordin's biography of Oscar Hammerstein II notes that in 1917 Hammerstein wrote his first song, "Make Yourself at Home," for the production *Furs and Frills.* Mae was featured, and she reportedly liked Hammerstein so much she told him, "The theater ain't for you, kid. You got too much class!"

In 1977 Mae recalled neither the song nor the play. "But I haven't forgotten Hammerstein," she said, rolling her eyes. "I think I had a little thing with him. In fact, I know I did."

In *Sometime,* which had a score by Rudolf Friml and book and lyrics by Rida Johnson Young, Mae was featured as Mayme Dean, a flip chorus girl who had broken up the hero's marriage five years earlier. The stars were Ed Wynn and Francine Larrimore, a dramatic actress whose inadequate singing voice brought her replacement, Helen Ford, her first leading role on Broadway.

Mae's opening song, "What Do You Have to Do?," was pleasant enough, but in the second act when she slammed into "Any Kind of Man" and introduced the shimmy to musical comedy, she stopped the show cold. So cold that she interrupted the plot to make a speech and repeat her shimmy—which some reviewers insisted was an old-fashioned cooch dance in which she barely moved her feet.

If the shimmy was new to Broadway, it was not new to Mae. Seven years earlier, during a vaudeville date in Chicago, she visited the Elite Cafe on the South Side, where she saw black dancers doing the shimmy shawobble. She learned it and the next day added it as an encore. The manager immediately came running backstage and demanded its removal. But the following week, in Milwaukee, Mae tried it again, and again the manager came back, screaming she would get the theater raided. "What're ya gettin' excited for?" Mae inquired. "They're doin' it in Chicago." Off and on over the years she would tantalize vaudeville audiences with the dance.

For *Sometime* she had hired Joe ("The Boy with the Cigar and the Hat") Frisco, an eccentric jazz dancer, to help her perfect a version designed for maximum impact on blasé Broadway audiences. Thereafter she largely abandoned the dance to Gilda Gray, explaining she didn't want to become too closely associated with a fad. "When it passed, I'd be a back number. Me, I'm more perennial," she confided. "I may just go on forever."

"Most of us in *Sometime* thought Mae was just shocking," said Helen Ford, who later appeared in several Rodgers and Hart musicals. "Which was just what she wanted us to feel."

Helen, who only recently had married George Ford of the Ford Theater family of Washington and Baltimore, was easily embarrassed, and Mae delighted in quizzing her about her sex life. "I remember Mae's saying that maybe George was enough for me, but that she'd never marry the man she was going with. 'How am I gonna know I won't wake up some morning and want to throw him out?' she asked. 'Yuh know what I mean? But I gotta have a steady guy or I'd be sleeping with every fella in the cast.' That kind of talk continued until I learned not to blush; then Mae lost all interest in me and never said more than hello or good night," Mrs. Ford recalled sixty-one years later.

The day after *Sometime* opened nobody had a good word to say for the libretto and lyrics. There was grudging praise for Friml's music and some backhanded compliments for Ed Wynn. But Mae was heralded as "a new and diverting edition of the vampire [who had] all the assurance of a star performer" and as "an audacious young woman . . . tough, but fun."

The show ran until June 1919, making it the longest-running

musical comedy of the season and giving Mae exposure to segments of a great audience that previously had been unaware of her.

The actors' strike that summer kept the theaters dark, but when *Sometime* opened in Boston on September 7, Ida May Chadwick had stepped in to play a different type of Mayme Dean. Mae's vamp had vanished and Ida May was doing a Sis Hopkins country girl. She attempted no shimmy, and she and Frank Tinney harmonized on "I'm a Broadway Sinner and You're a Bowery Bum" in the spot where Mae had triumphed with "Any Kind of Man."

In April 1921 the Shuberts cast Mae in *The Whirl of the Town,* giving her billing above the title alongside Jimmy Hussey and Georgie Price. Her joy at reaching stardom was tempered by the fact that *The Whirl of the Town* in another form had already met with ignominious failure, despite the efforts of Hussey, under the title *Tattle Tales.* Now the Shuberts were sending it into Philadelphia for four weeks and Boston for two.

Hussey was still unhappy with the material, and Georgie Price miserable at the lack of it. The Shuberts were harassing him, attempting to force him to break the contract he'd signed when they were having problems with Al Jolson and Eddie Cantor. Now that Jolson and Cantor had returned to the fold, they wanted to cancel Price's deal. Although he received a star's salary, his dressing room was three flights up. In Act I he entered in blackface, hung around like an extra and exited without delivering a line. In the first-act finale he joined other cast members in white face. Act II found him in blackface again, but he was given neither a word of dialogue to speak nor a note of music to sing. The Shuberts anticipated receiving his notice, but for six weeks Price showed up faithfully to fulfill the demeaning duties and to collect his fat paycheck.

Hussey was under equal pressure, trying to evoke laughter from material lacking both wit and humor. So desperate were the producers that they persuaded Mae to renege on her vow to abandon the shimmy. The high spot of the production was unquestionably "The Trial of Shimmy Mae." In Philadelphia Mae wriggled with abandon to the delight of the audience.

But when the company moved to Boston, the Shuberts' representative, A. Toxin Worm, decreed no shaking would be tolerated. Mae bowed to his edict, but the show drew disastrous reviews, and the closing notice was posted. On the final night Mae decided to give Bostonians a view of her shimmy. Somehow Worm learned of her plan and stationed himself near the lighting board. The moment she prepared to go into the deleted dance, he signaled the lighting man to plunge the stage into darkness. Outraged, Mae sought out Worm to complain someone had censored her.

Apparently unfazed by this second failure, the Shuberts recast, revamped and rechristened the show *The Mimic World of 1921*, opening it on August 17 at their Century Promenade in New York. Hussey accurately prereviewed the offering by walking out just before the premiere, leaving a gap that Mae, Cliff "Ukulele Ike" Edwards, El Brendel nor any of the other principals could fill. Even the Shuberts' recruitment of James Barton to burlesque a prizefight proved useless. Jack Dempsey, the heavyweight champion of the world, who happened to be in the audience, was lured to the stage to officiate as referee and stole many of the notices.

Mae looked Dempsey over and didn't overlook some thrilling possibilities, even though he seemed shy. Not so shy, however, that he didn't propose she star opposite him in *Daredevil Jack*, a film he was considering. In the test they made together, she said, "Listen, Champ, hold me tighter. I can take anything you can throw." This declaration led to several fulfilling private sessions before Mae's jealous manager torpedoed the film project.

The Mimic World lasted only four weeks, but it made an indelible impression on at least two members of the audience—humorist Robert Benchley and dramatist Marc Connelly. Fifty-six years later Connelly recalled vividly at least part of the proceedings:

"The Century Promenade was located atop the old Century Theater that had been built with the idea of having something in terms of theater that approximated the Metropolitan Opera. It would offer a certain amount of elegance with boxes separating the elite from the riffraff. It fell on its face.

"The theater went through a series of ventures before the Shuberts decided to make the Century Promenade Roof a rival of the *Ziegfeld Frolics* on the Amsterdam Roof. The Shubert show turned out to be a very poor imitation. They tried to do it on a dollar and a half. And that was not quite the way with which you could compete with Ziegfeld and reach the clientele he was able to attract.

"One night Mr. Benchley and I went together to see something called *The Mimic World of 1921,* and we both memorized the chorus of a number that was a memorable tribute to Shakespeare.

"The scene was extraordinarily tasteful. They used a typical Shubert backdrop that had apparently been out on the road in half a dozen Shubert productions and hadn't been pressed in God knows how long. Its sky had about a thousand wrinkles in it, and in front of that backdrop were two quarter circle hedges. In the opening between the hedges, on a pedestal, was a very fine bust of Shakespeare that couldn't have been bought for less than twenty-five cents from a pushcart on Hester Street. And that stood there in glorious isolation while a young man in a dinner jacket came out and sang a song called 'Shakespeare's Garden of Love.' The chorus, which is what I remember and Benchley remembered until he died, went as follows:

> *There's Hamlet*
> *And Ophelia*
> *Romeo and Juliet*
> *Desdemona*
> *And brave Othello*
> *Their love*
> *We shall ne'er forget.*
>
> *There's Portia*
> *And proud Bassanio*
> *Immortal as the stars above*
> *And they're blooming*
> *Through eternity*
> *In Shakespeare's Garden of Love,*
> *In Shakespeare's Garden of Love.*

"And as though in the realization of a dream," Connelly continued, "the characters of Shakespeare's plays came across the stage, re-created, just making brief appearances. And among them in another verse was Cleopatra personified by Miss Mae West, who did a typical Cleopatra grind with her hands in front of her eyes as she came across. And Mr. Benchley and I were able to keep from falling off our chairs as we enjoyed that spectacle of Shakespeare's Garden of Love.

"That was the first time I ever saw Miss West onstage, but it was an unforgettable sight. She certainly made the most of it because she created her own very vivid concept of Cleopatra. Her grind was very, very graphic and very interesting. Caught the true spirit of Egypt."

Mr. Connelly did not remember Mae's Shifty Liz in "Times Square After Midnight," her French vamp in the Café de Paris scene or a portion of the show simply designated as "An Interlude with Mae West," which included a black-wigged imitation of Nazimova.

Mae, however, remembered everything well, including J. J. Shubert's remark that her personality was so exciting other female performers didn't want to appear in the same presentation with her. The implication was that she became the only woman in the show. This claim must have come as a shock to Ann Toddings, whose performance the *Evening Post* singled out:

> In previous entertainments of the kind—the midnight affairs— there has always been one woman who dominated the scene and *The Mimic World* is no exception to the rule. This time it is Ann Toddings, a very pretty girl, who is mighty good to look at, who has sufficient singing ability for the occasion and is a graceful dancer. . . .

In this review none of Mae's contributions was mentioned.

The Mimic World lasted only as long as it was propped up by theater ticket agencies' "buys," a guaranteed sale spanning four weeks. Then the ill-fated production went down for the third and final time.

4

Career-minded as she always was, Mae still found time for the sexual intrigue she enjoyed almost to the end of her life. In 1912, less than a year after their marriage, she saw to it that Wallace went on the road, first in vaudeville, and then into musical stock in Duluth, Minnesota, with Lew Fields. When Fields went broke, Wallace helped him raise enough money to get the troupe on the road again and didn't return to New York until the fall, when he was booked into the Salivan chain of restaurants with his song-and-dance single.

He tried in vain to contact Mae. Sometime before her September 30 opening at Hammerstein's, Mae and Tom Gray dropped in at the Faust, where Wallace was working, and she casually introduced him to Gray as "an old friend." On the bill was Ted Lewis, "The Tragedian of Jazz," whom Mae asked to play "Good Night, Nurse" so Wallace could hear a song written expressly for her.

During the evening Wallace recognized that his wife had become more mature and sophisticated. When she took him aside and suggested he team with handsome piano player Harry Richman, he finally understood she had little further use for him professionally. Even so, he couldn't refrain from inquiring when they could get together. Mae casually replied whenever he wished. Later that evening Wallace told Ted Lewis Mae was his secret wife. Lewis warned him to keep a close watch on the lovely lady if he wanted the marriage to survive.

There followed a series of trysts during which Mae repeatedly explained that her career would always receive priority over love and marriage. When Wallace pressed for more of a commitment, she reminded him, "I never said it was anything but physical."

At the end of 1912 Mae showed up at the Garden Restaurant, located at Broadway and Fiftieth Street, where Wallace was currently appearing. Her sister, Beverly, was going to open at the Bijou as a single in early January, and Mae, thinking that Wallace and Beverly might make a good team, invited him to attend. After seeing her performance, Wallace, unimpressed, dreaded going backstage, but when he appeared in Beverly's dressing room, no mention was made of the partnership. Instead, the two sisters began haranguing him to call off the marriage.

Soon Mae changed tactics, asking him to help her finance a home in Richmond Hills. He agreed, but when they went to his bank and Mae saw how meager his checking account was, she told him to keep the money, saying, "You need it more than I do."

Later she once more approached him about the possibility of teaming with Beverly. He yielded reluctantly. Rehearsals lasted through hardly one song, "Kiss, Kiss, Kiss." As Wallace and Mae demonstrated it for Beverly, their personal chemistry put the song over. When Beverly substituted for Mae, the excitement disappeared, and so did any prospects for the act.

Shortly after, Wallace declined an offer of $250 a week to appear in an American revue in London, on the grounds that he would certainly lose his wife if he went abroad. Remaining in New York, he staged several miniature revues with some success. Then, in a desperate attempt to regain equal professional stature with Mae, he invested all his savings in a revue production for which he not only commissioned original music but also undertook the staging and choreography. It opened at Reisenweber's Café and was a dead flop.

As Wallace continued to phone the house Mae had purchased in Richmond Hills, Mae's parents and Beverly—although only the latter had been told rumors of the marriage were true—

refused to give him any information about Mae. Down on his luck, he agreed to teach tap dancing to Paroto, an entertainer who had introduced Americans to the Apache, a violent knockabout dance that originated in the Parisian demimonde. In exchange, Paroto instructed Wallace in his specialty. The deal proved a profitable one for Wallace, who used his newly acquired skill to give private lessons to society women. Eventually he Americanized the Apache into a rag doll dance which he performed until retirement in the late 1930's.

The one lover of Mae's who finally forced Wallace to admit his marriage was a sham is identified in Mae's autobiography as Mr. D, a headliner she met while appearing at a theater in Detroit. She described him as a "terrific personality . . . with sensual Latin charm . . . [and] a hit wherever he played." He was, according to her, so smitten that he voluntarily demoted himself to conduct her orchestra so they might travel the circuit together.

Mae appreciated his sacrifice but felt no responsibility to remain faithful. When she became indisposed, Mr. D obtained the services of a doctor for her and then stepped in to headline in her place. "His mistake was the doctor he called was as excitin' and magnetic as himself," Mae said. "So I needed the doc's services quite often 'n' my recovery was unusually slow. Naturally I didn't get a bill, know what I mean? Truth is, he gave me a big diamond. I told Mr. D my mother sent it to me."

The overly protective D seems to have been kept so busy trying to ward off other suitors it is difficult to imagine how he even found time to lead the orchestra. Meanwhile, Mae recalled he was bothering her to marry him. She couldn't tell him she already was married and, anyway, had no interest in monogamous relationships.

Mr. D's jealousy of his rivals increased to the point where Mae feared his frustration would erupt into bloodshed. She said in her autobiography she solved the problem by persuading her agent, Frank Bohm, to book a road tour for her, leaving Mr. D behind. Fantasy? Part yes, part no. Mr. D's full name was Guido Diero. In 1910 Max Hart booked him on the Orpheum and Keith circuits as the first accordionist ever to play big-time vaudeville. In his advertisements Diero described himself as "originator and master of the piano accordion, a new and novel instrument." He also claimed to have taken out a $50,000 policy with the Hartford

Insurance Company "to protect his fingers." Presumably this was a publicity stunt rather than protection of his hands against Mae's envious lovers.

By 1914, like Mae, Diero was under the management of Bohm, and far from serving as Mae's orchestra conductor, he commanded top billing and was praised in review after review as an accordionist of exceptional ability, the greatest heard in New York until then. He was powerfully built, with heavily muscled shoulders and bulging biceps. His big hands gave him an octave and a half reach on the accordion. He had bold features, large eyes, wavy black hair and a sensuous nature that projected across the footlights. Mae might easily have coined her "tall, dark 'n' handsome" to describe him. He had everything she demanded in a lover—if just one had been enough.

Why, then, did she go to such extremes to camouflage his identity? Perhaps because she violated one of her principles. She always claimed she never "fooled around" with married men. Not only was the lusty Diero married but on February 25, 1914, he was arrested on a warrant for nonsupport of his wife, who lived in Spokane, Washington. Years earlier he had married to avoid prosecution on a statutory offense. Even after learning of his marital background, Mae continued the romance.

Ordinarily she quickly would have dropped anyone in such a predicament, but she was more emotionally stirred by Diero than any other man she had ever been involved with. They continued not only their affair but also their professional association as Bohm booked them to costar on Loew's circuit. In December of that year Mae and Diero took out an ad in *Variety* with a big photo of each:

FRANK BOHM
PRESENTS

DIERO	MAE WEST
THE MASTER OF THE	THE ORIGINAL
ACCORDION	BRINKLEY GIRL
The Incomparable In His Line	A Style All Her Own

Engaged jointly as headline features

40 weeks	Loew's Circuit
	Season 1916–1917

WISHING THE ENTIRE WORLD A MERRY CHRISTMAS
AND A HAPPY NEW YEAR

But the joint bookings were not to be fulfilled because Mae enjoyed sexual variety, and there were available to her many sturdy, well-muscled, clean-living acrobats on the various bills she played.

Jack Durant, whom she met at Fox's Folly Theater in Brooklyn, recalled, "She wanted me to leave the Dancing Shoes act to go with her. Said she'd pay me double what I was getting. I talked it over with Tiny Turek, the girl who owned the act. She told me to go if I wanted to, but once Mae'd had me and the novelty wore off, I'd be out of a job. I couldn't see it."

Dancer Dave Berk of Berk and Broderick had a brief, torrid affair with Mae during the Diero period, and then they went different ways. When he saw her at a Pittsburgh railroad station a few years later, she was sitting on a baggage cart, swinging her pretty legs nonchalantly. Berk went up and spoke. Mae looked him over and then asked, "Say, where do I know you from?"

During her affair with Diero, whenever they had encountered Wallace, she had snubbed her husband. On one occasion Wallace lost his temper and shouted he would never speak to her again. "I felt Diero had won," he said.

Ironically, once Wallace had turned on Mae, she and Beverly made a trip to his sister's house in Long Island searching for him. They obtained no information.

By chance, soon after, Wallace, strolling along Broadway, heard Mae's distinctive voice calling to him. Seated in an expensive automobile and gorgeously gowned and bejeweled, she beckoned him to her.

At her side was a tall, beefy Irishman who was older than Mae by fifteen years and bore a striking resemblance to her father. Atop his melon-shaped head sat a derby. Around his neck were a winged collar and a bow tie, and even though seated in the back seat of the car, he clasped a cane with an elk's tooth embedded in it. It stood between his legs like a menacing phallic symbol. "You knew he wasn't a nobody," Wallace observed.

Mae introduced her companion as "Mr. Timony," and James Timony informed Wallace that Mae had told him about their marriage. He called attention to her expensive apparel and jewels and suggested Wallace could only be excess baggage in the life of a woman who was headed for stardom. Wallace, seemingly a little slow on the uptakes, later said he then realized he had been nothing more than one of a succession of men in Mae's life.

Timony handed him an engraved card and requested that he come to an office at Forty-second Street and Broadway the following morning. Next day Wallace proved no match for Timony, who raved about Mae's beauty, her talent and future and discounted Wallace as a man and a performer. He meekly agreed to Timony's plan to institute divorce proceedings in secrecy. Shortly afterward Beverly came up to Wallace in the Chesterfield Hotel lobby and thrust some documents she claimed were divorce papers into his hand. Wallace angrily shredded them.

In the weeks that followed, he suffered an emotional collapse. Twenty years later Wallace would say: ". . . In speaking to my sister of the situation, I referred to Catherine the Great, who loved many men, one man at a time. Maybe Mae was inspired by her. She was a spirited woman who would fight for the possession of anything that she wanted, and if she wanted it real bad, she would move all obstacles in her path. Once she had it, she would crush all life from it—destroy it, so to speak, whether it was man or beast."

Timony, who was in Mae's thrall, would have been astonished at Wallace's observations. He saw her as Helen of Troy, Cleopatra and Duse rolled into one. They met through her mother, who was a client of his law firm.

In many ways he was the ideal man for Mae. He was a big, beefy ex-football player. No longer a strapping, unmarked youth, he had a slightly over-the-hill quality that, to Mae, added to, rather than detracted from, his sex appeal. If Diero inspired "tall, dark 'n' handsome," it may have been Timony who elicited "You're no oil painting, but you're a fascinatin' monster." And if he played Beast, he treated Mae as Beauty—praising, encouraging, reinforcing, deferring to and pushing her on toward what they both regarded as her place in the sun.

Not everyone took Mae's talent seriously. Marc Connelly recalled that while still a reporter on the *Morning Telegraph*, he used to visit Timony's office on the east side of Forty-second Street and Broadway. "Jim was a prosperous lawyer—a professional Irishman, the son of a Tammany politician. And very attached to Miss West," Connelly said. "I used to see her come into his office and she came in with the assurance of Bernhardt, I must say. Feathers, oh, my, yes, an enormous amount of feathers—and confidence."

In Mae's cast of pivotal lovers Joe Schenck helped her develop performing skills. Frank Wallace provided her with a passport to sexual freedom by putting her needs and wishes above his own and never demanding his full rights. Guido Diero proved not only an exciting lover but also a springboard to increased stature in vaudeville. Now, in 1916, Jim Timony was prepared to abandon his law practice to devote himself to her career. He would be the catalyst that would enable her to blend her outrageous personality with the hallowed tradition of the legitimate theater.

5

The Broadway theater in the twenties functioned on two levels: literate drama, family comedies and musicals constituted one, and salacious plays and risqué revues the other. Timony originally envisioned Mae as the star of prestigious productions, but Mae's natural bent would carry her toward the notorious.

A rash of "dirty plays" already had caused the Producing Managers' Association to create a panel of 300 volunteers from which juries could be drawn to judge a production's acceptability. Theater people hoped these juries would head off censorship and police raids. Even Sholem Asch's serious dramatization *The God of Vengeance,* which dealt with the evils of prostitution and had been staged in Berlin in 1910, drew a condemned rating. The producer justifiably defied that ruling and continued the run.

Despite the play juries' efforts, the trend toward bolder and tawdrier productions continued. *Ladies of the Evening, The Virgin Man, A Good Bad Woman* and *I O U a Woman* were typical of plays whose titles telegraphed their intention to shock.

In 1922 Mae announced she was writing *The Hussy* in collaboration with Adeline Leitzbach, whose credits included vaudeville sketches, silent movie scripts and plays. Nothing further was heard of the project for several years, for Timony recognized the lack of potential in *The Hussy* and began searching for another idea or script.

In 1924, while representing John J. Byrne of East Orange, New Jersey, in a lawsuit, he was surprised and delighted to find his client was coauthor of a play, *Following the Fleet,* which seemed a strong possibility for Mae. For $300 plus a $10 hat for Byrne's wife, Timony bought the rights from Byrne and his shadowy collaborator, Ted McClean. Once in control of the material, Timony turned it over to Mae and Adeline Leitzbach for a rewrite.

In Mae's reminiscences this project had an entirely different origin. According to Mae, after the Shuberts announced they were searching for a play in which to star her, Matilda urged her to begin writing a role for herself. "My mother was always behind me, pushin' me, believin' in me ever since I was little. She said, 'Dear, you always fix up all your characters so much that I know you can write your own play.' The trouble was I didn't have an idea."

The way Mae told it, inspiration struck one day when her driver, encountering a midtown traffic jam, took one of the less crowded streets along the waterfront. There she spotted many prostitutes and sailors, including one heavily rouged and mascaraed whore who caught Mae's imagination. The woman looked as if she'd slept in her skirt, the heels of her shoes were run over and she wore a ninety-eight-cent turban atop which was at least $300 worth of bird of paradise feathers. The woman had a sailor on each arm, and as the car was passing, she threw back her head and gave what Mae described as "a bum's laugh."

Mae could not forget the scene, and she even dreamed about this fifty-cent prostitute with the bird of paradise turban. She couldn't understand her obsession. (Later, when she became interested in extrasensory perception, Mae concluded the Forces were informing her that this was the woman she had been born to play.)

Then, so her story went, she was seized by a writing frenzy, scribbling dialogue and scenes on napkins, the backs of envelopes, the white space in newspaper ads—any odd scrap of paper that came to hand. She assembled her output and let Timony's secretaries type it up as *The Albatross.* Mae's mother and Timony read her work and liked it so much they wanted to produce it themselves, but Mae felt obligated to show it to the Shuberts. Not wanting to impose upon their friendship, she assumed her mother's middle name and combined the first two letters of her given name with the last two of her surname to create the pseudonym Jane Mast.

The manuscript was assigned to a reader, who, J. J. Shubert confided to Mae, leaned toward Shakespeare. It was read and rejected. Mae's mother and Timony enthusiastically undertook to produce it. They approached several directors, who had the temerity to suggest that they guide Mae in rewriting the script to provide more conventional construction. One also assured Mae that she had made a fatal dramatic error in bringing a jazz band onstage so she could sing and dance. "You'll never recapture the audience for the serious stuff," he told her.

Finally, the play was submitted to Edward Elsner, who, Mae wrote, was already recognized for directing such diverse talents as the Barrymores, Gaby Deslys, Maude Adams, Pauline Frederick and Julia Marlowe. Hearing his credentials, Mae thought he might be too highbrow. His appearance did nothing to reassure her. He wore an agony cape, a long shroudlike garment which was ordinarily restricted to melodramas. She was repelled by his "very thin lips like surgical scars," which he drew back to reveal "dry teeth."

"Luckily he'd broken his glasses so he hadn't had a chance to read my play," she told a friend. "I offered to read it to him. That came easy to me. After all, I wrote it." Elsner proved an enthusiastic audience. "He was a gay old dear," Mae said, "so he was open to fresh ideas and experimentation. After readin' two acts, I asked if he wanted to hear the third. 'N' he said, 'Every word, every syllable of it!'" Mae knew then that she had found her director. Through Elsner, Timony and Matilda involved C. W. Morganstern, for whom Mae had worked at the Family Theater in Pittsburgh. Morganstern, an aspiring New York producer, and Timony formed the Moral Producing Company (!), enlisting as angels for the venture businessmen Max Kolmes and Harry Cohn. (This was not the same Cohn who would head Columbia Pictures.)

Elsner told Mae that all stars had a special aura, but she had something unique. He could describe it only as a sexual quality. He kept talking about how she exuded sex, sex, sex. *Low* sex.

"The way he said it, it sounded like the best kind," she said. He kept repeating this until Mae came up with a new title. "I'm gonna call my play *Sex*," she informed Elsner.

"If we only dared."

"I'll dare."

She said Elsner predicted her play would change the American theater. He felt it was new, fresh, just what Broadway had been waiting for. Mae admired his direction. According to her, he would simply say that at a certain point something was needed and she would come up with it. What he did, she later realized, was to prod her into thinking of the unexpected.

"Good theater," she wrote in her autobiography, "is not what is expected, but what surprises." She surprised even herself when she unintentionally developed her trademark. She was swaying and moving her hips when she asked Elsner what to do to heighten a particular scene. He told her just to continue what she was doing—rotating her hips. That was easy for her since she wore eight-inch platform shoes to give herself height and the swaying helped her keep her balance.

The show was scheduled to try out in New London, Connecticut. Opening night was discouraging. Approximately eighty-five people showed up, and it looked as if the title had been a miscalculation on Mae's part. She insisted on herding patrons from the balcony down into the orchestra with the rest of the audience. Even so, she managed to get few of the expected laughs. Timony was so discouraged he suggested they pay the theater owner for the house and use it for rehearsals rather than performances. But the manager refused to agree to this arrangement.

Next afternoon, when Mae arrived at the theater, a line of sailors snaked around the block, waiting to get tickets for the matinee. The fleet, having discovered her play, packed the house. Such a mob appeared for the evening show that the manager brought in kitchen chairs and then sold standing room to the overflow.

The sailors liked not only the title but also the story, which dealt with a Montreal prostitute, Margie Lamont, who followed the British fleet. In the first act she becomes involved with a suave New York blackmailer. This city slicker lures a member of New York's old society into his apartment, slips knockout drops into her drink and, after compromising her, begins to extort large sums of money from her. Margie, who is the proverbial whore with a heart of gold, pities the socialite and arranges her escape—only to be accused by the woman of being a part of the blackmail scheme. Heart of gold or not, Margie turns vengeful. In retaliation she seduces the society woman's naïve young son, who proposes marriage. Then, at the last moment, Margie proves herself a sweet kid after all. Though it hurts her, she renounces the society boy and follows the fleet to Trinidad.

Seeing the sailors' reaction, John Cort, who had come up from New York, insisted on paying off Earl Carroll's production of *White Cargo* to rush *Sex* into the theater he owned on Sixty-third Street. How had the tryout turned from a flop to a hit overnight? Explained Mae: "Mouth-to-mouth advertising—which is the best kind."

No metropolitan newspaper would accept advertising including the title *Sex*, a word Mae said previously had been used only in conjunction with such unerotic phrases as "the fair sex" and "the opposite sex" or in medical books. She claimed the management was able to place ads in *The New York Times* and other newspapers only under the discreet listing of "MAE WEST in THAT CERTAIN PLAY."

That was Mae's story, and she told it and retold it until she undoubtedly believed it herself. But on April 28, 1926, two days after the opening, the following ads can be found in *The New York Times:*

63rd	**SEX**	with MAE WEST
DALY'S		
Street		
Eves. 8:30		Mat. Wed.
		& Sat. 2:30

and by July the management had been emboldened to add:

"BIGGEST SENSATION SINCE THE ARMISTICE!"
MAE WEST
in
SEX

According to Mae, the New York premiere was "a blockbuster with the audience," but the reviews described the audience as loosing "self-conscious guffaws" and "whooping, indeed a little more happily in those sadder moments when the affair degenerated into the moralistic and heroic."

Mae also related in her memoirs that after Walter Winchell mentioned her in his column, she "was a star in the legitimate theater." She omitted any reference to his review in which he called *Sex* "a vulgar affair . . . amateurish in script and cast . . . and relies on its sensationalism to cash in." (Oddly, *Sex* received a seal of approval from the play jury.)

How, one might ask, did a man who had directed the Barrymores, to say nothing of demure Maude Adams and brazen Gaby Deslys, make such a botch of things? He didn't. Elsner's earlier background lay in vaudeville, where, in 1917, he had written, directed and lighted a sensationalized dramatic sketch, *The Notorious Delphine*, whose story line bore a curious resemblance to the old tearjerker *Madame X*. In 1925 he directed *Cousin Sonia* on Broadway and followed it with *The House of Ussher* in January 1926, his last play before *Sex*. He was far from the distinguished director she later passed him off as.

Despite negative critical response, *Sex* began drawing at the box office, and a legal squabble developed over who deserved credit or discredit for its authorship. John J. Byrne filed suit in federal court, accusing the Moral Producing Company, Mae West, James Timony, producer Morganstern, John Cort and the 63rd Street Theater Ltd., Inc., of plagiarizing *Following the Fleet*. Byrne attempted to obtain an injunction preventing further performances and asked $500,000 damages.

Timony responded that he had bought only an idea from "the boy author," as he condescendingly referred to Byrne, for development by the Moral Producing Company. Mae, on the other hand, in her deposition stated the idea had been hers, that she had given it to Byrne, including the title, and had ordered him to write something on the order of *Rain*. But, she said, the results "so disgusted" her "with the obscenity and profanity" that she was forced to rewrite it completely. To add to the confusion, Adeline Leitzbach then popped up to claim she had collaborated with Mae and admitted that they had merely rewritten Byrne's script.

The case dragged through postponements and delays until March 1927, when Judge Charles W. Goddard handed down a dismissal of Byrne's suit, basing his decision on the odd puritanical premise that since both *Following the Fleet* and *Sex* were "probably designed for salacious appeal," no writer of a play of this nature could expect any support "when he does not come into court with clean hands."

The question of authorship in limbo, a row developed over financing. On July 16 Harry Cohn and Max Kolmes attempted to throw the Moral Producing Company into the hands of receivers, asserting that in return for investments they had received 40 percent of the company's stock but never had been able to gain access to the books.

With so much internal agitation and external scorn, it is surprising the play survived. But in its first week this cheaply put-together production earned a modest profit on its $8,000 box-office gross; by the fourth week the show was grossing $14,000; by the seventh, $16,500. *Sex* was the only production in a theater located above Columbus Circle to survive into the fall. Explaining its success, Mae said, "Everyone wants to write plays about a man 'n' women or men 'n' men. But my style is a woman among men—just the reverse of what's always been written, see? I found I showed to the greatest advantage when I kept the other parts straight and exaggerated my own."

In November, after *Sex* had run approximately thirty weeks, the *Daily Mirror,* the *Graphic* and other newspapers stepped up their campaign against it, sniping away at the play's tawdry situations, lurid lines and general sleaziness in an attempt to provoke police action. Behind the scenes Mae and Timony fervently hoped the newspapers would succeed. "Jim, that pinch would make headlines clear across the country," Mae said. She foresaw that people who never went to the theater would come out of curiosity. But *Sex* ran on and on at Daly's, showing no signs of closing or being closed. To relieve the boredom, Mae undertook a new project.

Disciplined by the long run and cut off from sexual adventure by the possessive Timony, Mae distracted herself by scribbling bits of dialogue for a new comedy-drama. For subject matter she drew on a group of female impersonators and chorus boys whose witty remarks, imitations of her and camping captured her fancy. When she took some of them to meet her mother, Matilda liked them as much as Mae did. "They'd do her hair 'n' nails and she'd have a great time," Mae said.

For her central character, she drew upon her acquaintance with a divorced man, the father of a child, who confided he was bisexual. Mae, who had been completely comfortable with the stereotyped mincing homosexual, had shrunk from this man's advances. Even as she did so, she became increasingly aware of the stresses to which society subjected such nonconformists. She decided to dramatize the subject.

After the script for *The Drag* had been assembled, Timony read it and envisioned even greater promotional possibilities and financial rewards for the new play than for *Sex*. Once again he approached C. W. Morganstern to serve as nominal producer and Edward Elsner to direct.

In a 1978 issue of *Studio* magazine, Tom Fulbright wrote of Mae and Timony's visit to "a dimly lit Village hangout for chorus girls and boys. . . . Word got out she was casting a play about homosexuals . . . and those kids really turned it on. . . . She did not stay long and before she left borrowed an order book from the waiter and personally wrote passes for everyone present, telling them to see her show [*Sex*] the following night and then stay for a regular tryout. Believe me, that is power when a star can write out 'Admit 1' and have over fifty people admitted to her play."

Although Mae's intentions may have been serious, her approach was decidedly sensational. Rehearsals began at Daly's 63rd Street Theater with a cast of twelve principals and an indeterminate number of female impersonators. Rumor was that Elsner had assisted with the construction and technical development of the play. It opened with a discussion between a doctor and a judge about the cause of homosexual orientation, not unlike the introductions included in pornographic films "to give them redeeming social value." But the vaudeville performer in Mae's nature was far stronger than the pamphleteer. The discussion was shallow, and she swiftly moved on to material she instinctively knew would intrigue and shock audiences.

In the first of these scenes, several characters simply got together to "dish the dirt" about others in the play, referring to males as "she" and "her" and using lines Mae had heard around dressing rooms for years. The second and, to 1920's audiences, most shocking episode involved a homosexual making a pass at one of the heterosexual males. The *pièce de résistance* was a big drag ball—which reviewers later compared to a nightclub revue—during which all types of males, including a cabdriver in women's clothes, sang, danced and camped.

Broadway was soon talking about *The Drag*'s unconventional rehearsals. *Variety* reported: ". . . Elsner permits the Our Sex [drag queens] to cavort and carry on as much as they like. Results are more natural and spontaneous." It was suggested that if admission could be charged for the rehearsals, most of the production's costs could be paid off before the out-of-town tryout.

The world premiere of *The Drag* was scheduled for Stamford, Connecticut, on January 28, 1927, but when the theater manager learned the nature of the attraction she had booked, she canceled the agreement. Timony and Morganstern scrambled around and finally arranged for their company to share the first three days of a split week with Minna Daily's Burlesquers at Poli's Park Theater in Bridgeport.

Everything possible was done to insure the success of the play. To attract crowds, the management inserted a two-for-the-price-of-one coupon in the city's newspapers; the manager of Poli's Park called a press conference to announce that *The Drag* was "clean and earnest" and had received the local police censor's seal of approval.

For those who weren't looking for "clean and earnest" theatrical fare, billers plastered the city with three-sheets describing the offering as "A Homosexual Comedy" and "The Male Version of *The Captive*," the latter a drama about lesbianism.

Across the street, positioned so that riders on the railroad caught a clear view, was an enormous banner reading: THE DRAG by the author of *Sex*. MORE SENSATIONAL THAN *RAIN* or *THE CAPTIVE*.

Nonetheless, Mae, Timony and their cohorts were uneasy about the play's reception. When asked why no theater had been booked in Manhattan, Timony said that all future plans depended on how the show went opening night—and opening night went very well indeed.

The Park Theater began turning away would-be customers at seven-thirty, causing Mae and Timony to regret the two-for-one lure. That the audience was on the rowdy side was blamed on the fact that most of them were burlesque regulars who traditionally gave "nance humor" a raucous reception. During the scene in which the homosexual made advances toward the straight male, one middle-aged couple banged up their seats and stamped out of the theater. It was the lone example of public outrage. Applause at the final curtain was encouraging.

One newspaperman reported that when he stopped in a restaurant, first-nighters could talk of nothing but the strange carryings-on at the Park. Only one or two patrons, who had assumed Mae was appearing in her own play, were disappointed. James B. Sinnott, secretary of the New York Police Department, after seeing the show in Bridgeport, declined to speculate on what action New York police would take if *The Drag* ventured into Manhattan.

The play's *succès de scandale* encouraged the company to move to Paterson, New Jersey, for further tryouts. The day before the troupe arrived there Chief of Police John Tracy issued a statement reassuring his constituents that all offensive lines and actions would be cut and that a representative of the department would monitor each performance. The Paterson engagement was financially successful and without incident.

No serious problems arose until February 10, when the show was about to open at the Opera House in Bayonne, New Jersey. Outside, Police Chief Cornelius O'Neill's reserves kept order among the block-long lines of people waiting to buy seats, while inside, O'Neill announced to a full house that the play was banned and that patrons should obtain a refund.

Faced with this prior restraint, Timony and Morganstern threatened to obtain an injunction to prevent further harassment, but several events discouraged the producers from pursuing this course. *Variety*'s Bridgeport review was virulent. "The whole play is a cheap and shabby appeal to sensationalism, done without intelligence or taste . . ." wrote *Rush*. Later he observed:

> This whole venture is without justification and merits the un-
> qualified condemnation of the public, the theater and the au-
> thorities, not to speak of calling for the prompt intervention of the
> police. . . . This reporter doesn't believe Mae West wrote it. It has
> all the earmarks of being the work of a boss hostler in a livery
> stable.

In addition, John S. Sumner's Society of Prevention of Vice warned New York's playboy mayor James J. Walker that if *The Drag* opened in New York, he would interpret it as an invitation to invoke censorship. Mae's narcissism allowed her to remain untouched by the savage attacks on her work. "Every knock is a boost," she maintained. "It makes me better known." In her mind there was no difference between notoriety and fame. She boasted that the production had earned back its investment in Bridgeport and Paterson and that she and Timony had acquiesced to demands they not bring it to Manhattan because it would "upset the city."

In truth, they had their own reasons for closing the show. They needed to devote their attention to a far more pressing problem.

6

Throughout its run *Sex* was subjected to harassment from bluenoses. Growing increasingly aware of the appeal of the forbidden, Mae and Timony did everything in their power to tantalize theatergoers without actually bringing down the wrath of the police.

They let it be known unofficially that they had supplemented the "original script" with a "number two version" which was milder and used whenever they were under scrutiny by reformers. Mae, who gloried in any kind of intrigue, delighted in tweaking the nose of authority, while Timony became arrogant. When, after a six-month Broadway run, a *Variety* mugg asked him one evening which version the company was using that performance, Timony, fully aware that he was speaking to the press, smirked and said, "The original."

Mae attempted to attract repeat attendance by varying the double entendres from performance to performance. She also tried to think up ways to lure more women into the audience since the play was attracting an approximately 80 percent male clientele.

District Attorney Joab Banton grew increasingly angry over the publicity and rumors surrounding various "dirty plays" that were on Broadway. Still, Mayor Jimmy Walker, who had chosen an actress for his mistress, restrained the DA from taking any drastic steps. Then, in February 1927, when Mae was in her forty-second week as the star of *Sex*, Walker left for a Cuban vacation.

Acting Mayor Joseph B. "Holy Joe" McKee harbored none of Walker's tolerance for human weakness and gave Banton the signal to proceed with the crusade to banish nudity and obscenity from New York stages. Beginning on February 5, plainclothesmen began monitoring performances of several productions, and on the ninth the police burst into the theaters where *Sex*, *The Captive* and *The Virgin Man* were playing and arrested various actors, producers and directors.

Herded into a Black Maria, Mae found other performers so fleet of foot that all seats were filled and she was obliged to stand during the ride downtown. Accustomed to her own chauffeur-driven limousine, she was still seething while waiting to be booked.

To make matters worse, actors from *The Captive* and *Sex* started casting aspersions on the merits of each other's productions. Eventually Mae and Helen Menken, a distinguished dramatic actress who played a lesbian in *The Captive*, exchanged insults, which reached a peak when Mae exhibited unexpected prejudice by sniffing, "Well, at least we're normal!"

After a night in the Jefferson Market Women's Prison, Mae was released on bail, looking forward to the increased business she was certain would materialize in the wake of the scandal-filled headlines. Nor was she disappointed. In spite of promises of local authorities that the play would not be raided again that week, attorneys for *Sex* wisely obtained a Supreme Court injunction against interference. Timony ordered the box-office personnel to hold onto seats regularly allotted to cut-rate brokers. Before curtain time the tickets had been snapped up at full price. When a police captain, a lieutenant and seven uniformed officers showed up at Daly's that night to raid the play, the restraining order stopped them.

On Tuesday, the fifteenth, at a hearing in the West Side court, the attorney for Mae, producer Morganstern and twenty other actors in *Sex* rejected a proposal for "implied immunity" in return for withdrawing the production. *Sex* continued running under the Supreme Court injunction restraining the DA's men. To avoid proceedings that would have interfered with the evening performance, Sex's attorney abandoned plans to fight for dismissal of charges. Bail was continued. Thursday, the seventeenth, Supreme Court Justice Bijur accepted the application of Sex's representatives for the case to be heard by a jury rather than by three judges, and on the twenty-seventh he ordered trial by jury in general sessions. His reasoning: twelve men from different walks of life would be in closer touch with community standards of morals and decency than three judges.

Three days later the grand jury indicted not only Mae, Morganstern and twenty actors but also Timony, the Moral Producing Company and John Cort and his theatrical corporation. The charge: producing an immoral show and maintaining a public nuisance.

Commenting on the accusations, Mae said she thought Sex was "one of the cleanest shows on Broadway. There's no nudity and no obscene language. . . ." She admitted some script changes had been considered but insisted the original lines had been retained.

At the request of the prosecutor the trial was delayed until March 28. Meanwhile, on the twenty-first, Sex voluntarily closed its eleven-month run. Spokesmen for the defendants said their decision partially was based on Judge Goddard's prejudicial remarks in dismissing John Byrne's plagiarism suit. Mae's ill health was also given as a reason. Morganstern said, "Miss West is tired out after a year's work in the play. She was particularly unnerved by developments of the past months and is in need of a rest."

Mae was unavailable to the press. But at the trial she laughed and seemed untroubled by the prosecution's claim that in return for immunity, she had offered to testify before the grand jury that Timony had turned over the presidency of the Moral Producing Company to Morganstern shortly before the raid in an attempt to escape arrest. Nor did she exhibit concern when Assistant DA James Garrett Wallace again accused her of altering and spicing up the script after the play jury had accepted it and she assumed authorities had relaxed their vigilance.

For her court appearances Mae changed costumes daily, favoring a variety of black satin numbers—some with georgette tops and satin panels, others with bugle beads—modish, fur-trimmed, wraparound coats and cloche hats or turbans. Timony was dapper with a fresh flower in his lapel each morning.

During the parade of witnesses for the prosecution Mae frequently glanced at the ceiling incredulously, whether the testimony came from the disgruntled author of *Following the Fleet*, John Byrne, singed financial angel Harry Cohn, who claimed he'd objected to "the language and Mae's coochie dance," or playwright Adeline Leitzbach, who complained that although her name had appeared on the copyright claim registration as author, it had been absent from all advertising.

Sergeant Patrick Keneally of the Mid-Town Vice Squad provided the comic highlight when, aided by copious notes, he proceeded to recite ribald lines and mimic postures and deliveries of the actors. Spectators also laughed when Mae demonstrated her humility by modestly looking at the floor as her lawyer made favorable comparisons between *Sex* and other works—such as *A Tale of Two Cities, Hamlet* and the Bible.

During the trial Mae and her codefendants behaved as if they felt certain of acquittal—especially after John Cort was exonerated on two counts before the case went to the jury and charges against Morganstern and the Moral Producing Company of maintaining a public nuisance were dismissed.

Their mood changed, however, when the jury returned for clarification of whether it was necessary to find the entire performance corrupting to the morals of youth in order to convict. The judge ignored the question of possible redeeming social value and ruled that isolated lines and stage business could be regarded as sufficiently corrupting to warrant conviction.

As the jury filed out to resume deliberations, Timony reached into his pocket, extracted rosary beads and began silent prayers. Leading man Barry O'Neill fidgeted and grew red-faced, while Mae put up a brave front, uttering a series of soothing reassurances that they would all be acquitted.

Approximately five and one-half hours later the jury returned a guilty verdict on the count of producing an immoral play. Sentencing was set for April 19. While information was taken and arrangements were made for bail, tears welled in O'Neill's eyes, and he buried his face in his hands as a compassionate Mae soothingly rubbed his back.

Outside the court Assistant District Attorney Wallace complacently told the press, "This verdict vindicates the theory that dirty plays successfully can be prosecuted before juries and the stage can be kept clean without censorship."

Mae told newsmen, "If anybody needs a dirty play, they ought to call Wallace for suggestions! He brought our conviction. *Sex,* as given at Daly's 63rd Street Theater, was a work of art."

Mae, Timony and Morganstern were sentenced to ten-day jail terms—and she and Timony were fined $500 each. *Sex* had operated at a break-even point of $2,200 weekly, after which there was a sixty-thirty split with Cort and 10 percent to Morganstern during the eleven-month run. (Cohn and Kolmes had been bought out.) For their 30 percent, Mae and Timony averaged $2,700 a week. Toting up her profits and estimating she had reaped $1 million worth of free publicity from the trial, Mae concluded, "Considering what *Sex* got me, a few days in the pen 'n' a five-hundred-dollar fine ain't too bad a deal."

Given one day's credit for the night she was incarcerated preceding her transfer to Welfare Island plus one day off for good behavior, she served only eight days. Mae's account of her experiences in prison was so embroidered with Westian fantasy no one could hope to determine what actually happened. But if her stay accomplished nothing else, the mandatory shower under the watchful eye of the prison matron and the subsequent physical examination should lay to rest the persistent rumor that for sixty years Mae masqueraded as the world's most successful female impersonator.

The way Mae told it, the warden quickly perceived that rough cotton underwear was too abrasive for her delicate skin and ordered that she be allowed to keep her silk teddies. He also assigned her to a private room and took her riding in the evening. On her second day there she claimed that he asked her to visit other women prisoners who were fans of hers. Mae felt she couldn't refuse.

Characteristically she converted a humiliating experience into whimsical publicity. Contemporary newspaper reports had Mae assigned to the laundry, but she later told reporters it was the library—where she dusted books. "They was in such bad shape and so dull that I wrote an article for *Liberty* magazine. Knocked down a thousand bucks for it. I donated that check to the prison to found the Mae West Memorial Library," she said. "Wonder whatever happened to it. I heard that when they had some big-league hoods servin' time over there, they tore up my books 'n' burned 'em to fry the steaks they had sent in. To do a thing like that shows a lack of class."

Seemingly there was no stopping her. She amused the press by finagling an invitation as guest of honor at a Welfare Island charity luncheon sponsored by the Women's National Democratic Club in association with the Penology Delinquency Division of the New York Federation of Women's Clubs.

While incarcerated, Mae began scribbling bits of dialogue and remembered jokes ("He may have been a halfback at Notre Dame, but he's a fullback to this dame") to be fitted into an exposé of beauty contest promoters and contestants that would serve as her next vehicle. She came up with a promising title—*The Wicked Age*—which turned out to be the only promising thing about it.

The show went into rehearsal with a skeletal script the first week in July. Mae, as was her custom, encouraged performers to improvise material, which, if it pleased her, she kept in. The story told of the adventures of a headstrong jazz baby, Bridgehampton's Babe Carson. Defying her puritanical aunt and uncle for forbidding her to visit a roadhouse, Babe tosses a wild party in their home. When they return to find couples engaged in hot petting all over their living room, they throw Babe out.

In the second act Babe gets drunk and enters a beauty contest, hoping to embarrass her relatives. In spite of the promoters' schemes to cheat her out of the title, Babe triumphs.

The third act finds Babe living in New York, cashing in on her celebrity by endorsing elixirs for the liver and the kidneys and enjoying an active love life. As one critic pointed out, these activities apparently made her so prosperous she kept a private jazz band around her apartment when she felt like singing such numbers as "Baby's Kisses" and "You Can Neck 'Em."

Actress Wilva Davis, fresh from Minnesota and playing her first professional role, found rehearsals bewildering. Fifty years later she said with bemusement, "The setup was unusual. These strange characters who had put money up kept coming in with Mr. Timony. We got the impression they were big-time gangsters. And that was funny because Mr. Timony prayed a lot. One minute he'd be living it up with these rough characters. A few minutes later he'd be off in the corner somewhere saying his beads.

"Miss West was always pleasant but aloof. After all, she was the star, and that was the tradition in those days. And Edward Elsner was the director, but this was sort of the end of his career. He wasn't young, and I got the impression he'd given up. He'd suggest something to Miss West; then she'd go over and they'd whisper until he'd cave in and give her what she wanted. Always—except in the scene where she won the beauty contest. He insisted on draping her with a shawl because, you know, she was pretty plump. He was firm about that."

If rehearsals were unpromising, the pre-Broadway tour was disheartening. The production staggered along receiving withering attacks, partly because it challenged puritanical attitudes and partly because it was theatrically inept. The Long Branch (New Jersey) *Daily Record*'s pithy review consisted of twenty-five words: "Gross, disgusting, tiresome, utterly futile vulgarity, without a single excusing feature or reason for being. The Broadway theater management is to be pitied, not blamed."

A less self-involved personality would have been destroyed by the savagery of the New York notices. The *Evening Post* dubbed Mae "the matronly jackanapes," while the *World* described her as a "cheery, pudgy, straw-headed little figure with a hoarse voice." The *Tribune* tolerantly noted: ". . . if viewed as the Cherry Sisters used to be viewed . . . that is to say, so terrible that it is actually funny, it might even amuse many for whom it was evidently not intended." The *Times* dispatched the production, saying it was "in the best Mae West school of playwriting and acting—that of just saying one word after another with no regard for any sort of technique and less for common sense."

After the fourth week the show closed, and Mae's plans to recast and redirect it came to nothing when Equity refused to allow reopening without posting new bonds.

The genesis of *Diamond Lil,* as Mae told it, was her recollection of another, slightly more elevated whore than the one who sported bird of paradise feathers. This second prostitute, who also had a bum's laugh, worked Coney Island. Her technique was to throw back her head and laugh raucously to attract attention; then, having established eye contact with prospective clients, she'd slip cards to those who looked well heeled. Mae often said she became obsessed with these characters but was lazy about creating plays around them. Had her mother not prodded her into action, she might never have turned out the scripts. That was Mae's story. And since *Diamond Lil* would quickly have been forgotten without benefit of her dazzling personality, she has, in a sense, a moral claim as a cocreator of the play.

But the truth is that writer-director-actor Mark Linder had written and appeared in a Bowery sketch called *The Frame Up* in a touring burlesque unit, *The Passing Revue*, in 1915. Mark and his brother Jack, an agent for vaudevillians, decided that an expanded version of the sketch had the potential of a Broadway hit. Mark called the three-act comedy-melodrama *Chatham Square*.

Jack sent the script to Laura Tintel of the Paul Scott Agency, and Tintel contacted Timony. He was enthusiastic, but Mae was leery about associating herself with the Linders because they were small-time showmen. When she finally agreed to meet them, she announced she had written a play with a similar setting and style and suggested combining the two scripts. To secure her services as star, Mark agreed to split the royalties fifty-fifty. Mae added gag lines and at first suggested retitling the script *Diamond Dora* but sacrificed alliteration and changed it to *Diamond Lil,* in a sentimental nod toward her father's pet name for her mother—Champagne Til. Contradicting Mae, *Variety* noted that a Diamond Lil, who had hailed from Chicago and sported a diamond in her front tooth, had been a denizen of the Bowery and Chatham Square district in the 1890's.

"The Linders got a break when they hooked up with me," Mae asserted with her usual modesty. "I'm the one who brings people into the theater." Recognizing her strength, she saw to it that she got what she wanted in terms of production. At auditions she was smitten by an actor named Jack LaRue. Having heard the role of Juarez, the Spanish villain, was available, LaRue had studied a Spanish-English dictionary before going to read for Mae. After throwing around a few newly mastered Spanish words, he played a hot love scene with her which she enjoyed. At the end of it she complimented him, "Not bad. Not bad. In fact, you could be plenty sensational."

The Linders and Timony were reluctant to meet LaRue's salary, but Mae insisted on having him. "The funny thing is," LaRue later admitted, "she could have had me for practically nothing after our first—uh—encounter. I was in love with her and didn't particularly care who knew about it."

LaRue wasn't the only one. The production was 50 percent financed by Owney Madden, a big-time bootlegger who dabbled in show business. Although a racketeer, Madden was the most amiable of men socially and enjoyed the company of showpeople such as Mae and Fanny Brice. Occasionally even Cole and Linda

Porter accepted his invitations to dine at a gangster restaurant downtown. They saw only the good side of his chameleonlike personality.

Like many other underworld characters, he found Mae physically attractive and was amused by her quick wit. "I don't know why mob guys all seemed to go for me, but they did," she mused. "And since a lot of 'em were tall, dark and hairy, I liked them, too."

One of Madden's boyhood friends, who now worked for him, was George Raft. During the run of *Diamond Lil* he regularly dropped by the Royale to pick up his boss's share of the cash. Mae liked what she saw. He had black hair, shiny as patent leather, a sharp, slightly sinister face and the grace of a panther.

She invited him into her dressing room, and their affair began. Timony, who continued to guard her with watchdog ferocity, was unable to scare off the mobster's courier as easily as he did acrobats, actors, cabdrivers and others who caught his mistress's wandering eye. Mae and Raft had strong sex drives, and they fulfilled their desire—one way or another—in her dressing room, hotel rooms, Owney Madden's sleek bulletproof black Packard, elevators and even a broom closet. "It was love on the run with half the buttons undone," Mae said airily. "The results were like a high-speed film—blurred but excitin'." Looking back on their affair from the 1970's, Mae admitted, "He was one guy I woulda married—if I coulda."

In spite of the play's eventual success, the rehearsal period of *Diamond Lil* was fraught with difficulty. During the first two weeks three directors came and went before an experienced middle-aged man named Ira Hards took over. He had made his debut under the aegis of Charles Frohman in 1903 and was fresh from successfully directing *Dracula* on Broadway. He proved equally adept at pacing the company to the star's demands and creating memorable stage pictures in his blocking of the crowd scenes with which the play abounds.

One member of the cast was Harold Garry, later Gary, who went on to enjoy a long career in the theater, earning acting awards on three continents, including a Tony for his performance in Arthur Miller's *The Price* on Broadway. *Diamond Lil* marked Gary's professional debut. "I never went to acting school. I learned from other actors," he said. "And I always give Mae

West credit for teaching me never to take the tempo from any other actor. Once you attain a pace, you keep it. In other words, if I'm playing a placid character who has occasion to become angry, I must get angry in placid terms, not in terms of the man I'm arguing with. It's a kind of subtle thing, but I learned it from her."

Gary was hired to play the Bowery Terror, a saloon bouncer, and to understudy Jack LaRue's Spanish lover. "The original play was by Mark Linder," Gary says. "It was based on actual people out of Suicide McGurk's Hall, which got its name because so many girls committed suicide there. It was a nest of white slaves, pimps and thieves. Linder wasn't a literary talent, but he knew how to translate what he'd seen to the stage.

"He wrote it as a sketch and expanded it. Then she began rewriting the script, and before you knew it, she'd appropriated it. As she rewrote, she obscured her character's connection with the white slave ring for obvious reasons. Of course, she gave herself a lot of boyfriends. She made Lil one of those improbable women no guy can resist."

Diamond Lil opened for a shakedown at Shubert's Teller in Brooklyn, earning an impressive $8,000 during the traditionally lean Easter week. It came to the Royale on April 9, 1928. This mixture of comedy and melodrama was seasoned with prostitutes, madams, dope pushers, addicts, shoplifters and uptown slumming parties—to say nothing of songs and dances. In spite of her early stand against being responsible for her sister, Mae again acceded to her mother's plea and cast Beverly (who briefly had adopted the stage name Osborne) as the distraught young girl who had been "ruined" and whom Mae comforted by telling her, "When a girl goes wrong, men usually go right after her." Again, Beverly's fondness for champagne interfered with her performing and caused another temporary rift between the sisters.

"I'm one of the finest women who ever walked the streets" and numerous other witty lines delighted critics, who were reluctant to admit they had enjoyed the play but found it impossible to resist Mae's high-voltage personality any longer.

The New York Times finally conceded Mae was "a good actress." The *World* described her as "a mighty figure in the fashions of those days [who] played her rough, hard-boiled beauty with a sort of phlegmatic quietness, almost a sulkiness, that was far more telling and effective than the loud pseudo, out-of-the-northwest-corner-of-the-mouth methods of many actresses when they essay a tough character." Percy Hammond, who once had called her "the world's worst actress," raved:

> The result of Miss West's reformation is that the Theatre Royale is crowded at each performance of *Diamond Lil* with persons anxious to encourage a conscience-smitten transgressor in her desire to be meritricious [*sic*]. It is one of the "hits" of the waning season and vies in money-making values with the most prosperous output of dramatists who have never been in jail. Miss West, its star and author, recently under lock and key, is now more admired by her public than is Jane Cowl, Lynn Fontanne, Helen Hayes or Eva Le Gallienne.

Among the weekly critics, Charles Brackett's response in the *New Yorker* was more tempered:

> As you can see, this isn't even dime-novel material. It's Hearst Sunday Supplement stuff. Miss West has, however, been uncannily clever in choosing her period. With no attempt at historical accuracy, *Diamond Lil* takes a certain flashy brassiness which reached a climax in the underworld of New York about that time as few subtler playwrights could have done it. Pure trash, or rather impure trash though it is, I wouldn't miss *Diamond Lil* if I were you.

Of all the reviewers, Robert Garland of the *Evening Telegram* placed the most glittering jewel in Mae's critical crown. He pronounced:

> So regal is Miss West's manner, so assured is her artistry, so devastating are her charms in the eyes of all red-blooded men, so blonde, so beautiful, so buxom is she that she makes Miss Ethel Barrymore look like the late lamented Mr. Bert Savoy.

After *Lil*'s premiere Mae became an authentic star on the legitimate stage instead of a freak attraction playing principally to male audiences. Society leaders, intellectuals, sports personalities, newspaper writers and vaudevillians mingled with other Broadway habitués who dropped backstage to drink near beer out of the working tap in the saloon set. Ironically the world's wickedest woman abstained or sipped health drinks.

Mae greeted her visitors still wearing her stage makeup and her Gay Nineties garb. She was polite to everyone but encouraged the most outrageous characters to remain, shrewdly storing away impromptu quips and humorous or colorful behavior for later use.

Although she enjoyed these backstage soirees, she was sometimes puzzled about the identity of her guests. Since she read little except material that might provide ideas to incorporate into her productions, she was unfamiliar with many of the celebrities who arrived. Her friends were amused, but not surprised, one evening when that superb light comedienne Ina Claire, the toast of Broadway, sent word she was coming back. So informed, Mae shrugged. "Okay. Send her in. But who is she anyway?"

Another evening British producer C. B. Cochran, actress Constance Collier and the newly established playwright-actor-songwriter Noel Coward visited. Cochran attempted to talk to Mae about allowing him to present *Diamond Lil* in London, but she was more interested in touting him on to her newest creation, *Pleasure Man*, which was trying out in the Bronx. When Cochran persisted in returning to the subject of *Lil*, Mae turned her attention to Coward. "Noel," she said, "you'll be crazy about the story of my new one. There are all these drag queens and this guy, the lead, who—" Cochran interrupted and again attempted to talk about his possible presentation of *Lil*. Exasperated, Mae turned on him, crying, "But you don't understand! In this show, I got seventeen *real live fairies on stage!*" Her visitors bade Mae good-bye and left in silence. Halfway down the alley, the dignified and somewhat grandiloquent Collier broke the silence by saying, "What I like about her is she's so reee-uhl!"

On one occasion Harold Gary brought Jack Dempsey backstage to renew his acquaintance with Mae. Mae and Dempsey were so obviously glad to see each other that Gary left quietly, closing the door behind him.

Next day both Timony and Joe Skinner, one of Mae's lovers who was in the cast, were angry at Gary for bringing the former heavyweight champion around. That evening, during the sham fight between Skinner and Gary, Skinner began throwing real punches, and a genuine fistfight broke out. Mae witnessed it from the wings and after the curtain came down said, "Keep it in, boys! Keep it in!"

They had no opportunity. When Timony saw Skinner's reaction, he became suspicious and fired him. "The upshot was I got Teddy Klein, who changed his name to Teddy Lawler, Skinner's job," Gary says. "And before you knew it, Miss West had him in the kip, replacing Skinner, alternating with Jack LaRue, George Raft and a few others—when she wasn't busy with Timony."

During the run of the play Mae arrived at her dressing room around 2:00 P.M., matinee or not, to attend, so she said, to her writing, business correspondence and other career duties. She demanded total privacy. Timony was happy, thinking she was concentrating on her playwriting. Mae was happy because she could meet her lovers with no worry that he would intrude. She had impressed upon him that even so much as a "hello" disturbed her concentration and made it impossble for her to do any creating that day.

She sincerely believed sex was good for her health, and her health was of prime importance to her. She never drank more than an occasional glass of beer and smoked cigarettes only when a role called for it. "She was on a health diet before Gloria Swanson ever heard of one," Harold Gary said. "You never saw her in nightclubs. She was a very private person. Really a woman of many paradoxes, complications and contradictions. Selfish? Yes. Generous? Yes. Pearl Regay, the star of *Rose Marie* and other musicals who was down on her luck, told me Mae paid all of her bills and never let anybody know it. And old fighters held her in high regard for her financial help. She was like a queen to them.

"But all those things wouldn't have meant anything if she hadn't been able to deliver when she got onstage. As a professional I have utmost respect for her professionalism. She knew what she was doing onstage. And she did it every performance."

As *Diamond Lil* gained increasing stature, Mae grabbed more and more credit. She even became embroiled in an argument with Robert Sterling over the show's theme song, "Diamond Lil." When Sterling refused to name her as coauthor, she retaliated by dropping the number and substituting "Heart of the Bowery."

In a *Variety* interview she contended she alone deserved writing credit for her hit. "Anyone could tell I wrote *Diamond Lil*," she said. "I only go into a play where I can be myself and strut my stuff. I know how I want to walk 'n' talk, show off my figure 'n' my looks.

"I bring one man after another into the play to revolve around me, and no one else can. I have five men in love with me in *Diamond Lil,* and most authors can't keep up one love interest."

Jack Linder responded, "We let her do some rewriting and gave her 50 percent of the royalties to get her as the star, but Mark wrote the script." Linder also boasted that he owned the play, had Mae under contract and held the lease with the Shuberts and Chanins for the theater.

Linder was contradicted soon after when he tried to bring Mae before the Equity Council on charges of unprofessional conduct. The council advised him to settle his differences with Mae privately since Equity regarded her as part author and a principal stockholder. As the feud continued, Mae began declaring Mark had not written a line of the play. On one occasion she called him into the presence of a *Variety* reporter and browbeat him into saying he was responsible only for "atmosphere and local color."

"Local color and atmosphere." She sniffed. "There ain't any way you can copyright them."

As Mark was leaving, she said, "The Linders want to stick their names on anything because they never got such a break before. And after I get rid of them," she correctly predicted, "they'll never do another worthwhile thing."

With all the controversy swirling around her, Mae found it difficult to concentrate on filling out the skeletal script of a play she called *Five-a-Day*, *The Stage* and finally *Pleasure Man*. The producer, Carl Reed, Lillian Russell's former manager, described it as "the saga of the coffee and cake vaudeville circuit." The sparse story punctuated with variety acts told of a compulsive Don Juan whose "love 'em and leave 'em" style led to his murder.

During the first week of rehearsal no parts were permanently assigned. Cast members played whatever role they wished. The first three or four days resembled an open-end audition. Occasionally Mae or the director would ask an actress reading the leading woman to take over as the slavey. Often Mae would speak to someone privately, and soon he or she would disappear.

Not everyone was so unfortunate. Alan Brooks was selected for the title role. Stan Stanley, a former vaudevillian, waved a long, thick document for photographers as Mae announced she had placed him under contract and professed to be dumbfounded that the Shuberts or Ziegfeld had overlooked this major talent. One lucky novice was chosen to play half of a married ballroom dance team. It was this innocent young beauty whose ambivalence about her planned tryst with the Pleasure Man would make her and her husband suspects in the castration-murder.

In 1928 the actress was happy to be cast, but half a century later her feelings had changed. After an initial phone call requesting an interview for this book, the woman had her telephone disconnected. Reached a month later, when service had been reinstated, she reluctantly agreed to talk, but only on condition her name be omitted.

The Ingenue said, "I was in *Pleasure Man,* but these days most of my friends don't know anything about my connection with that notorious production. At the time Miss West was known as the World's Wickedest White Woman, but she insisted upon strict decorum between men and women backstage.

"The production setup was most peculiar. There was no script and at first no sides. They handed us scraps of paper from time to time, and eventually these worked into sides. But mine had nothing for me at the climactic moment in the third act when I slipped away from the big drag ball downstairs and went upstairs to Alan Brooks's room for a rendezvous. There I found him dead, sexually mutilated. This was the infamous castration scene.

"My problem as an actress was that I had to return downstairs and tell what I'd discovered. But none of my lines had been written. The first time we came to that moment in rehearsal, I said, 'Miss West, I have no words. What do I do? What do I say?'

"She said, 'What would you do?'

"I said, 'It's not something I've thought about, but I suppose my first impulse would be to call the police, then I'd hesitate, frightened my husband might be accused.'

"She said, 'You're on the right track, dear. Go on with it.'

"I did, and whatever I said was kept in. I had to develop that most important scene without help from a writer or director.

"When I finished, she came over to compliment me. She said, 'I noticed how you expressed emotion through your hands while you were still. You're a very fine actress. And we'd never conflict because I don't play 'good.' You're the sympathetic type, not a sex personality like me.'"

The Ingenue laughed. "It was a ramshackle production. Our producer was having financial problems. He let the director go, and Miss West came over to rehearse us after her performance in *Diamond Lil.* We'd go from eleven-thirty until two or three in the morning.

"I was very naïve when I joined the company. I didn't know anything about homosexuals or drag queens until then. There were four, I recall—small, very dainty men. I don't see many of that type today.

"The leading one we called Leslie Queen or Queenie in the play. His real name was Lester Sheehan. He'd been a dancer who supported the famous Dolly Sisters in the past. But his drinking and—well, I won't venture what he was taking—were out of control during *Pleasure Man*. One night he wouldn't rehearse for the stage manager, and he had a major role. When Miss West arrived, they told her. She went over and began talking in a soft, sympathetic way. 'Queenie, dear, what's your trouble?' He said, 'Oh, if I could just scream, if I could just let out a big one!' She looked into his eyes as if screaming were the most sensible thing she'd ever heard of and she said, 'Do it, honey. Go ahead! Scream your head off.' She knew how to handle him because he let out a screech and in a matter of minutes was ready to rehearse."

The Ingenue recalled that Mae seemed attuned to understanding perverse behavior. "Once during a rehearsal break, Miss West was rummaging in her purse and shoved several letters in my hand. 'From my fans,' she said.

"I opened one and read a few lines. I said, 'Oh, this is horrible! Disgusting! This—this man is a degenerate!' She just smiled and said, 'I don't pay no attention. But if you're going to be a good actress, don't shut yourself off. Study all types. I get some of my best ideas from letters like this.'"

Discussing Gay Liberation with Christopher Stone in the *Advocate* in 1975, Mae cited *Pleasure Man* and *The Drag* as evidence of her longtime acceptance of it. "I was fighting for Gay Rights before it became fashionable," she said. "Way back in the twenties, in New York, I got ahold of the police and started explaining to them that gay boys are females in male bodies. That's Yogi [*sic*] philosophy—take it or leave it.

"The police were really rough on homosexuals then. I said, 'Now look, fellas, when you're hitting one of them, just remember you're hitting a woman.'

"That straightened them out. They stopped beating up the gay boys.

"In those days all the chorus boys were gay. But the producers never gave speaking parts to known homosexuals! If a gay boy got a job and did so much as this [her wrist goes limp] he would be fired.

"So I helped a lot of gay boys along. I gave them parts."

84 /

Yet Mae seemed to equate homosexuality with transvestism. And although she related perfectly to the flamboyant homosexual's life-style, when she discovered that a relative with a macho image was homosexual she became distraught and disassociated herself from him.

Pleasure Man opened at the Bronx Opera House (not in Bridgeport, as Mae claimed in *Goodness Had Nothing to Do with It*) on September 17, 1928. The metropolitan papers regarded the premiere as a tryout and did not cover it, but Jack Conway of *Variety* attended and headlined his review:

OH, MY DEAR, HERE'S MAE WEST'S NEW SHOW,
GET A LOAD OF IT AND WEEP.

After rapping everyone connected with it, Conway concluded:

The party is the payoff. If you see those hussies being introduced to do their specialties, you'd pass out. One Sylvan Repetti was just too adorable as a snake dancer and stopped the show. The host sang a couple of parodies, one of them going, "When I Go Out and Look for the Moon," now I ask you? Another guest very appropriately sang, "Balls, Parties and Banquets," and I ask you again.

The thing ran two hours-and-a-half. It needs plenty of cutting and rewriting, but will it get the pennies? You and I should have a piece. . . . That West girl knows her box-office, and this one is in right now. It can't miss and if you think it can, hope you get henna in your toothbrush.

But don't miss it, because you must see it to appreciate the strides that we girls are making. You can't possibly imagine it. And go early, for some of the lines can't last.

Pleasure Man moved to the Boulevard Theater in Jackson Heights and from there to Broadway's Biltmore Theater, where it opened October 1. Although no harassment had taken place during the tryouts, after the premiere New York's Finest herded fifty-four actors, many still in stage makeup and clutching opening-night bouquets, into Black Marias, which headed for the West Forty-seventh Street police station, notorious for its violence and brutality.

Some of the cast treated the raid as a joke, shouting to friends, "Beat it, Mary, before Lizzie Law grabs you, too!" Others were angry. The Ingenue recalled taking the raid calmly. "I felt I had

/   85

done nothing reprehensible," she said. "And I was confident Miss West would take care of us."

The Ingenue's confidence was not misplaced. Jeffrey Amherst, who was then assigned to the police beat by the New York *World*, colorfully described Mae's response in his book *Wandering Abroad:*

> Suddenly the doors were flung open and in swayed all five feet nothing of Miss West herself, just having finished her play *Diamond Lil* at the Royale Theater.
>
> Her hands on her hips, she planted herself firmly in front of the Police Captain's desk. "Had she written the play? Was she responsible? Had she not been warned not to open on Broadway?" he asked.
>
> Calmly she gazed at him, took her time and replied, "Don't ya read ya noospapers?"
>
> "Are you going to provide bail for all these people?" he asked.
>
> "Somepin' of the sort," she answered with the maximum of insolence and turning on her heel she swayed out, the photographers' lights flashing and the company applauding. . . .

Mae's attorney, Nathan Burkan, a distinguished lawyer specializing in theatrical cases, not only applied for bail but also petitioned for and received a temporary injunction from the Supreme Court preventing the police from interfering with further performances.

Equity Council hurriedly met and dispatched warnings to cast members they would be placing themselves in jeopardy by appearing unless the temporary injunction was made permanent. *Pleasure Man* was being prosecuted under Section 1140-A of the Penal Code, which made conviction possible if any portion of an attraction could be proved indecent.

From the vantage point of the 1980's, when pornographic films, plays and books are readily available even in small Bible Belt cities, the critics reacted hysterically to a sniggering but harmless production that owed its existence and appeal to the unreasoning repression that had for so long gripped the United States.

It serves little purpose to do more than suggest the tone of the reviews. Robert Littell of the *Evening Post* moaned: "But it is smeared from beginning to end with such filth as turns one's stomach even to remember." And Gilbert W. Gabriel, usually a reasonable man, thundered in the *Sun:* "No play in our time has had less excuse for such a sickening excess of filth. No play, I warrant, has set out more deliberately to sell muck by the jeerful."

Mae told Thyra Samter Winslow: "People want dirt in plays so I give 'em dirt. See? They can be dull at home, but in the theater they want excitement. They want to feel, not think."

The Ingenue and the rest of the cast had faith in Mae and her lawyer, so after missing one performance, the entire company returned for the Wednesday matinee. "The house was packed in spite of or because of our reviews, just as Miss West predicted. And the audience loved the show," the Ingenue said. "Well, just imagine our surprise when we got to the big drag ball and Lieutenant James Coy raced down the aisle. He called for the houselights to be turned up, identified himself as an officer and said he was placing us under arrest. We thought he was acting illegally."

Unaware that the temporary injunction had been vacated, the actors emitted catcalls, booed and gave the police the raspberry. One transvestite, stepping to the footlights in full drag, delivered a tirade against police oppression and the muzzling of free speech—only to feel a huge hand muzzling him as he was dragged from the stage and slammed into a paddy wagon.

"That second arrest, the police got out of line," the Ingenue said. "They wouldn't let the drags change into male clothing, you see. Miss West was very fond of this one boy, Gene Pearson, the Male Jeritza. He'd been in vaudeville and evidently came from a very nice family. He had a fine soprano voice and sang 'Ah! Sweet Mystery of Life.' So of course, he was in costume. When we got to the bullpen at the station, he said to me, 'Honest, I don't know what to do with this fan,' and I said, 'Well, give it to me and I'll carry it.' He did, and I distinctly heard one detective say to another, 'Do you think *that's* one, too?' Gene and I had to laugh, and I thought, 'Well, it's the first time there's been any doubt as to what I am.' But I suppose it proves you're judged by the company you keep.

"Of course, it wasn't all laughs. Leo Howe, the Bird of Paradise, asked me to talk to Lester Sheehan, or Queenie. It seemed he was drinking and was already on parole for dope, so he could have been in danger of going to the Tombs. I sat down beside him and asked him not to do anything to make it worse for anyone. And he promised."

The headline-happy Coy's plot to have the fifty-four actors, still in costume, arraigned in night court was foiled by Mae's swift arrangement of bail, and everyone was released. But the play closed two days later. With no trial date set 1928 became 1929. Mae was still appearing in *Diamond Lil* and bickering with the Linders. She also was distracted by her mother's failing health.

Then, early in 1929, after forty weeks on Broadway and an average weekly gross of $15,000, Jack Linder suddenly announced he was sending *Diamond Lil* on tour. The succession of battles between Mae and Linder had until this point been fought to a draw. But Linder's decision to close the show provided Mae with an opportunity to join with the Shuberts to force the Linders to sell their 16 percent of the production. The Shuberts then installed their own producer.

Under the new management Mae went on the road with *Lil*. Almost immediately she was plagued with a series of brief, excruciatingly painful abdominal attacks. These occurred sometimes once a week, sometimes for several days in succession. After one such bout she entered the hospital for tests but left against her doctor's advice, refusing to consider exploratory surgery that would have disfigured her alabaster skin.

She and Timony began investigating metaphysics as an approach to curing her ailment. Although from time to time she had dabbled in palmistry, tea leaf readings, tarot cards and séances, she had indulged in these activities merely to divert herself. Now she became serious about venturing outside the conventional field of medicine and inquiring into the discipline of mind power.

Timony somehow met and introduced her to Sri Deva Ram Sukul, who claimed to be from India and identified himself as "President and Director of the Yoga Institute of America." Mae was immediately impressed. The *sri* was a clean-shaven, dark-complexioned, extremely thin young man whose most memorable feature was two enormous dark brown eyes that mirrored his empathetic nature.

She briefly described her condition to the *sri* as he sat directly in front of her. He seized her hands and intoned a short Hindu prayer. Then he asked her to stand, positioned himself behind her and firmly pressed his strong hands against her abdominal wall for two or three minutes. "I'm sure you'll be all right now," he quietly assured her. "I think you're cured." The pain, he informed her, had been caused by someone who was envious and wished her bad luck. Before he departed, he presented her with some literature to study and refused payment, saying that to do so would lay him open to charges of practicing medicine without a license.

In her autobiography Mae said she fought the *sri*'s approach as illogical and sought to retain her belief in "the now and the here." But her interest in the metaphysical was aroused. She admitted, "I felt I had touched the hemline of the unknown."

On a more worldly level Mae's career flourished wherever she played. In Chicago, billed as "The Most Talked About Star in the World," she remained fourteen weeks at the Apollo, before transferring to the Great Northern for several weeks more. Then she moved to Detroit, where she drew big grosses and the wrath of Mayor John C. Lodge. He threatened to close the show and arrest Mae—not for her performance but for an advertising herald made up to resemble the *Police Gazette*. Lodge claimed if it fell into the hands of children, it would corrupt them. His well-publicized ire resulted in enormous headlines and even bigger grosses.

September arrived with the *Pleasure Man* trial still in abeyance, so Mae took a swing around New York's Subway Circuit with *Lil*, expecting the court case to be called the first week in October. She was thankful to be in New York, which gave her the opportunity to spend a great deal of time with her mother, whose increasing frailty was causing Mae deep concern. By concealing her pain and pretending she felt stronger every day, Matilda allayed Mae's anxiety.

Persuaded her mother was recovering and learning the *Pleasure Man* trial had been further delayed, Mae took *Lil* to San Francisco's Curran Theater early in November 1929. After an initial spurt of enthusiasm the play settled into an unexceptional run—affected no doubt by the economic conditions that had produced *Variety*'s famous October 30 headline: WALL STREET LAYS AN EGG.

During the San Francisco engagement Mae was shattered when her father wired her that Matilda's condition was again deteriorating. Mae was so emotionally distraught she simply walked through her part when she opened at the Biltmore in Los Angeles in mid-December. Critics were unimpressed, and attendance was sparse. After two unprofitable weeks Mae persuaded the Shuberts to send the company to Jackson Heights, Long Island. Dissatisfied with the treatment her mother had been receiving, she wanted to explore any available therapy.

Over the years Mae's relationship with her mother had remained remarkably close. When Mae ran afoul of the law, Matilda attended her trial daily and, if possible, undoubtedly would have served her sentence for her. Upon Mae's release from jail Matilda was there, with Beverly in tow, to welcome her. By inclination Matilda was in no way the typical interfering stage mother. However, Mae's regard for her and her judgment kept her at the center of Mae's life, and Matilda was discreet enough never to intrude or comment upon Mae's love affairs. Mother and daughter were, in fact, almost a family within a family.

Mae's father, sister and brother were astounded by the sheer willpower Matilda demonstrated when anticipating a visit from Mae. She would drag herself out of her sickbed, dress, do her hair and make herself up to camouflage her true condition.

Catering to Mae's sweet tooth, Matilda saw to it the kitchen always was stocked with chocolate eclairs, spiced apple strudel and strawberry tarts, but she was wise enough never to teach Mae how to create such rich delicacies. Otherwise, her sex-symbol daughter might have become the fat lady at Coney Island.

Matilda downplayed her weakened condition so convincingly that one afternoon Mae brought along a couple of the boys from *Pleasure Man* who always had made Matilda laugh. The effort proved too much for her, and she had to return to her bed.

Although the rest of the family had accepted the doctors' diagnosis of terminal cancer of the liver, Mae characteristically responded to the unacceptable by evolving her own version of reality. The problem, she concluded, was that Matilda had dieted so strenuously she had damaged her liver. But, she rationalized, that was no reason to despair since the liver of all vital organs was the one most capable of repairing itself. She decided what Matilda needed was the help of the *sri*.

Mae and Timony searched for him in vain. As Matilda continued to fail, Mae showered her with new frocks, hats and purses she would never use. "It kept both of their spirits up," Beverly commented.

On Monday, January 26, 1930, when Mae was opening *Lil* at the Shubert Riviera at Ninety-sixth Street and Broadway, Matilda seemed in stable condition. Midway through the second act Mae was notified Matilda was dying. Timony urged her to refund the audience's money and rush to her mother, but Mae, in good trouper tradition, insisted on completing the performance before dashing to her parents' apartment.

She arrived just as her fifty-six-year-old mother died. Unable to accept the reality of the situation, Mae withdrew from her personal tragedy by falling into a faint from which the attending doctor had difficulty bringing her around. Although everyone concerned urged her to close the show to give herself time to adjust to Matilda's death, she insisted on returning to the stage Thursday night. After the final curtain she collapsed in hysterics. She repeated the pattern after Friday night's and Saturday afternoon's performances. Saturday night she had to be carried to her car and driven to the Harding Hotel, where she had engaged a suite.

Years later, with her customary penchant for exaggeration, Mae told an interviewer that the shock of her mother's "passing" (she had banished the word "death" from her vocabulary) caused her to lose her voice for three months. "I went to pieces," she claimed. "It took me three years to get over it—no, not to get over it, but to live with it." Mae would never admit her mother died of cancer. She always said it was pneumonia that had "taken her away."

The trial for *Pleasure Man* finally began in Judge Amedeo Bertini's General Sessions Court on March 14, 1930. Mae entered at 10:35 A.M. She had lost forty pounds since her mother's death, and her entire ensemble was black—a long black suit, a black straw hat atop her blond braid-ringed head and a black fox fur piece that hugged her shoulders.

She stood with one hand on her hip and fidgeted while the bailiff and the clerk performed their rituals. During the tedious jury selection Mae primly crossed her ankles and gazed into space. She sighed often and showed interest only when one prospective juror said he had seen neither *Sex* nor *Diamond Lil.* Then she stared at him incredulously but managed a smile as he added he was too busy ever to attend the theater.

Her interest picked up only when the subject returned to her. In questioning one prospective juror, Burkan asked, "Have you ever seen Mae West, the star of this case?" Mae continued to preen even as Assistant District Attorney James Garrett Wallace sarcastically noted, "Miss West is not the star of the case. There is no star in this case. She is the star of the show." And she beamed when Burkan replied, "Well, you billed her first on this court program. Gave her name the honor. You put her name first on the indictment."

When Wallace threatened, "We will prove that it would take the most confirmed pervert to write such a play," Mae smoothed one side of her hair and appeared unconcerned, as if she felt a derogatory remark about her was preferable to no remark at all.

By March 18 the jury had been selected from people who swore they harbored no prejudice against actors, female impersonators or impure drama and belonged to no antivice society.

Wallace conceded the play was a backstage type of show, but in his interpretation many of the male characters were sleazy, shrill-voiced creatures who dressed as women. Their presence and carryings-on had triggered police action against the production for tending "to corrupt the morals of youth and others."

Lieutenant James J. Coy, the first witness for the prosecution, wore a snug-fitting brown suit set off by a canary yellow tie and matching handkerchief in his breast pocket. He was zealous in his responses to the district attorney's questions. When asked to describe what he had seen, he leaped up, pulled his manly body to its full six feet, daintily placed his hands on his hips, turned on his heel, looked over his shoulder and said, "They behaved in a very effeminate manner." He gave minute details and flamboyant imitations of all the disgusting behavior by both men and women he had witnessed a year and a half before.

Early on Coy emerged as a figure of fun to the press and spectators alike. After he admitted to having been supernumerary in a play thirty years before, Burkan raised an eyebrow and said, "Oh, you were a chorus boy?" "No," Coy shouted. "I was just a part of a large assemblage. I stood on the stage for a big stage picture."

When Burkan asked whether Coy was familiar with Jimmy Durante's work in the Clayton, Jackson and Durante trio, Coy demonstrated his elevated sensibilities by dismissing them as "a tough vaudeville team—they push each other all over the stage, knock each other down, but there is nothing acrobatically clever about them."

Continuing his campaign to make the macho Coy appear foolish, Burkan baited him to again imitate the female impersonators. Coy pranced up and down, hands on hips, announcing, "They walk with their hands on their shoulders." The spectators howled with laughter. Wallace jumped to his feet and said, "I think you mean *hips*, Captain!"

Irene Kuhn of the *Daily News* cleverly captured the absurdity of the proceedings, reporting:

> Coy in a sense established the fact that *Pleasure Man* was a high-class show, for he could think of nothing but three or four syllable words to describe it. Nothing ever happened; everything transpired. The ladies and gentlemen of the cast were never dressed; they were attired. When they got to the acrobatic scene to which the police objected, Burkan wanted to know all about it. "Now about the female impersonator sewing on stage?"
>
> "Yes?"
>
> Burkan: "How could you see the needle and thread?"
>
> "Oh," vouchsafed Coy, "it was illuminous on the stage."
>
> Burkan wanted Coy to sing the ballad "The Queen of the Beaches" so the jury could determine for itself whether beaches rhymed with peaches, as the defense claimed, or ditches, as Coy testified. Coy flatly refused.

Other prosecution witnesses added little in the way of establishing guilt or evoking laughter. Postponements because of the judge's illness and a juror's "pressing business" slowed the trial's pace to a crawl, causing reporters to complain it had taken weeks to establish it was no crime "to have a soprano voice if you belong to the sex that is supposed to shave each day."

Defense witnesses were as outrageous as the characters Mae customarily devised. Pleasure Man Alan Brooks, in spite of his sensational castration-murder, swore he never clearly understood how he had been killed. Wally James, who identified himself as a married man from Long Island, actually insisted he had never seen any female impersonators in the play.

Acrobat Chuck Connors, self-styled son of "the mayor of Chinatown," testified he had never heard a derogatory slang term applied to impersonators because "I live with my sixty-five-year-old mother at the Hotel Langwell." Like many other witnesses, he insisted the material he and his partner performed had been used in vaudeville without shocking anyone. Connors, when asked whether the cast wore evening clothes, responded, "You mean nightgowns?" And his crooning of "Get Out and Get Under the Moon" was so horrendous Mae had to cover her mouth to keep from laughing. Next day the *Journal-American* reported "the defects were more musical than moral."

Texas Guinan, wearing layers of pancake, knee-length pearls and a mid-calf mink, showed up at the press table. Tex, a much-arrested speakeasy hostess-entertainer, famed for her greeting "Hello, sucker," said she had been hired by a newspaper to analyze Mae's behavior on the witness stand. "It feels strange to find myself on the opposite side of the rail," she confided. She flashed a smile at Mae but soon was frowning when Burkan decided Mae would not testify.

In their respective summations to the jury Wallace and Burkan charged witnesses from the opposing side with committing perjury. Burkan attacked "nightstick justice" and accused the police of "framed testimony." "They didn't go to see if a crime had been committed," he said. "They went to get Mae West—and they got her. . . . Police who testified here were vicious perjurers and this Courtroom has been defiled by their perjury. . . ."

Wallace responded that the witnesses for the defense rather than the police had committed perjury. Had the police set out to manufacture a story, he claimed, it would have been made of stronger stuff, with no loopholes.

After fourteen days of listening to testimony, the blue-ribbon jury was charged and began deliberations on the fate of twenty-four defendants after a motion had been made shortly before noon by Wallace to dismiss the indictments against thirty-four others.

Mae left the courtroom, looking subdued and somewhat depressed after listening to Judge Bertini's charge to the jury. He had urged them to reach a decision not only to protect the people of the state but also to clarify for professional entertainers what was prohibited as "immoral," "impure," "indecent," and "obscene." It was necessary only for the prosecution to demonstrate that parts of the play fell into those categories. If the jury found that any of it

> . . . tended to the corruption of the morals of youth or other people and you believe that beyond a reasonable doubt, based on the evidence of the case, then you may find these defendants

94 /

guilty under the first count of the indictment; that is, every person aiding or abetting in its performance.

In addition to what I have already stated I wish to say that discussions or dialogue offensive to public decency or having a depraved tendency are not privileged.

The people of the State of New York are anxious to have pure drama. We are anxious to have decent plays. Not alone the youth of this state but their elders are equally entitled to cleanness in spoken drama. . . .

In his charge the judge continued in this manner, making a covert plea for stage censorship. Yet weighted as his instructions were, the jury, which began deliberations at 11:56 A.M., was unable to agree, as Irene Kuhn put it, "whether Mae West's play was an indecent exhibition or an innocent little comedy."

At 9:50 P.M. the jury foreman reported he and his cohorts were deadlocked. Rumor had it that initially the jury was eight to four and on their final ballot seven to five for acquittal.

Mae was not in the courtroom at the time. Judge Bertini took the occasion to plead for censorship of plays, citing difficulties involved in representing in a court of law what was seen on the stage. Afterward Wallace announced that he probably would not seek a retrial.

MAE WEST BEAT IT, *Variety* exulted.

7

Free, Flaming Mae immediately hit the Fox vaudeville circuit with a scorching act that offended the chain's predominantly lower-middle-class, highly moral clientele. Refusing to censor herself, she quit the tour and returned to the Shuberts, who initially announced she would star in *Frisco Kate*. A week later they postponed that and substituted something called *The Racket*. When auditions began, actors spread word that the script actually was a revival of *Sex*.

Lyle Talbot, who was to have a long career in films, was sent to the Maxine Elliott Theater, where Mae was looking for a leading man. "There was Mae sitting in the front row with Jim Timony. Someone handed me some sides for the young sailor that Mae goes on the make for.

"She had this cockney stage manager who knew all the lines and stage business. He really played Mae West! And we had to do a very sexy scene!

"Well, apparently she thought I did pretty well because she got up onstage to do the scene with me. She was supposed to be seducing the guy, and I'll never forget how embarrassing it was. In the midst of my reading she gave me directions, 'Don't be bashful! Go ahead 'n' push in your middle! That's it, that's it. Grind!'

"I guess she was intrigued by the result because I was offered the part but turned it down because the salary was too small."

With an undistinguished cast the play got off to a rocky start at the Garrick in Chicago late in August but eventually managed an eleven-week run. Encouraged, the Shuberts booked a short midwestern tour to buy time until *The Constant Sinner,* Mae's 1930 novel, originally called *Babe Gordon,* could be turned into a playable script. Business for *Sex* or *The Racket* was spotty in smaller towns. Still, the company staggered along, earning a profit one week and going in the red the next. Nevertheless, because of the demise of big-time vaudeville and the deepening Depression, Mae was happy to collect the royalties on the play and her salary as the star.

"Mae West, who at the outset might as well be described as unique . . ."[1] . . . "brought her new show, *The Constant Sinner,* to the Royale last night, a melodrama nicely calculated to offend public taste and attract paying customers. . . ."[2] . . . "No burlesque show strikes a lower level of life and morals than does *The Constant Sinner.* . . ."[3] . . . "To the followers of *Diamond Lil,* however, it is pretty certain to come as a disappointment, for *The Constant Sinner* is not quite bad enough to be consistently funny, and not good enough to supply many melodramatic thrills. . . ."[4] . . . "It may be clumsy drama (it is clumsy drama, very clumsy) but it is written as if she knew what she was talking about, and Miss West acts it, as is her custom, as if she had been born and brought up among her characters. . . . The woman has flavor. Call it bad taste if you will, it remains nevertheless something definite and distinctly salable. There is enormous gusto in her playing. . . ."[5] ". . . "That she is an atrocious playwright and appears in her own dramas is her only failing as an actress. . . ."[6] . . . "She is so different from anything you have seen outside the zoo that you decide her impersonation is deliberately outlandish. When her various heroes ply her with jewels and admiration you suspect that they should be feeding her peanuts. . . . As a showwoman she is crafty and, I suspect, she knows as much about life as Balzac, Dreiser, Hugo, Samuel Shipman or Eugene O'Neill. At any rate, she is wise enough to surround herself with a company of real actors."[7]

1. *The New York Times*
2. Howard Barnes, *Herald Tribune*
3. Stephen Rathbun, *Sun*
4. Willella Waldorf, *Evening Post*
5. Arthur Pollock, *Brooklyn Eagle*
6. Howard Barnes, *Herald Tribune*
7. Percy Hammond, *Herald Tribune*

The Constant Sinner, with twenty-one scenes and a cast of fifty, had been put into rehearsal by the Shuberts on July 23, 1931, and opened its tryout tour in Atlantic City on August 24. The production proved so cumbersome that by its September 13 New York opening it had been pared to sixteen scenes, which were all the jackknife stage could accommodate.

Under pressure to come up with an added box-office draw, the Shuberts persuaded Mae, as Babe Gordon, to flirt with nudity on the stage, for the first and last time. She crossed the dimly lit stage wearing only a thin chiffon wrapper and changed into a dressing gown in view of the audience. "It wasn't my game," she said. "I didn't make a big thing of it."

Far more intriguing to Broadway audiences than this illusion of nudity (there was plenty of that in *George White's Scandals* and the *Ziegfeld Follies)* was the bold black-and-white romance which was one of the major love stories in the play. No collaborator surfaced to demand acknowledgment for having written the script, but Mae herself credited Howard Merling, who had played Eben in O'Neill's *Desire Under the Elms,* with suggesting she "mix the black-and-white theme."

She said Merling gave her "rich data about the high life and low down on Harlem—all about the speaks, the numbers racket, the clip joints, nightclubs, the fly characters, white and black." In 1929 she devised a plot. Babe Gordon's exploits included ruining her boxing-champion husband with her voracious sexual demands, carrying on a torrid interracial affair, selling dope in compacts over the counter in a department store, causing her black lover to be killed by his millionaire rival, allowing her regenerated husband to be arrested for the murder, persuading the millionaire to pay for the defense based on a husband's right to protect his home, and finally sharing herself with her millionaire paramour and her fighter husband.

Audacious as Mae was, still, she dared not in 1931 cast a black actor as Money Johnson, the Harlem policy king. She chose George Givot, whose previous experience was confined to a singing turn in vaudeville. Givot regarded his assignment as a bewildering bit of good luck. He said forty-six years later, "I still recall my first scene with some so-called white underworld characters. My opening speech as a professional actor on the legitimate stage was: 'Wait a minute, boys! I wanta talk to you. If I catch you passin' that junk in any goddamned compact—or in any other way—you're gonna heah from me. Now get that in yoah haids and keep it theah, because I ain't tellin' ya twice.' It wasn't the kind of relationship between blacks and whites you saw portrayed on the stage in those days."

Devising a makeup for Givot that looked convincing presented a problem. "Finally, we hit on an old-time makeup—Warrenson's Number Four. You put it on evenly, then patted it down with a white powder," Givot said. "Under the lights I looked fine, even alongside the twenty blacks Mae made J. J. Shubert hire for small roles and atmosphere."

For Givot's curtain call, Mae drew upon the female impersonator's traditional doffing of his wig at the end of the last act. Givot removed his half wig to reveal a generous strip of white skin which reassured audiences he was a Caucasian.

Mae impressed Givot with her theatrical ingenuity. "She was a woman with a lot of moxie, a lot of staunch self-confidence that you don't ordinarily find in an uneducated human being. She was educated on the streets, so to speak. Never went to school that I know of. But instinct is something stronger than education. She sold sex and nothing but. She had just begun to get some humor out of it, but she would do anything to project sex, literally and figuratively.

"She always was trying to get me sexed up during the cabaret scene. She told me some of the weirdest damn things. One story was about having this Greek come to her house for an afternoon of sex. There was humor in what she said. But she'd keep on talking until she'd get a certain look on her face—puckered lips, the moving tongue, the narrowed eyes—until she'd talk herself into an orgasm.

"Sometimes she'd say under her breath, 'Come down to my dressing room in your dressing gown between acts.' Now that's somewhat unusual—or was—for a star. I don't know how the hell you can publish a thing like that even today. Not that it hadn't happened to me with chorus girls. After all, I was a good-looking kid, but she was a star."

Givot said more did not come of their relationship because he was turned off by her mechanical attitude toward sex and Jim Timony's interference. "She used to say, 'Jim? He's nothing to me. We're just in business.' She said that he was a go-between for her and the Shuberts, that there had been a romance in the beginning, but it was over. Maybe so, but he sure did his best to scare everybody away."

Givot's understudy was a black actor named Lorenzo Tucker who had starred for Southland Pictures as "The Colored Valentino" in films made expressly for theaters catering to a black clientele.

Tucker, who in 1978 still bore a striking resemblance to the William Powell of *The Thin Man* period, explained how he was hired for *The Constant Sinner*. "It was rumored she was infatuated with me," he said, "but that's not true. She did have several black lovers. I think I knew them all. Possibly I was too light for her.

"I had an agent in the 1930's who used his office as a cover. Even in those days in Harlem there were colored racketeers who were getting a piece of the action. This fellow sent me down to the Maxine Elliott Theater. Sure enough, when Miss West saw me, she said she wanted me to play the headwaiter and to understudy George Givot.

"The understudy job upset everybody—Timony, the Shuberts, the director—but she got her way. Black men had never before been considered for romantic leads in white shows. But she insisted, and they outfitted me with everything but the nappy wig, which I didn't need.

"That's one thing I'd like to say about her: she was always strong for the colored. She went up to Harlem to Connie's Inn, the Cotton Club—all the places. At the Cotton Club she hired Paul Meers to do the African Strut. Another place she found Robert Rains for Liverlips, a wonderful part. She hired Rudolph Toombs for Mr. Gay, Hubert Brown as a waiter and Trixie Smith for the upstairs maid in the whorehouse."

In Mae's autobiography she paints *The Constant Sinner* as one of her major triumphs, requiring two box offices to accommodate ticket buyers. The fact is the play survived only as long as the eight-week ticket brokers' "buy" propped it up.

A combination of the Depression and antitrust rulings had forced the Shubert chain of theaters into receivership in 1931. Still, they decided to send this heavy production with a large cast and twenty-one stagehands to Washington, D.C., and Chicago. For the road Mae had a plan. Lorenzo Tucker was to play the headwaiter until after the Chicago opening, then take over the Money Johnson role.

"You have to give her credit," Tucker said. "Washington was totally segregated at the time. It took nerve to offer a black-and-white love story even if the colored man was a blacked-up white. The DA, a fellow named Rover, came to the theater and told Miss West it just wasn't going to happen in Washington, having blacks and whites on the stage together and a Negro kissing her. Even the Shuberts tried to get her to cut out those love scenes for Washington. Well, she was determined to have it done, and Rover said she couldn't continue. But she said, 'My play stays the way it is.' And she stuck to it, even though it meant a big loss and cancellation of the Chicago date where I might have got my chance."

Tucker feels Mae went as far as she dared at that time. "People now say that wasn't much. But I believe we have to look at folks like her with raised eyes and give them credit for their contribution," he said.

As *The Constant Sinner* brought Mae's six-year span of Broadway shows to a close, *Sex* and *Diamond Lil* clearly stood out as milestones in the evolution of the Mae West persona. *Sex,* in which she played her whore-with-the-heart-of-gold character seriously, brought a puritanical society face-to-face with the reality of the sordid underside of life. It also brought Mae an arrest, conviction and term in jail.

Among the reputable members of the theatrical community Mae was considered reprehensible. Yet, step by step, she brought forbidden topics aboveground, and, to the good of all, fought police censorship to a draw, making the guardians of public morals appear priggish and bigoted.

Following the scandalous impact she made with *Sex,* she floundered until she brought *Diamond Lil* to the stage. In *Lil* she discovered the key to the personality that would become indelibly, forever, Mae West—the woman who handled even the most audacious situations with humor and self-mockery. This ploy disarmed and enchanted almost everyone. Writer Marion Spitzer

Thompson recalled, "My original impression of Mae was that she believed all that sexy stuff about herself. But she began to recognize the value of self-kidding and began broadening it into parody. I think that explains her enduring hold on people's imaginations."

8

1932. Corner grocers closed shops and returned to street peddling to cut overhead. A lucky broker abandoned his seat on the stock exchange for a seat behind the steering wheel of a bus. Bootleggers prepared to switch from booze to bank robbery, kidnapping and narcotics. A social theory called Technocracy flourished briefly. Desperate ex-vaudevillians entered endurance contests, walking forty-five minutes out of the hour, twenty-four hours a day. The reward? A roof to shelter them, food for their stomachs.

Truth to tell, Mae's options were limited. Vaudeville couldn't afford her. Cabarets didn't appeal to her. Broadway productions diminished in number, and runs became shorter. Motion pictures with the advent of double features and free dishes prospered. But in youth-oriented Hollywood, fortyish sex symbols weren't getting any propositions.

George Raft, on the other hand, definitely had become a winner. The former gangsters' driver had parlayed winning a dance contest into an engagement at Texas Guinan's El Fay Club and a featured spot with the Old Maestro, Ben Bernie, a popular bandleader of the day. Raft's friends at first felt he had foolishly traded what he had achieved in New York to play gangster roles in Hollywood B movies. But by 1932 Paramount Pictures saw him as a potential replacement for Valentino. Luckily for Mae, Raft had never forgotten the flame she ignited when he was Owney Madden's bagman.

Naturally that's not the way Mae told it. According to her, the William Morris Agency received an offer of $5,000 per week— which she agreed to accept.

The truth is producer William Le Baron was concentrating on giving Raft, who had attracted a strong following in seven films, including *Dancers in the Dark* and *Scarface*, every opportunity to display his full potential in *Number 55*, later retitled *Night After Night*. One of the perks Le Baron had granted him was consultation on casting. Raft was enthusiastic about Constance Cummings, the leading ingenue who had been labeled "Miss Wholesomeness" by a newspaper reporter. He also liked feisty Wynne Gibson and that comic grande dame Alison Skipworth but hesitated at the suggestion of Texas Guinan as Maudie Triplett. "Tex might be great," he told Le Baron, "but I know a woman who'd be sensational. Mae West."

On January 16, Mae and Timony set out by train for Hollywood, determined to give films Mae's best shot, and if that didn't work out, they would have had a nice vacation. Four days later, when they debarked in Pasadena (no real star rode into Union Station in Los Angeles), Mae set newspeople straight by telling them, "I'm not a little girl from a little town here to make good in a big town. I'm a big girl from a big town who's come to make good in a little town."

She and Timony went from Pasadena to the Ravenswood, an apartment hotel located on Rossmore, an extension of Vine Street. The William Morris office had chosen it because of its proximity to Paramount Studios. Whatever other reservations Mae may have had about Hollywood, the apartment was not one of them. She furnished it like a white-and-gold cocoon, and it became her chief residence for the rest of her life.

After a week of sitting around, Mae tired of sightseeing and waiting to read the script. Nor was her mood improved when Louella Parsons ran this item:

The buxom blonde Mae West, fat, fair and I don't know how near forty has come to Hollywood. It's a contract the plumpish Miss

West holds in her two fists. The contract is with Paramount and it calls for an important part in Louis Bromfield's novel "Number 55." Miss West will be featured. . . .

To keep Mae occupied and in an amiable mood, the Paramount publicity department arranged some gallery sittings and also persuaded Muriel Babcock to interview her for the Los Angeles *Times.* After an introduction emphasizing early negative responses by theater critics, Miss Babcock described meeting the star at the studio:

> She wore a big, black droopy picture hat, a tiny jacket of scarlet red over a summer print dress. There was a huge rock on one finger of the right hand, a diamond collar around her left wrist and an enormous diamond necklace about her neck. To these eyes she looked at least 20 pounds lighter than on the occasion of her last visit to Los Angeles in December, 1929, in the rowdy, roaring melodrama of the 1920s, *Diamond Lil.* She is, in truth, she said, only 10 pounds lighter. She tips the scales at 120 and two years ago could not possibly have been more than 130, which caught the eye. . . .
>
> Will she put Mae West, unadulterated, and her rowdy mannerisms on screen? Will she indulge in all the bodily calisthenics which have made her quite remarkable on stage?
>
> "It will not be necessary," she thinks. "The screen doesn't require as much acting of a certain type. The camera catches the slightest facial expression, the slightest twitch of the eye. What you must make emphatic on the stage you can suggest in a less obvious manner on the screen. . . ."
>
> In pictures, she is to appear in *Night After Night.* She will play a lady of no character.

Finally, the script arrived. Mae, who was accustomed to other cast members extolling her beauty, talent and general superiority for several minutes before she entered, was appalled that no one hailed her entrance and that she didn't appear until halfway through the fourth reel. Worse still, as written, Maudie was a colorless minor character; one which, in Mae's opinion, could be played by any utility actress.

With Timony she stormed into the office of Al Kaufman, one of studio head Adolph Zukor's chief aides. She told him that she hadn't worked long and hard to turn herself into a character woman. She offered to refund her salary and go back to New York. Kaufman informed Le Baron of Mae's revolt, and Le

Baron, recalling Mae's flair for creating dialogue, urged her to rewrite the character to show off her talents to full advantage. Since the scenes were already structured, he was certain not much harm could be done. Mae, meanwhile, set out to endow the role with a maximum of Westian witticisms and double entendres.

From the first moment of her screen appearance outside Raft's nightclub, wearing her floor-length white gown, wrapped in her personal white furs and jewels, Mae set a fast pace. Having noted the other actors were playing their scenes in a slow style, she abandoned her own slow-'n'-easy delivery for a zingy tempo.

Mae's rapid delivery proved unnerving to veteran Alison Skipworth, who had reached the age where the slightest change in a scene threw her. She complained to no effect. Finally, she told director Archie Mayo that Mae's timing was ruining the characterization she was creating. Then, turning to Mae, she drew herself up imperiously and announced, "You forget I've been an actress for forty years." To which the unruffled Mae smilingly replied, "Don't worry, dear. I'll keep your secret."

In Mae's first scene she mocks her personal notoriety by asking a trio of admirers to leave. Don't they know her daddy doesn't allow her out after 9:00 P.M.? Then she reassures wives in the audience that they have nothing to fear from her by urging her married suitors to forget about her and go home to their wives.

When the doorman responds to her knock by asking who is there, she replies, "The fairy princess, you mug!" He tries to turn her away, but she pushes inside, announcing, "No sale, no sale! I'm gonna see that guy tonight." As she approaches the hatcheck girl, Mae drops her wrap. The girl, overwhelmed by the glitter, gasps, "Goodness, what beautiful diamonds!" Mae then delivers the line that launched the most discussed screen debut of all time: "Goodness had nothing to do with it, dearie."

Mayo insisted upon ending the scene as soon as Mae had uttered her line. Mae was determined to have the camera follow her up the long stair, providing, she said, an opportunity for the audiences to respond fully to the dialogue. No one could dissuade her. Finally, the matter was tossed into the hands of Emanuel Cohen, executive vice-president in charge of production. He agreed to film it Mae's way.

Mae's best sustained sequence is with Alison Skipworth, a

stumpy girls' schoolteacher. The form the dialogue takes is that of the traditional crossfire, fast-talking double act. It reflects Mae's vaudeville training. A hung-over Skipworth awakens in the late afternoon to find she's slept through her class for the first time, and she fears she may be fired for her previous evening's dissipation. Mae breezily comforts her, telling her she's wasting her time, that a gal like her could make thousands in Mae's racket, one of the best in the world. Jumping to a conclusion, the bewildered Skipworth tries to hide her shock and agrees Cleopatra and Du Barry certainly made contributions. But doesn't Mae think her a bit old for that kind of thing? "Say, listen, dearie, you got me all wrong," Mae replies. "Why, I got a string of beauty parlors." What she has in mind is for Skipworth to act as hostess for a new one she's opening in New York, "The Institute de Beaut."

In synopsis or even in script, the material suggests uninspired situation comedy, but as rendered by two superlative comediennes, it is transformed into a hilarious exchange which is equaled only by Mae's two brief introductory scenes in the picture.

Night After Night opened October 4, 1932. Reassessing it in the 1970's, Kevin Thomas wrote in the Los Angeles *Times:* ". . . Miss West . . . injects a natural note that shows up all the sappiness and artificiality of the contrived romance between Raft and Miss [Constance] Cummings. . . ."

Only the public makes a star, as producer Samuel Goldwyn and his unsuccessful actress protégée Anna Sten were to discover. Often it takes the public to recognize one, too. In advertisements Paramount allotted Mae billing after Raft, Cummings and Wynne Gibson. In fact, she was really fifth since the credits read: "and ALISON SKIPWORTH."

George Raft neatly capsulized what had occurred in his autobiography. "It was her [Mae's] first screen appearance and her cleverness on the stage was a new kind of thievery to me," he said. "She stole everything but the cameras."

Paramount was in deep financial trouble, having gone from an $18 million profit in 1930 to a $21 million loss in 1932. After Mae's debut the moguls talked of continuing the association, but with the studio on the verge of bankruptcy, they wanted to hedge all bets. They saw difficulty in fitting her into leading roles that would meet censor approval, and they fretted lest she be a one-picture novelty.

While the movie executives waffled, Mae converted *Diamond Lil* into a novel, hoping it would surpass the popularity of the widely read *Constant Sinner* and become a hot property for films.

Asked by a skeptical reporter if she didn't use a ghostwriter, Mae admitted her secretary researched background, looked up synonyms and typed the finished product but claimed that was the extent of his participation. She declared, "Anyone who has read anything of mine can always spot my style if my name is on the title page or not. It's distinctive, individual and easy to identify."

Paramount, meanwhile, found it simpler to create a suitable vehicle for rotund Kate Smith, the sensation of radio. So confident was the studio of the hefty, wholesome Kate's appeal that it budgeted her film at more than a million—an enormous investment in Depression days.

Not until the Paramount mailroom was inundated with fan letters for Mae and 5,500 theater owners rebooked *Night After Night* did the company recognize the impact of Mae's performance. Still, it was leery about presenting her in *Diamond Lil* on several counts, including a reader's report, stating: "We don't think Miss West's play would make a good picture. The period—the Gay Nineties—would be all wrong for the movie-goers who are college students, teen-agers, and children."

"It's easy to see why Kate's project moved while Mae's was stalled," said Teete Carl, then assistant head of publicity. "Kate Smith seemed like the easiest imaginable commodity to sell. You know she had this big radio program that always opened with 'When the Moon Comes over the Mountain'; then she'd say, 'Hello, everybody. This is Kate Smith.' *Hello, Everybody* seemed like a title with a lot of promotional possibilities. So the studio got all enthused about capitalizing on it and her popularity."

But Mae kept pressuring Paramount to proceed with *Lil*, reminding them that a pretested play couldn't be such a poor bet. The studio decided to go ahead but with a title change. After considering *Diamond Lady*, *Honky Tonk* and *Ruby Red*, the studio finally settled on *She Done Him Wrong*.

As unit publicist the studio chose Bill Thomas, the newest man on the lot. His only previous credit in films was the successful

"Panther Woman" promotion for *Island of Lost Souls*. "They weren't sure what they had," Thomas said. "Nobody gave a crap about her when she arrived. Hollywood didn't think she was any big thing. She was just set for two or three scenes in Raft's picture. But neither I nor anybody else suspected Mae was going to rescue the studio. I mean, who could know? I'm sure Universal didn't know Deanna Durbin would save them with *Three Smart Girls* either."

Lowell Sherman was assigned to direct. Socially eminent John Davis Lodge announced he was abandoning his law practice to play opposite Mae in this story of "a romance between a detective and a woman of the underworld." And John Bright was hired to do the screenplay.

Bright, who had written four pictures for Cagney and one for Bette Davis, came to the project in a typical Hollywood way. During a heated exchange with Warner production chief Darryl Zanuck, Bright volunteered to throw his boss out the window. Instead, Bright himself went out the front gate.

That night he encountered his new agent, Myron Selznick, at the popular Clover Club and reported the incident. Selznick listened and asked gleefully, "Did you connect? Did you break his leg? Did you throw him out the window?" Bright admitted he had been overpowered by Zanuck's stooges and Zanuck had said he'd never work in Hollywood again. "Why, that prick!" Bright quotes Selznick saying. "You're going to be working by tomorrow. Tomorrow hell! Tonight!"

Half an hour later Samuel Goldwyn, who was at the club, had agreed to pay Bright $1,500 a week to write the script for the Barbara Stanwyck version of *Stella Dallas*. Bright went to Selznick's office next day to confess he couldn't write soap opera, even high-class soap opera because it would look and sound like a *New Yorker* parody. "Would you do it for twenty-five hundred dollars?" Selznick inquired. Bright explained he *couldn't*. Whereupon Selznick picked up the phone and called Paramount, where he set the deal for Bright to write the screenplay for *She Done Him Wrong*.

"I'd seen *Diamond Lil* in New York and enjoyed it enormously for the same reasons I enjoyed a play called *The Drunkard* that ran for eleven years in Los Angeles. Both were terrible plays—so terrible they were funny. But there was a plus for *Diamond Lil*— that was this extraordinary personality of Mae's, which has its roots in rebellion against Puritanism. The titillation of the madam or whore—or both," Bright says.

He recognized the play's structure, which dated from the 1880's, with the traditional chord-in-C entrance for the star. He made his first mistake at a meeting with Mae and Le Baron in assuming Mae also realized this. His second was to mention that certain changes were necessary. Mae bristled, and Le Baron diplomatically explained that films were a different medium from stage plays and that Bright would simply structure *Lil* for the screen without damaging her script.

As Bright began tinkering with *Lil*, Mae demanded—and received—approval not only for scenes and lines but also for word changes. "It was a terrible tug-of-war, but I acted upon a long-held theory of mine that in motion pictures what is important is not ability as an actor or actress but personality and image. She had those. There had never been a stage constructed that she couldn't dominate. She knew every trick in the trade of scene stealing. And she had the scene stolen anyway—because she had control of the script."

Bright estimates that a comparison of the play and the film would reveal 50 percent of the dialogue was hers, 50 percent his. "But in every instance where I came up with a line, I'd say to her, 'I remember a crack you made the other day and I put it in the script. Do you think it fits?' She always remembered saying it and gave her okay. So that's the way I got my lines in.

"I did that on the advice of our director, Lowell Sherman. He said, 'Don't do anything on your own. Give her credit because she'll claim it anyway.' It was a sophisticated technique that came from a man twice my age, and I thought it good pragmatic advice. Most stars, despite all their arrogance, are quite humble before writers because they do realize they need us badly. But not West."

Bright made his most serious miscalculation in discussing how the scene in which the Salvation Army officer rejects her should differ from the way it had been handled in the play. He had observed that in the presence of people Mae considered ladies and gentlemen, she used polysyllabic words and became almost a caricature of a lady. But when working with fellow professionals—even so cultivated a man as Lowell Sherman—she used longshoreman language at the top of her voice. "I think it's absurd to say 'shit' in the presence of your maiden aunt from

Keokuk. But Mae herself indulged in some rather good street talk. And in explaining the internal drama of the scene as I'd changed it, I said to her, 'It must have happened to you sometime, Mae. You got hot rocks for some joker. It didn't work out. And you gave the heat to another one who didn't realize he wasn't the one who'd raised your temperature, and he felt great.' I thought I was talking her language. But she jumped to her feet and said, 'You are the most obscene son of a bitch I have ever known.' And I said, 'Thanks for the Good Housekeeping Seal of Approval.'

"It was the wrong thing to say. Because her house in the Ravenswood with the mirrors on the ceiling and the stream of black and white prizefighters, wrestlers and muscle guys was the talk of the town. She was furious because I'd hit on something. The usual criteria of wanting a full relationship with someone you're having sex with simply didn't apply to her because she was only interested in fulfilling her sexual narcissism. That was the only way she communicated with men—by fucking them. That was the extent.

"Any other communication was business. She had no communication with women at all—except maybe Edith Head, who did her costumes. It was all narcissism and she didn't give a damn who was on top of her. She was only interested in watching herself in that mirrored ceiling."

After their confrontation Bright could do nothing to please Mae. Finally, he went to Le Baron, who told him that Mae demanded he be fired or she would walk off the picture. "I had three scenes to write, three days' work at most if I was lazy," he said. "But Mae wanted to destroy my sole credit, so she demanded my head. Le Baron was unhappy about it, but with costs already rolled up, he couldn't afford to antagonize her. So he brought in a man I'd worked with briefly at Warner's, Harvey Thew. Harvey is a nice man, but he's always been totally housebroken. He came in and did the scenes I'd outlined. So the credits to *She Done Him Wrong* are 'Screenplay by John Bright and Harvey Thew.'"

Before Bright left Le Baron's office, he told his boss, "Bill, you're right in replacing me in this instance, but if you allow this process to continue, the tail is going to wag the dog. Because this most extraordinary personality has in one appearance caught evangelical America with its hand in its pocket, and if you give her power, she'll ruin the studio. She may be a great personality, a unique personality, but she can't spell 'cat.' She knows nothing of construction. She couldn't hold down a writing job on a radio soap opera." Le Baron said he thought Bright was right, but his hands were tied.

Ironically the invitation "Come up 'n' see me sometime"—the line most often associated with the film—was never uttered in that picture, although upon meeting the Salvation Army captain, Mae did ask, "Why don't you come up sometime 'n' see me?," adding "I'll tell your fortune." But after the catchphrase swept America, she included both "Come up 'n' see me sometime" and "You better come up 'n' see me sometime" in her next picture, *I'm No Angel.*

Other memorable Westicisms—some from the play, others new—include her wisecrack to a man who admires a nude painting of her hanging in Gus Jordan's saloon: "Yeah, I gotta admit that is a flash, but I do wish Gus hadn't hung it over the free lunch." She confessed when asked if she'd ever met a man who made her happy, "Sure. Lots of times." She described the Salvation Army captain as "tall, dark 'n' handsome." And when the captain accused her of being a bad girl, she replied insinuatingly, "You'll find out."

Mae insisted that her first starring vehicle include songs, as had most of her plays. She performed "Pretty Baby," "Frankie and Johnny," "A Guy What Takes His Time" and "Easy Rider." Censors apparently were unaware that "easy rider" was street slang for "pimp."

One canard has been repeated often enough to be so generally accepted that even the subject himself no longer bothers to deny it. Mae circulated several versions of the story. A synthesis of them is that she had just come out of the casting office having unsuccessfully appraised the photos of available leading men— none of whom appealed to her. Then she spied a tall, dark, exceedingly handsome young man—"the best-lookin' thing I'd seen around, yuh know what I mean?—walkin' along. 'Who is that?'" she asked.

Producer Al Kaufman is supposed to have said, "His name is Cary Grant. He's never made a movie. We just use him for screen tests."

"If he can talk, I'll take him," Mae claims she replied. In point of fact, Grant was no test actor, but he always remained a

112   /

gentleman, never contradicting Mae's version. On occasion he has said he believed she had seen him at the Friday night boxing matches and had heard favorable reports on his work opposite Marlene Dietrich in *Blonde Venus* from director Lowell Sherman.

His other credits included a small part in *This Is the Night* with Lili Damita; *Sinners in the Sun* with Carole Lombard; *Merrily We Go to Hell* with Sylvia Sidney and Fredric March; *The Devil and the Deep* with Tallulah Bankhead, Gary Cooper and Charles Laughton; and the aforementioned *Blonde Venus,* which moved Mordaunt Hall of *The New York Times* to write: "Cary Grant is worthy of a much better role than that of Townsend." Which is what Mae provided him with, although technically Owen Moore was her leading man—both on film and in private. Still, there is no denying Mae propelled Grant to stardom.

She claimed Edith Head as another of her discoveries. After seeing some of her sketches, Mae requested that the relatively inexperienced designer do the costumes for *She Done Him Wrong* —which was probably just as well since Mae had her own ideas. "I changed the fashions on two continents," Mae once said. "At the time Garbo was the rage. Then I come along. Busts were visible, waists went in and Edith Head became one of the biggest designers in Hollywood."

Miss Head has always recalled their first association whimsically, saying, "In the 1930's costumes didn't have anything to do with real life. The poor working girl was smothered in furs, and Mae West wore a simple black velvet festooned with rhinestones and ruffles when she met Cary Grant in the park."

Worried about the budget, Paramount executives held a conference with Mae to discuss the schedule before shooting began. Her request for a week's rehearsal was resisted on the basis of cost, and her contention that the film could be shot in three weeks if prerehearsed brought tolerant smiles at her ignorance of the time required to shoot a period costume picture. However, her will prevailed, and to the delight of the financially harassed company, *She Done Him Wrong* was completed in eighteen days on a budget of $260,000.

Unit publicity man Thomas's previous experience as a theatrical press agent for the Pantages Circuit helped him establish an immediate rapport with Mae. For other publicists, it was difficult to fit her into a comfortable niche since even when her ideas were good, they were unconventional. The publicity department was mostly staffed with former newspaper reporters who looked askance at some of Mae's promotional stunts, but Thomas, who had scrambled to grab space for vaudeville, understood her immediately and she, him.

At one point Mae called Thomas with the idea of having a life-sized cardboard figure of herself made for lobby display. The sign beneath it was to read: SEE MAE WEST AS SHE REALLY IS!

The figure was to be fully clothed, but her garments were to be hinged so that they could be folded back until she was revealed only in her bra and panties. Thomas tried hard to sell the idea to his superiors, but it was rejected on grounds it would prove too costly.

He had better luck with other schemes, such as the catch line "The gal with the hourglass figure that makes every second count."

Mae seldom objected to any of Thomas's maneuvers, and when he appeared with a sheaf of publicity clippings, she would smile and reach for them, asking, "What'd I say funny today?"

As she grew increasingly impressed with Thomas's work, she would often tell Timony, "Drop a little for Bill," and Timony would hand over a $20 gold piece or two. Sometimes it was considerably more. At that time Paramount had a tie-in with Old Gold cigarettes. In return for a star's testimonial, the tobacco company bought billboard and newspaper space to publicize itself and the star's latest film. Old Gold offered Mae $1,500 for the endorsement. She turned it down on the grounds that she didn't smoke.

Thomas reported her decision and took off for his Hermosa Beach weekend retreat. Upon arrival he found a message ordering him to return to the studio immediately. New York was determined not to lose out on the promotion for *She Done Him Wrong,* and it was Thomas's duty to change Mae's mind. "They worked until noon on Saturday in those days," he said. "I told her how important New York thought the promotion was, how important it was to me. 'If I don't deliver . . .'"

"So it means a lot, huh?" Without waiting for him to answer, she picked up her eyebrow pencil and signed the agreement. Then she said, "You keep the fifteen hundred. But don't go around tellin' everybody. They'll think I'm a soft touch, see?" "That was the kind of dame she was," he added.

Later, when Prohibition was repealed, Thomas grabbed free

newspaper space by having Mae challenge Gary Cooper to a beer-drinking contest. (She and Cooper had had a couple of assignations in her dressing room until Timony discovered what was happening and persuaded the front office to order Cooper to stop seeing her.) Thomas also arranged a testimonial with Mae posed on a keg of beer and a line he remembers as "Mae West says drink beer and you'll get curves, gals."

He often dropped by the Ravenswood to discuss ideas, sometimes to dissuade Mae from a plan he considered ill-advised. As Christmas approached, he was appalled to see she had had a nude painting of herself reproduced on her Christmas card. Inside, Thomas recalls it said something like "Come Up and See Me Sometime. Merry Christmas, Mae West."

"I told her she couldn't send those. She kept asking what was wrong with them, and I finally thought I'd convinced her," Thomas said. "Then she came up with a substitute. I think she sent a few of them before we got to her. On the card Santa was collapsed in a chair and the caption read: 'Santa Comes But Once a Year—Too Bad!'"

When Thomas read that evangelist Billy Sunday was in Los Angeles, he saw an opportunity to tie together Mae and religion. He contacted Sunday's publicity man and arranged for the evangelist to visit Mae on the barroom set. Then he invited Paramount Newsreel plus all the syndicated movie writers.

The stunt was scheduled for 8:00 A.M. with *She Done Him Wrong* shooting to start at 9. Billy Sunday arrived at 7. Mae already was in her dressing room. "I don't know if anyone realizes what she went through to get ready, but it was a *big* deal," Thomas said. "I kept saying, 'Mae, Mae. It's eight o'clock.' Then eight-thirty. Pretty soon it was ten to nine, and Sherman came in with his long cigarette holder, sees us filming and stalks out again—headed for the front office.

"Now Le Baron sent a message he wants me. Kaufman wants me. Well, I figured, hell, I'm in so much trouble now I'm going to finish this stunt. At ten o'clock I did. My attitude was if I get fired, I'm not going to have any problems getting another job.

"I went to Le Baron's office, and Sherman was there. 'How dare you go on Mr. Sherman's set and hold up the whole company? Whatever gave you an idea to do such a thing?' Le Baron yelled at me. I turned sarcastic. 'Oh, I was just having a little fun out there,' I said. 'All kinds of fun. Of course, I made the newsreel, the syndicates and all that. But that means nothing to the picture.' With that Lowell Sherman said, 'It's not this young man's fault. It's that blond bitch! She's always late anyway,' and he put his arm around my shoulder and we walked out."

Lowell Sherman was a stage actor who had dabbled in films since 1920 and had begun directing them after the advent of sound in 1930. His attitude toward the play was the same as John Bright's. Sherman had told Bright that Mae was a great personality, but for him she lacked sex appeal. He naïvely predicted there would be no conflict between the star and him, saying he wouldn't waste his creativity on this movie because he knew the impact of the film depended entirely on Mae's wonderful flamboyance and exhibitionistic self-love. "In the social sense," he told Bright, "it will be the great American wet dream."

In spite of his earlier prophecy of a peaceful relationship, Sherman found himself increasingly intolerant of his star's foibles, especially her late arrivals on the set. But he knew how to deal with her. One morning he ordered every available impediment stacked at the entrance. Flats, furniture, lighting and sound equipment plus a tangled mass of cables made passage virtually impossible. All hands were warned against assisting the star. When she arrived, Sherman ignored her and continued talking to co-workers. With great difficulty, increased by her Gay Nineties garb and platform shoes, Mae picked her way onto the set, muttering imprecations under her breath—but thereafter she arrived promptly as long as they worked together.

On several occasions when Mae and Sherman clashed, she would retreat to her dressing room. Early on Bill Thomas had discovered that looking at publicity photos acted as a tranquilizer. So Sherman would call Thomas to ask him to mollify the angry star. Thomas would grab a group of portraits and hurry to her dressing room to tell her he had a commitment from *Photoplay* or some other magazine and ask her to choose a pose. "She'd start looking and mmmmmming and ahhhhhing until you could actually see her calming down," Thomas remembered. "At just the right moment, I'd say, 'That one you've chosen is great. I've got to get it over to the magazine, but I'll walk you over to the set.' And over we'd go."

Even as *She Done Him Wrong* neared completion, the studio regarded it with ambivalence. In preparing advertising copy,

Arthur Mayer, a Harvard graduate known for his erudition and impeccable taste, nevertheless chose a provocative portrait of Mae to be airbrushed to emphasize strategic points where she was already amply endowed. Beneath it his advertising streamer read: HITTING THE HIGH SPOTS IN LUSTY ENTERTAINMENT.

He sent a copy to studio head Adolph Zukor and, when no objection was heard, ordered full distribution of the material. Then Zukor called him in. "Mr. Mayer," he said, "I thought you were such a fine gentleman. In these times with grosses what they are, how could you send out a dirty word?" Mayer attempted to defend his slogan and his reputation, but Zukor would have none of it. "Lusty." He moaned. "How could you use that word at such a time? With low grosses and the censor—" Mayer cut in to explain that "lusty" was a derivative of *lustig*, a German word which connoted zestful, vigorous, full of life. "Don't give me your Harvard education," Zukor snapped. "One look at that dame's tits and I know what 'lusty' means!"

Luckily for Paramount, *She Done Him Wrong* was the success they needed, for the much-vaunted Kate Smith picture was a flat failure. Teete Carl can still quote one reviewer who began his criticism with "The title of Kate Smith's picture is *Hello, Everybody*. It should be titled *Hello, Anybody*. Talk about shooting deer in the balcony."

She Done Him Wrong benefited when Paramount switched its promotional focus to it from *Hello, Everybody*. At the end of January Mae arrived at Grand Central in New York just as commuters were jamming the station. Awaiting her and Timony was a horse-drawn victoria which caused a traffic tie-up for blocks as it rolled toward her apartment on Central Park West.

When the picture was released in February 1933, Mae received a barrage of love letters from film critics. Fans clogged sidewalks around the Broadway Paramount, where she was appearing in person. After drawing a $58,000 gross for the first week, she moved to the Brooklyn Paramount for seven days, then broke a precedent by returning to the Broadway Paramount, where she drew $40,000 during the bank holiday.

In the face of big city grosses, some doomsayers predicted the film would flop in smaller towns. Mae disagreed, explaining that no matter where people lived they were fascinated with sin. Speaking of the characters she played, she said, "There are some people who can get away with anything. The worse they are, the

/   117

better you like them." Personally, Mae said, the only good woman she could recall in history was Betsy Ross and all she ever made was a flag.

Viewed by standards of a half century later, *She Done Him Wrong* was innocent entertainment compared to prime time TV programs. While theatrical films later would routinely portray frontal nudity and simulated sexual intercourse, only one perfunctory kiss is included in *She Done Him Wrong*—and that near the end of the film. That there is an abundance of violence seemed, in 1933, beside the point. It simply inspired one critic to write admiringly of Mae as the screen's first lady gangster.

To make male gangsters palatable to the public, screenwriters sentimentalized them throughout the picture, then had them gunned down in the last reel to pay lip service to the triumph of moral order. Mae played it tough but leavened the characterization with humor instead of sentimentality. Because she implied her character was not to be taken literally, the self-parody made a happy ending possible. At least for the moment—because if the moviegoer thought about the character's past, he could hardly escape the premonition that one man would never suffice, even if that man was Cary Grant.

Mae's impact was deemed sufficient by the New York *World-Telegram* to run a five-part series entitled "This Westian World." She was credited with bringing back curves, popularizing falsies and making jeweled shoe buckles fashionable. Even *Vogue* found space in its glossy pages to salute her influence. And to her delight, she replaced the farmer's daughter as middle-class America's most ubiquitous presence in dirty jokes.

She also finally won over Louella Parsons. In early 1932 the columnist questioned whether movie patrons would take to Mae, causing Mae to ask, "Why shouldn't they like me? Wouldn't you like it if you were gettin' a Cadillac for the price of a Ford?" At the time Louella was unimpressed, but she now conceded:

> When all's been said and done, Paramount's biggest bet is Mae West. I don't even except Maurice Chevalier, Gary Cooper, Fredric March or Marlene Dietrich. Box-office talks and Mae West has been a sensational success in *She Done Him Wrong*. Feverishly, and madly, the whole scenario personnel is trying to get another story that will keep Miss West's popularity at par.

While the writers struggled to find a new vehicle for her, 786 theater owners across the country rebooked *She Done Him Wrong* as a first-run attraction. It eventually grossed over $3 million, and when *Variety* announced the top box-office pictures of 1933, it headed the list. Which only proved that what Mae had said to the Salvation Army captain also applied to supposedly puritanical America—"I always knew you could be had."

9

In a community where box-office grosses command professional respect, Mae could by no means be ignored. The astonishing international success of *She Done Him Wrong* earned her grudging acceptance by the Hollywood establishment. She was taken up, granted at a distance, by such solid citizens as Will Rogers, Helen Hayes and Mary Pickford. Rogers described her as "the most interesting woman in Hollywood." Helen Hayes posed with her for a publicity shot, and Mary Pickford, after initially condemning Mae's influence, visited her at the studio. Mary reputedly told Mae she was one of her favorite actresses. Genuinely touched, Mae responded by praising Miss Pickford's lovely face. To which Little Mary replied, "But I have no sex." Apparently having used up her supply of compliments, Mae nodded. "Not on the screen anyway." Still, the mutual admiration society flourished, and eventually Miss Pickford suggested the Mississippi showboat sequence in *Belle of the Nineties.*

So successful was Mae that every studio from MGM to Monogram began developing West clones. White or black, imitators were thought to be box-office attractions. At Warners' even the distinguished dramatic actress Ruth Chatterton was directed to drop her refined diction and adopt a Westian earthiness, while the Michaux Pictures Corporation, catering exclusively to black audiences, came out with a series of films starring Bee Freeman, who was billed as the "Sepia Mae West."

Nor were attempts to commercialize on Mae's appeal limited to Hollywood. The Continental Bus Company paid a West look-alike and her black maid $150 to travel from New York to Los Angeles with overnight stops in major cities as a promotional stunt for bus travel. And in London, Madame Tussaud's added a wax likeness of Mae to those of Du Barry, the Queen of Sheba and Helen of Troy.

Oddly, Paramount's bosses didn't know quite what to do with the real Mae West. They considered adapting *Sex* for the screen, announced *Barnum's Million Dollar Beauty* or *I'm a Million Dollar Beauty*, then abandoned all plans to concentrate on *Czarina*, a dated Broadway hit, to be directed by that master of light comedy Ernst Lubitsch. It quickly became apparent neither of these individualistic artists would compromise, and the project was forgotten.

During a stay in New York Mae had confided to writer-publisher Lowell Brentano that had she not become an actress, she would have enjoyed being a lion trainer. The King of Beasts excited her, and she yearned to climb into a cage to order them around, dominate, even hug them.

Brentano quickly wrote a treatment or screenplay—exactly which is not clear—entitled *The Lady and the Lions*. Mae liked the atmosphere and locale but felt character development and plotting left a lot to be desired. However, she was enthusiastic enough to have Paramount buy the property and give Brentano screen credit for "Story Suggestions."

Harlan Thompson, a Broadway playwright who was under contract to Paramount, was assigned to develop the script. His widow, Marion Spitzer Thompson, recalled, "Harlan *wrote* the script. He did meet with her. How much she contributed I don't know, but she moved in, as she always moved in on everything, and got credit for the story, the screenplay and dialogue. Harlan received the ambiguous billing 'Continuity.'"

According to Bill Thomas, it is easily understood how Mae received the credit. "In those days writers were under contract, getting a weekly salary, damn good money," he said. "The Writers Guild hadn't been formed. Everyone was under one roof, so when a guy finished a script, the producer would give it to someone else to do a little polishing. Some writers like Eddie Moran and Blackout Eddie Welch worked on most scripts. Jack Wagner was a 'Why-don't-you-try-this?'-man on the set.

"Until the Screen Writers Guild was formed, there wasn't much pride of authorship. Nobody raised a stink about it. If anyone did, the next day his ass would be on the street. And where the hell would he go for another job? So there's no mystery how Mae got major screenplay credit. Any big star—Dietrich, Garbo or Crawford—could have demanded and got it. Who was going to jeopardize his job for a script that passed through that many hands?"

In addition, writers assumed they were creating ephemeral entertainment. Nevertheless, they did resent the system. As work on the script progressed, Thompson was annoyed to find himself forced to listen to Timony, who, uninvited, sat at the writers' table in the commissary every day and talked obsessively about Mae. One noontime he was telling everyone what a great woman, great singer, great writer, great all-around artist she was. At last Thompson could tolerate Timony's monologue no longer. Fixing him with a steady gaze, he said, "Jim, the trouble with you is you're always blowing your own strumpet."

As preparations began for *I'm No Angel,* as *The Lady and the Lions* had been retitled, Mae summoned Bill Thomas to discuss the publicity campaign. Thomas informed her that he had been promoted and placed in charge of advertising and exploitation. Mae asked who was assigned to her new picture. "Blake McVeigh," Thomas said. "He just finished working on *Hello, Everybody.*" "Oooooooooh," the superstitious Mae moaned. "Don't mention that name! It's like whistlin' in my dressin' room."

Like all performers, Mae had seen too many stars flare and burn out. To protect herself, she avoided situations, objects and persons believed to bring bad luck. She also tried to appease the Fates by doling out money to those who were down on their luck. When a *Variety* reporter learned she had contributed $25,000 to the Motion Picture Relief Fund, she said, "It's true, but you can't print it." In addition, she gave thousands to the Catholic Church to aid unwed mothers and donated her old limousines to convents because, she said, "It depresses me to see nuns riding on buses or in Fords."

Old-time actors could be sure she would find a bit for them in her films. Edward Hearn, whose reputation had been tarnished by his female impersonations in *The Drag* and *Pleasure Man,* made token appearances in most of Mae's films, beginning with *I'm No Angel.* Dan Marakenko and his wife, featured dancers who could find no bookings after the demise of big-time vaudeville, called on Mae in New York, where she was making an appearance with *She Done Him Wrong,* to ask if there might be anything for him in Hollywood. Mae sized him up and casually said that if he and his wife ever came to the West Coast to give her a call. He did, and within twenty-four hours he was set at $300 a week to play the ringmaster in *I'm No Angel.*

Returning to Manhattan for personal appearances with *She Done Him Wrong,* Mae met Libby Taylor, a former black actress, who was working as a barbecue cook in Harlem's Black and Gold. Sensing Miss Taylor would make an excellent straight woman, Mae put her into the act she was doing to promote her current vehicle. They worked so well together Mae took her to Hollywood to appear in the next two West films.

Miss Taylor, Louise Beavers and Hattie McDaniel all played Mae's maids at various times. Phyllis Klotman of the Afro-American Studies Department at the University of Indiana has pointed out: "Although in subservient positions and acting often as foils for Mae West's barbed one-liners ('It's not the men in your life, it's the life in your men!'), they were more handmaidens/confidantes than typical mammy maids. The world of Mae West was a great deal more democratic than the big house environment whether pre- or post-emancipation. . . . In *I'm No Angel,* she had an entourage, partially presided over by Gertrude Howard of 'Peel me a grape, Beulah' fame. Not a great deal was made of it, but Mae's conversations with her confidantes indicate that these women do have a life of their own. . . ."

Loyal, thoughtful and generous though she often was, above all, she remained the tough-minded pragmatist any star must be to survive in the entertainment field.

While preproduction work on *I'm No Angel* was under way, Mae spent her spare time at the Al G. Barnes Wild Animal Circus headquarters in Los Angeles, storing impressions, cutting up jackpots with circus veterans and, especially, talking with animal trainer Mabel Stark. Miss Stark, a former nurse, was, like Mae, fascinated with the big cats. Her specialty was wrestling tigers, and most of her body was covered with scar tissue from wounds she had received, sometimes from a vicious animal, more often from playful ones. Mae confided that Miss Stark was the only woman in the world she'd consider trading places with, to which Miss Stark replied, "We'll switch. I wish I were Mae West."

Filming on *I'm No Angel,* with grandiose settings, eye-catching costumes and a splendid supporting cast, began July 11, 1933. Cary Grant was again opposite Mae, this time playing the type of suave charmer that was to become his trademark. The story opens on a small-time carnival-circus. Tira (Mae) doubles as a cooch dancer and wild animal trainer, while on the side she indulges in luring horny chumps to hotels to relieve them of their money. After Slick (Ralf Harolde), her pickpocket ex-lover, supposedly kills a Dallas chump, Tira decides to go straight. She works up a daring stunt, putting her head in a lion's mouth, a feat that takes her from the tall-grass circuit to Madison Square Garden.

Tira's beauty and daring attract the attention of blue-blooded Kirk Lawrence (Kent Taylor), who showers her with gifts accompanied with cards containing such sentiments as "To Tira, who can tame more than lions."

At the urging of Kirk's snooty fiancée, Alicia (Gertrude Michaels), cousin Jack Clayton (Grant) attempts to persuade Tira to leave Kirk alone. Tira, attracted to Clayton, agrees. They fall in love, and she decides to leave the big show. Her boss plants Slick, clad in pajamas, in Tira's apartment, where Clayton discovers him and concludes Tira is being untrue to him.

Clayton drops her. Enraged, Tira sues him for breach of promise, demanding a million dollars, and wangles permission to represent herself in court. She wins by exposing the true character of Slick, and Clayton capitulates, paying her the million.

As the film ends, he tells her he believes she really loves him and he finds her more fascinating than ever. "Well, I get better as I go along," Tira assures him as she tears up his million-dollar check. "You've got a lot of other things to make a girl happy," she informs him. When he asks what she is thinking about, she replies, "The same thing you are."

This bare plot gives no hint of the richness and rhythm of the actual film as it emerges under Wesley Ruggles's direction. A case can be made for *I'm No Angel* as the best of Mae's films on several counts. It is more cinematic than *She Done Him Wrong*. The songs include "I Want You, I Need You," "They Call Me Sister Honky Tonk," "Goin' to Town," "No One Loves Me Like That Dallas Man," and "I'm No Angel." The dialogue sparkles with a barrage of verbal wit. "You just tell me about my future," she says to a fortune-teller. "You see, I know all about my past." In answer to how she acquired so many beautiful things, she replies, "It's a gift, honey, it's a gift!" She advises, "Take all you can get and give as little as possible," counsels, "Find 'em, fool 'em and forget 'em." Asked whether she believes in marriage, she responds, "Only as a last resort." She boasts, "When I'm good, I'm very good, but when I'm bad, I'm better." Asked by Clayton if he can trust her, she replies, "You can. Hundreds have."

As Tira, Mae played a hard-bitten but fascinating broad who, finding herself with what she assumes to be a corpse in her hotel room, wastes no sympathy on the supposed victim but concentrates on having the body removed. It was a part she had played often and well during her stage career, and it was especially effective in contrast with the characters of café society. Her earthiness, overstated beauty and novel slant on life could be expected to intrigue the blasé males already impressed with her bravery in the lions' den. That Tira proves to be a whore with a heart of gold is perfectly in keeping with the script's stock characters.

Cary Grant once said that making two pictures with Mae was like taking a crash course in film acting. "She instinctively knew everything about camera angles and lighting, and she taught me all I know about timing. For me she was the right person, who came along at a crucial point in my career. Those two pictures gave me the kind of showcase every actor dreams of."

Kent Taylor, the second lead in *I'm No Angel,* said, after his retirement, he would gladly have accepted the assignment for nothing. "I want to tell you I've worked with a lot of greats— Carole Lombard, Hedy Lamarr, Crawford, Lana Turner. And all those dames sure as hell could have taken a lesson from Mae."

Prior to *I'm No Angel* Taylor had often tried to introduce a few humorous characteristics to the saps he played. "I was tired of doing the conventional character," he recalled. "During a scene I'd fix the star with an 'I'll-bet-you'd-make-a-hell-of-a-lay' look and the director would yell 'cut' and tell me I couldn't get away with it. That's how times have changed. But our director, Wesley Ruggles, never bothered me about it because Mae was doing the same thing.

"She was a hell of a gal. She gave me a signed picture: 'To Kent, If you're half the man I think you are, you'll do.'"

That line, originally an ad lib, was incorporated into the picture. "In one scene I was wearing tails and a white scarf," Taylor remembered. "During the take she removed the scarf from around my neck and wrapped it around my rear end, pulled me close to her and really gave me the old dry screw. I responded. I was at an age, believe me, if I hadn't had makeup on, you'd have seen me blushing, and the cause of the blush, I'm sure, inspired her ad lib."

The chemistry between Mae and Taylor was evident to a fan magazine writer who reported in *Silver Screen:*

> Director Wesley Ruggles was putting Mae and Kent Taylor through a snappy scene. . . . Mae turned on the heat. . . . Mr. Taylor began to burn. . . . She gave him the Westian eye business—down on his shoes, his ankles . . . now on his third waistcoat button, now his tie . . . the eyes. . . . That's the sexiest eyetrick in the world, if you really want to know. Marlene Dietrich's left to right eye shift is like a bottle of sarsparilla in an absinthe shop compared with it.

(Despite attempts of fan magazine writers and columnists to instigate a feud between Mae and Dietrich, the two sex goddesses wouldn't rise to the bait.)

The most novel scene in the film is the one in which Mae enters the lions' cage, puts the beasts through their paces and, as a climax, pries open the mouth of one of them and thrusts her head between its jaws. It was assumed around the studio that a stunt woman would be used, but Mae, in her fascination with the big cats, vetoed the plan and insisted on performing the trick herself. Afterward she learned that earlier the same morning one of the cats had mangled its trainer's arm.

Various film historians have claimed that Mae's appearance in the cage was achieved through a process shot and that the story of the trainer's mangled arm originated in the publicity department. When asked, Teete Carl, who was no longer associated with publicity or anything else at Paramount, vigorously denied the allegations. "Mae went into the cage and did the stunt, and the trainer had been hurt that morning. The studio gave her protection as they would any valuable piece of property by strategically positioning marksmen instructed to kill any animal that began acting up. It probably is true that the cat in whose mouth Mae stuck her head had been tranquilized, but it still took a lot of courage to go in there." (In 1976 Paramount police lieutenant Fritz Hawkes recalled guarding the closed set. He claimed that Mae not only performed the feat in the film but also put her head in the lion's mouth at the wrap party since that scene was the last one filmed.)

Like the action in the lions' den, almost everything else progressed smoothly during the shooting of the picture. Mae was good-natured and thoughtful, but firm in dealing with executives, other actors and Ruggles. "There was a real sweetness about her," Taylor reminisced. "But you'd no more think of crossing her than you would an army drill sergeant."

I'm No Angel's world premiere was held at the Oriental Theater in Chicago on October 4, 1933, grossing $4,800 between six o'clock and closing, setting a record for an opening at that house. Paramount quickly renegotiated Mae's contract and on October 13 signed her to a new eight-picture pact, for two films a year.

When *I'm No Angel* opened in Los Angeles, Edwin Schallert reported in the Los Angeles *Times* that the picture drew one of the largest street crowds ever to gather outside Grauman's Chinese Theater. Upon her arrival at the premiere, Mae quipped, "It's nice to be in a place where they take your footprints rather than your fingerprints," which earned her the most tumultuous ovation Schallert had ever observed. "Mae West is more than a star. She is a phenomenon. They come once in a generation of movie going," he said.

In addition to praise from the newspapers, trade papers and newsweeklies, *I'm No Angel* and Mae attracted attention from unexpected sources who analyzed her popularity.

William Troy, in the *Nation,* found the picture

of a great deal of interest, although of an oblique and rather intellectual nature. . . . It is another astonishing example of the phenomenon of personality in the theater. From the moment that Miss West issues from her tent . . . we are completely subjugated by personality. Miss West's acting style is at once both traditional and burlesque. Unfortunately there is a certain confusion possible here because one means both that Miss West's style is in the tradition of American burlesque, or "burlycue," and that it is a burlesque of that tradition. Whatever one may think of that tradition, it must be granted that Miss West has brought it to its classic culmination. One may use such a word as classic because of the extreme objectivity in which Miss West recognizes and employs her materials. So perfectly does she now sum up in her own person—her speech, gestures and carriage—the main elements of her tradition that she no longer requires a story or even a backdrop. She would be effective on a bare concert stage.

Then, going on to explain her vogue among those who felt it necessary to justify enjoyment of "vulgarity, crudeness and irrepressible gusto," Troy wrote:

The reason these people can appreciate her with such safety is to be found in her own special care to make them feel that this is after all something just put on, a broad joke, a burlesque of burlesque. By a tone of voice or an expression of the eyes, Miss West makes everything seem all right. And thus by making possible an intellectual defense for its perhaps unconscious response to her very real and great energies she enables her audience to save its face.

John Mason Brown observed of Mae's career:

These unregenerate Thaises of the Tenderloin that Miss West loves to play—and plays so grandly—move in a world that has little or no relation to real life. . . . She has no inhibitions. . . . There is something delightfully anachronistic about Miss West; something that belongs to the frontiersman's idea of fun, to the days of free-lunch counters, and yet that has about it the imperiousness of a vanished race of regal sirens. . . .

The truth is Miss West is that rarest of all species among contemporary artists. She is pre-Freudian. . . . Her approach to what Mr. [Percy] Hammond has dubbed the "obstinate urge" is as simple as her dress is ornate. To her sex is sex, and that is all there is to it, or, for that matter, to life. . . . To misquote George Ade, she is a bad girl who needs no help. . . .

Warming to his subject, Brown continued:

She shakes speeches out of her mouth as if they were dice being rolled with terrifying deliberation from a box. Her sentences writhe like serpents. Vocally, she is a hoochie-koochie artist. . . .

Her exploits as a saleswoman of sex benefit by being exaggerated until they belong to the mock-epic class. Both as an authoress and as an actress, she continues the Paul Bunyon tradition.

Brown wrote that she seemed to recoil and comment on her speeches while playing them seriously. "She makes passion palatable to a puritan public by making even its intensity ludicrous." To him, her heroines were "so unreal they do not matter." That by her extravagance she was making palatable the message that women as well as men were sexual creatures and doing it in a humorous way, Brown seems first to endorse and then to deny.

Forty years later in Jon Tuska's *The Films of Mae West,* Tuska came to terms with the content of her characters in general and Tira in *I'm No Angel* in particular. He observed:

> There is a moral philosophy in this picture, despite the fact that it was originally criticized for moral lassitude. That philosophy has to do with the admission of woman's sexual nature, no less legitimate than man's. It has to do with the comic overtones of lust, greed, vanity and their basic futility. But more than any of these, it has to do with what it is, precisely, that attracts both men and women and cements them into a social order, what brings them genuinely closer to each other rather than what divides them. In her personal relationship with people around her . . . Tira embraces all of life and all of man, without hatred or pettiness, but with wit, tolerance, equality, and with personal capability, mastery of herself and her world, the world in which she lives and, by extension, the world in which all of us must live.

While high-, middle- and lowbrow critics concurred on the artistic merits of *I'm No Angel,* its commercial success was even greater. It grossed $85,000 in the first week of its New York run and $75,000 during the second week, compared with $52,000 for rival Jean Harlow's *Bombshell.* Eventually the film, which was produced at a cost of $225,000, earned more than $3 million at a time when $500,000 was a satisfactory return. "Virtue has its own reward, but not at the box office," said Mae, who then asked, "Why should I go good when I'm packin' 'em in because I'm bad?"

Not everything was perfect, of course. Custom had it that reigning stars turned out for each other's premieres, lending glamour to the event and attracting personal publicity for themselves. When *I'm No Angel* opened in Hollywood, following the awesome success of *She Done Him Wrong*, a kind of spontaneous boycott developed among most of the major stars. It can be attributed to envy of Mae's swift climb and to the fact that some people were genuinely scandalized by her.

Mae's response was: "There may not have been many picture people, but the society crowd turned up, and that's my idea of a house. That set a lot more tone than the gang that let the business get into the shape where there was talk of turnin' theaters into office buildings or parking lots, know what I mean?"

Perhaps the only top Hollywood home Mae was invited to in the early 1930's was the Hunt Strombergs'. Mae and Kitty Stromberg, wife of the distinguished MGM producer, had met and become friends at the Assistance League, to whose thrift shop Mae donated her gowns. Mae was intrigued by Kitty's stockmarket acumen while Kitty enjoyed Mae's wit. Mae dined at the Strombergs' frequently and, according to Hunt, Jr., always assumed the occasion was formal, even though the other guests seldom dressed for dinner.

"Mae was considered low-class because it was rumored she hung around with blacks, wrestlers and fags. But none of that bothered Mother," said Hunt, Jr. His most vivid recollection came from once eavesdropping on an upstairs extension when his mother invited Mae to dinner. Mae said she would be delighted to come but requested a favor. "There's a most attractive man you and Hunt know. I'd like you to invite him for me. Joe Schenck."

"So my mother called Joe, who was a big shot with Twentieth Century-Fox. He was a pudgy, gross, little man. He said he couldn't dine but would come after dinner. Well, when my parents had small evenings of ten or twelve, they still hired an eight-piece orchestra. I wasn't old enough to be at the party, but I peeked from the top of the staircase.

"Joe arrived shortly after dinner, and I can still see him and Mae dancing the tango, doing the dips. She seemed mesmerized by him. I don't know whether anything came of it, but it was obvious she had a crush on him. They looked like Beauty and the Beast."

Whether or not she was invited to the homes of industry leaders was of no consequence to Mae. From the beginning she was completely happy in her unpretentious apartment. On the outer door was a minuscule triangular opening, through which callers could be scrutinized, and the numeral 611. (She regarded the apartment as a good-luck retreat since 6 + 1 + 1 equals 8, which she believed to be her lucky number. Later she managed to have her dressing room, her telephone number and her license plate incorporate variations of 8.)

The decor of the apartment remained the same during her entire tenancy, and the furniture always reflected the personality of the owner. No one ever doubted that Mae had seen to "the decoratin'" which struck one writer as "early French candybox" and another as "late wedding cake."

There was an entrance hall, a living room, two bedrooms, two baths, a kitchen and a tiny breakfast room. The living room, on the small side, was crowded with white, cream, beige, gold and pale pink furnishings. Between two front windows was a mirror surrounded by a shell of Venus. The mirror, slightly curved, produced the illusion of added height and reduced weight. All coffee tables had mirrored tops backed with gold instead of silver to produce a glowing reflection. "It cheers you up when you look in one of those tables. You get the feelin' you're in the money," Mae explained. On the floor were three polar bear rugs, one of which she claimed was the "largest retail polar bear in Hollywood." She dismissed a visitor's description of a larger one shot by the late director Woody Van Dyke with "I ain't got time to have mine shot to measure."

Against one wall was a huge white sofa, with cushions and whoopee dolls scattered about. The room was filled with enormous arrangements of artificial flowers and numerous favorite photos of the occupant at different stages of her life. A white-and-gold grand piano dominated all.

The guest bedroom, originally occupied by her brother, John, was done entirely in white, except for a mirrored wall and a gold plaque of a sword. Mae's bedroom-dressing room suite also reflected the essence of the owner. The furnishings were Louis XIV. Like the living room, it carried a white, beige, gold, pale pink and mirrored scheme. The quilted headboard stood beneath the famous mirrored ceiling which Mae had installed because, as she explained, "I like to see how I'm doin'."

She described her bedroom as "royal." It had been inspired, she said, by the great ladies of the eighteenth century who received callers in their boudoirs, which she believed gave the occupant of the bed a psychological advantage. "You're lyin' there perfectly comfortable 'n' the guys are fidgetin.' There's a lot of good mental thought behind that."

If Mae's bedroom aroused the most curiosity, the closet-sized kitchen drew hardly a mention. Mae recalled venturing in there only a couple of times. "I did make coffee once," she said, "after sendin' out for instructions. But then I got otherwise involved in somethin' more interestin' and forgot to turn off the heat. Well— I never turn off the heat."

The only time she actually cooked occurred shortly after she and Timony arrived in Los Angeles. Having been detained at a meeting, he arrived at his own apartment at the Ravenswood past the dinner hour and knocked on Mae's door to ask what was in the icebox. She looked, saw a carton of eggs and some leftovers and decided to try her hand at an omelet. To the dozen eggs she added some creamed onions, boiled spinach, stewed tomatoes and half a pound of butter and poured the mix into a frying pan. Timony told her it was the best omelet he ever had eaten.

Timony was more glutton than gourmet. His sister said that as a young man he would devour an entire ham by himself. In Hollywood he would spot a hot dog stand, send the chauffeur around the block and be waiting with two hot dogs in each hand and two more stuffed in his coat pockets when the car returned. It is hardly surprising that on the Coast he ballooned to 280 pounds. By then Mae was fond of him and relied on him, but any romantic feelings she may have harbored had been long extinguished. Still, he guarded her zealously, threatening her suitors while she continued to encourage them.

Depending on their point of view, people arrived at conflicting opinions about Mae's relationship with Timony. John Bright wryly concluded it was nearly perfect. "He was one of her eighteen thousand lovers while she was young, but like most con men, he conned himself into thinking he still meant something special to her. He was a friend, but the friendship was based on a con woman's respect for a super con man."

Co-workers Teete Carl and Bill Thomas of the Paramount publicity department, who might have been expected to see him from the same vantage point, disagreed. "I never got into their private life, but he knew everybody in the department whether or not they had anything to do with Mae," Carl said. "A lot of ideas originated with him. He was for anything that furthered her image. He was a great manager, he really was, and she appreciated him."

Bill Thomas, on the other hand, believed that from the time she made her hit in *Night After Night* she looked upon Timony as a respected but outmoded relic. "I don't know what he contributed to her stage career, probably a lot. She certainly seemed fond of him, but he was like a big collie dog following her around. I liked Jim, even though he'd boast what he could do and he really had no authority professionally. He couldn't even okay tie-ins. Now Murray Fiel from the William Morris office had some influence. She'd listen to him, but not to Jim."

Whatever his status, Timony still shared many interests with Mae. They liked going to men's restaurants for rare steaks. They were racing enthusiasts and avid boxing and wrestling fans. Mae's enthusiasm for the fights was so great that in 1932 and 1933 she held ringside seats at the Olympic Auditorium on alternate Tuesdays, the Pavillion in Santa Monica on Wednesdays and the American Legion Stadium on Fridays. At the end of the evening she and Timony would settle their private wagers before leaving the halls.

At these boxing matches, whenever she spotted a fighter who interested her, she'd give a secret signal to Morrie Cohen or Sewey Welch, bookers who were good friends of hers. The prospect then would be brought around to be introduced. Mae took it from there.

As her financial position improved, Mae backed a number of fighters. "I'd always had the inclination from the time I saw my father fight," she explained, estimating that by 1932 she had attended 2,000 matches. Once, when someone asked whether she had ever seen the great champion Jack Johnson, Mae responded, "No, but he came up to see me several times."

When Mae met Max Baer, the attraction between her and the heavyweight champion of the world was immediate and mutual. One day out of the blue Baer phoned from the lobby of the Ravenswood and Mae invited him up. They talked for a while. "Then he said he was curious about my famous bed. One thing led to another 'n' we were soon in it," Mae recalled. When their lovemaking was over, Baer went to the window, pulled up the shade and stood there naked, waving to somebody down the street at the El Royale apartments. Mae asked what he thought he was doing, and he replied he had won a $500 bet with his agent, who had opera glasses trained on her bedroom window. Mae loved telling the story on herself.

One of her agents was sometimes delegated to approach a man who had caught Mae's attention. In the early 1930's Jack Durant, the husky ex-acrobat, was working in films and living at the Ravenswood. One morning, as he entered his apartment after a sunbath, his phone rang. It was Mae's agent, who explained Mae had invited Durant to escort her to the fights at the Olympic. He agreed, and at seven-thirty Mae's chauffeur drove Durant to Paramount to call for her.

Durant wondered whether she would mention trying to hire him from the Dancing Shoes act at Fox's Folly fifteen years earlier. He was never to know. After greeting him warmly, she began humming under her breath and continued to do so even during the bloodiest fistic exchanges. Annoyed, Durant broke in to ask, "Do you dance as well as sing?," thinking his little joke might remind her of their earlier encounter. But she neither laughed nor stopped humming until they were back at the Ravenswood in the elevator. When they reached Durant's floor, Mae said, "You're comin' up with me." Durant did.

Entering her apartment, she told him to make himself at home. Shortly after, she reappeared wearing only a sheer negligee. "Do you like what ya see?" she inquired. Irritated that after giving nothing of herself all evening, she expected him to perform stud service, Durant replied, "Yeah. Not bad for an old girl," which caused Mae to begin throwing things.

Ducking, Durant went into a series of one-line imitations of Clark Gable, Herbert Marshall and other film stars. His performance dissipated Mae's anger and eventually broke her up. "Listen, between pictures I could take you out on a personal appearance tour, doing your imitations. It'd be a sensation."

"Yeah," Durant replied. "I can just see the billing: 'Mae West and Her Men.'" Mae ordered him out.

Perhaps because he represented a challenge, Mae continued seeing Durant. Columnists Harrison Carroll, Jimmy Starr and others built up a romance in the newspapers. Privately they kept inquiring what Mae did in bed. "When I kept telling them I didn't know, they began accusing me of being queer. So I finally told them, 'Yeah, she's the greatest.' But I never touched her," Durant confided years later.

Lovers were plentiful, but there were, inevitably, some like

Durant who failed to respond and others who tried to take advantage of her.

One handsome black singer who appeared at a small nightclub in Los Angeles developed a reputation for his skilled sexual technique. According to his story, Mae sent word she was willing to receive him. The singer, who had grown up on the streets, was earning about $400 a week but squandered much of it shooting craps and playing poker. So he supplemented his salary by going to bed with any woman willing to pay. He assumed Mae was aware of the arrangement when he went to the Ravenswood. As he was getting dressed, he casually asked for his present. He said Mae looked aghast, then said she'd forgotten and asked what he wanted. An old Harlem gag was: "I need a new pair of shoes, baby," and he used it. Mae got out of bed, promising he would get them. A moment later she reappeared wielding one of her platform Wedgies and conked him over the head. Her outrageous response took him by surprise. He burst out laughing and left without the customary "little gift."

Of the men who rejected Mae several types can be identified. There was the macho man who was turned off by her reversal of roles, making him the pursued and her the pursuer. Neither did she appeal to the man who required a shrinking-violet, Madonna type. She repelled men who were intimidated by healthy vulgarity. The same was true of those who wanted a relationship in addition to intercourse. One such fellow commented, "I didn't want to be a male sex object. With her it came through loud and clear that you could be a combination of Einstein and Cary Grant but you would mean nothing if a well-built fighter with a crooked nose, cauliflower ears and the IQ of an ape appeared."

10

Paramount, elated by Mae's success but fearful that she might prove a nova instead of a star, rushed her into a fourth film. The picture was briefly announced as *That St. Louis Woman* then changed to *It Ain't No Sin.* The two Bills, Thomas and Pine, heads of advertising and exploitation at the studio, quickly capitalized on the title. Their first step was to purchase fifty African parrots. "There were no tape recorders in those days, but we had a record made repeating, 'It ain't no sin,'" Bill Thomas recalled. "We had a guy feed and water them for two or three weeks. Twenty-four hours a day all they heard was: 'It ain't no sin.' We bought fifty beautiful gilt cages and had Mae write messages to send along with the parrots to the biggest exhibitors and columnists. We were all set to ship them when notice came that the title was changed to *Belle of the Nineties.*"

Teete Carl maintained the parrots were worth every penny and hour spent on them. "I invited the major wire services over to listen to them. As a matter of fact, I think we grabbed more space about the failure than we would have if the stunt had been successful. Newspaper guys always loved to write about anything that made press agents look sappy. Then after the two Bills got rid of the birds, we got a lot more space spreading the story they'd been released in South American jungles which echoed with cries of 'It ain't no sin!'"

When casting began, Paramount announced that George Raft would play opposite Mae. Raft objected. He said a man could be had the first time by mistake, but if he let himself be had the second time, it was his own fault. "Let's face it," he told Emanuel Cohen, "this picture will be ninety-nine percent Mae West and one-half percent Georgie Raft." To his surprise, Cohen agreed and borrowed Roger Pryor from Universal. Johnny Mack Brown as the southern sugar daddy and John Miljan as the double-dealing nightclub owner were delighted with their roles. But half of Paramount's female contract players called in ill or claimed to be overworked until C. B. De Mille's daughter, Katherine, was cast as Miljan's mistress.

Belle of the Nineties is a complicated tale of Ruby Carter, "Queen of the Entertainers from St. Louis," whose affair with the Tiger Kid, a fighter, is broken up by his manager. Ruby accepts a New Orleans engagement at Ace Lamont's Sensation House. Ace makes a play for her, but Ruby prefers Brooks Claybourne, who bedecks her with diamonds. Ace signs Tiger Kid to fight the Champ in a boxing match he's promoting. He also persuades Tiger Kid to rob "a lady blackmailer" of her diamonds. It turns out to be Ruby.

Meanwhile, Ace bets on the Kid, Claybourne on the champ. In the twenty-sixth round Ruby surreptitiously adds knockout drops to Tiger Kid's water bucket. Claybourne recoups his gambling losses, and Ace is ruined. The Kid accuses Ruby of slipping the mickey to him, but she cons him into thinking Ace did it, and the Kid *accidentally* kills Ace. Then Ruby *accidentally* sets fire to the Sensation House. And the picture *accidentally* ends with Ruby and Tiger Kid's marriage.

Ludicrous as the plot sounds, it is peppered with some well-remembered Westian lines. Told a painting is an old master, Mae replies: "Looks more like an old mistress to me." She confides, "A man in the house is worth two on the street," and explains, "I'm just gettin' even with two guys that are so low they could walk under that door without taking their hats off." She acknowledges, "It's better to be looked over than overlooked." Asked if her method of acquiring jewels didn't unnerve her, she replies, "No. I was calm and *collected*." Responding to a suitor's recital of her physical assets, she cries, "Wait a minute! Wait a minute! Is this a proposal or are you taking inventory?"

The picture also benefited from the contributions of director Leo McCarey and Duke Ellington and His Orchestra. McCarey, who had served his apprenticeship directing comedy shorts and then a Marx Brothers movie, believed that highlighting Mae's personality in each scene or musical sequence superseded the importance of a logically developed story. The musical numbers, particularly, retain their effectiveness, illustrating Mae's show-manly instincts in insisting that Paramount hire the Duke Ellington Orchestra instead of using black extras to mime numbers prerecorded by studio musicians.

"My Old Flame" is first introduced simply by having a request that Ruby sing her favorite song. Then, throughout the picture, the song is used as background music to underscore the emotional ties that still exist whenever Ruby and the Kid meet during their estrangement. "Memphis Blues" is given an innovative treatment, and there is the diverting "When a St. Louis Woman Comes Down to New Orleans." Although not entirely successful, "Troubled Waters" mixes the Negro spiritual with New Orleans jazz and melds them in counterpoint. The impact is heightened by McCarey's and cinematographer Karl Struss's surrealism to express the emotions of the music. Still another number, "American Beauty," sung by Gene Austin, is the excuse to introduce Mae in a series of camp costumes. It is a tribute to the soundness of the conception of the number that it retains interest after numerous imitative presentations—some serious, others satirical. The effect is not unlike, but less sophisticated than, Rodgers and Hart's "In the Flower Garden of My Heart." "American Beauty" presents Mae in tableaus as a rose, a butterfly, a bat, a spider and the Statue of Liberty—causing critic George Jean Nathan to wisecrack that the latter might better have been described as the "Statue of Libido."

Actress Louise Brooks recalled that Travis Banton had a field day creating costumes that accentuated Mae's best points. (In the fitting room Mae would entertain him with details of her chauffeur's sexual performances, unaware she could be heard in the next cubicle by Mary and Letha, two old-maid Irish-Catholic seamstresses, who did some exceedingly erratic sewing.) "She was extremely sensitive and thoughtful as well as grateful to Travis for accentuating her bosom and waistline," said Miss Brooks.

Having heard about Banton's Chinese jade collection, Mae gave him an exquisite figurine for Christmas. Banton was impressed, especially since Marlene Dietrich had given him identical wristwatches on four successive Christmases.

Karl Struss recalled in 1978 that once *Belle of the Nineties* started filming, Mae always went to see the dailies. "I'd say she shared Irving Thalberg's view—use any technique you want, but make sure it makes the subject look beautiful.

"Leo McCarey, the director, was captain of the ship," Struss continued, "but I had full control of the crew—makeup, costume consultation, all different departments, including the all-important lighting to show off everything to best advantage. As executive officer I took all that responsibility from the director so he could concentrate on his idea of the script.

"I lit Mae depending on the angle. If she was looking from right to left, my key light was from the left side and vice versa. That makes the narrow side of the face brighter than the other side and narrows the whole face. It also puts the chin line in the shade." Whatever Struss did, Mae liked it, writing of him in a promotional book: "Karl is my cameraman and what he can do for a gal's curves is something to write about. He really brings them out in the right places. . . ."

Struss returned Mae's professional respect. He regarded her as her own best critic and director. He remembered the occasion when McCarey was directing promo footage to be sent to a convention in London. "We were shooting in the makeup department," Struss recalled. "After about ten minutes she said, 'Gentlemen, we're not going to get it today.' She knew she was just saying lines. She wasn't putting her personality in her stuff, and she realized it before McCarey did. She could feel the emotions and quips weren't flowing. The shooting was postponed a day. She didn't blame the script; she just waited until she could approach it in a relaxed way which gave her the sparkle she wanted."

Mae's personal life had taken a melodramatic turn in 1932. On September 27, her limousine had been damaged in an accident. Harry Voiler, a burly, wisecracking forty-two-year-old, who had first come into Mae's life when he was Texas Guinan's business manager, volunteered to drive her and Timony to and from the studio until their limo had been repaired. Voiler enjoyed his reputation as a check-grabbing man-about-town and a close associate of Mae's.

The evening of the twenty-eighth, after calling for them at Paramount, he drew up across from the Ravenswood, and Timony went into the apartment house, leaving Mae chatting with Voiler. Suddenly a stocky man, wearing a snap-brim hat pulled low over his forehead and his collar turned up to shade his face, leaped from a nearby hedge, his right hand stuffed in his coat pocket as if he held a drawn gun. He nervously demanded Mae's "poke."

Mae made a wisecrack, assuming this was a practical joke, but when the gunman barked, "Snap out of it, baby!" she realized he was serious. Aware that Voiler always carried a gun, she deliberately tossed her diamond necklace to the ground so that her assailant had to stoop over to retrieve it. But Voiler failed to act. When she fumbled at the clasp on her bracelet, the gunman threatened to pistol-whip her.

"All right, take it," Mae told him. "I can always get along without my diamonds, but I can't let anythin' happen to my face." She quickly turned over a bracelet, ring, wristwatch and brooch—all diamond-encrusted—and her handbag.

The gunman scooped them up, warned her and Voiler to forget what he looked like and escaped in a waiting dark green automobile. When Mae reproached Voiler for not drawing his gun, his excuse was that the risk to her had been too great. Mae's loss: $3,400 in cash and more than $12,000 in uninsured jewels.

The incident seemed so blatant a publicity stunt that some newspapers refused to carry the story and others buried it. But the Los Angeles Police Department took the robbery more seriously than the press. In the preceding months Carmel Myers, Jeannette MacDonald, Constance Talmadge and Helene Costello had also been robbed.

District Attorney Buron Fitts and the police department asssured Mae of an exhaustive investigation. Fitts assigned two crack detectives to the case. After a couple of days Voiler claimed he had received a call from the robber, offering to return the loot for $5,000. While Voiler was present, the gunman called Mae, telling her she could test the offer by retrieving her handbag in a nearby vacant lot.

Although the bag was recovered by the two detectives, one of whom was disguised as Mae, the demands were rejected. Voiler then reported another call lowering the amount to $3,000, but Mae also rejected that. Growing suspicious of Voiler, she persuaded Fitts to put a tail on him. After questioning a score of characters Voiler associated with, the two detectives booked Edward H. Friedman and held him incommunicado for thirty-six hours until he confessed.

Friedman appeared before a grand jury on December 4, testifying Voiler had approached him with the robbery plan and suggested he enlist a confederate. Friedman had chosen a Detroit gangster, Morris Cohen. On the afternoon of September 28 the three met between 1:30 and 2:00 P.M. and made plans for Friedman and Cohen to hide across from the Ravenswood about an hour before Voiler was scheduled to deliver Mae. Indictments were returned against Friedman, Cohen and Voiler, but Voiler and Cohen had already fled the state.

When word spread that Mae was appearing as a witness against Friedman, threats from the underworld became so ominous two armed police guards were assigned to protect her. Asked whether she was afraid, Mae replied, "Afraid? Not a bit! I owe this duty to my public. They believe in me. I'm just another citizen doing her duty." On January 22, 1933, her guards found a prowler attempting to enter her apartment at 4:00 A.M. and gave chase, but he eluded them.

After Friedman was convicted on two counts of second-degree robbery, Mae received further threatening calls. The police set up a close watch for any arrivals of out-of-town gangsters. And Mae, who had kept a life insurance salesman dangling for six months, suddenly bought a $100,000 policy. Not to be outdone, Timony took one for $30,000 on himself.

Mae also secretly engaged a personal bodyguard, an action that was to arouse all kinds of jealousy in Timony. The guard's name was Mike Mazurki, a young wrestler who had arrived from New York to work the California circuit. He had immediately attracted Mae's interest when she saw him stride into the ring in Pasadena.

"I was a nice-built kid," Mazurki said matter-of-factly, recalling their initial encounter. "The first time I was introduced to her she said, 'Oh, my God, how beautiful that is!' Morrie Cohen, the promoter, gave me an award as the most popular wrestler of the year, and Miss West presented it to me. She liked doing that."

Shortly after their meeting Mae called Mazurki to explain that some hoods had threatened to throw acid in her face because she'd cooperated with the police regarding her jewel robbery. "I'll want you around all the time, see. Take me to the studio. Be on the set. Watch for anybody tryin' to get too close to me and ruin my face, see?" she told him.

"That's how I started as an actor. All through *Belle of the Nineties* I dressed like an extra. I appeared in a few scenes and kept an eye out for any suspicious characters. I took her to work. I took her home. We'd go for rides. We got to be very close. And when the picture ended, she saw to it I got a credit—Mike Mazurki . . . Extra."

Their alliance continued for more than a year before Mazurki decided he wanted to return to the wrestling circuit. His decision was based partly on the jealous actions of his nemesis, Jim Timony. "He knew what was going on wasn't kosher," Mazurki recalled. "He was too old to do her any good. He could still manage her business, but he wanted to do more than that. A lot of times I'd be downstairs. He'd see me and tell me to get out or he'd call the police. I'd phone Miss West, and she'd promise to get rid of him and tell me to come back in half an hour. Then she'd send him on an errand. See, it got to him that she still had a love life. He couldn't accept these young guys coming up and making love to her, but that was her thing. She took wonderful care of herself. Watched her body all the time. She used to say, 'What keeps me in shape is sex.'"

Mazurki's relationship with Mae operated on a set of clearly spelled-out guidelines. Like most of her lovers, he was never allowed to call her Mae. "She told me, 'When we're alone, call me dear, darling or honey. When we're in public, call me Miss West.' She thought it showed respect."

After Mazurki left Mae's employment, it became increasingly difficult for them to meet without Timony's causing a scene. "When she was working, I'd get a call for a job at Paramount. Miss West arranged it, just like she arranged it that Timony had to be away on business during the lunch hour. That gave me an opportunity to go over to her dressing room. She always knew what time to expect him back, and about fifteen minutes before he was due, she'd say, 'You better get out of here quick.' Not that he was any danger, but he'd nag. 'What are you doing with that guy? Or that other one. They're no help to your career. They'll cheapen you.'"

Mae's cheapening herself was one of Timony's great fears. He saw the value of her interest in fights and even investing in fighters, which got her almost as much space in the sports pages as in the entertainment section. But as often as possible he accompanied her to the arenas. "He was afraid if he wasn't there, she might have mixed with all the fighters," Mazurki said. "He thought it would have hurt her reputation, and it would have, too. The way it worked when I knew her was if she saw a guy that appealed, she'd say to Sewey Welch, 'That last boy looked awfully good in the fight.' To Sewey that meant she had an eye for the fella. So Sewey would give the guy Miss West's number and let them take it from there."

Mazurki believed she preferred wrestlers to fighters on the ground that the worst that happens to a wrestler is that he gets misshapen ears or his nose and bones broken, but boxers often become punch-drunk. "Being punch-drunk wasn't important because it interfered with conversation but because it affected coordination," he said. "What she was looking for was a guy with a nice build. He didn't have to be too handsome. And this is something very few people know—what excited her was a fellow with a busted nose or a cauliflower ear. She liked to fondle it, nuzzle it, kiss it.

"She liked blacks as much as whites. You've heard of Gorilla Jones [William Jones]? I'm not telling things out of school. Gorilla Jones was a beautiful man, a boxer and a champion. Gorilla was kingpin for a long time there. He's at a point where he can't hear anymore. He wears a toupee, too. I see him around Cauliflower Alley—a club where all the old-time boxers and wrestlers hang out. He and Miss West still talked on the phone while she was making *Sextette*." (In a July 1974 issue of *Jet* an article by Robert E. Johnson discussed Mae's association with blacks. Johnson wrote: "Of all the blacks she has known, her relationship with Jones has been the most enduring. As his manager she charted a course that was climaxed with the middle-weight boxing title. As his financial adviser, she made it possible for him to avoid ending his career as a broken, boxing bum. . . ." Later in the article Jones says he was once offered $250,000 to film his story, making him Mae's lover. "That would be a lie because she was just my manager and friend," he said. Mazurki, who was in a position to know, dismisses Jones's denial of the affair.)

During Mazurki's reign Timony had to struggle harder than ever against the erosion of his power. Rumors spread that Mae was firing him. With two smash starring films behind her, she had the full attention of the William Morris Agency. Where Timony had once been essential, providing connections and guile to carry out their outrageous schemes, she now had the clout of a huge talent agency and a major studio.

In an effort to remain indispensable, Timony succeeded in wresting from Paramount Mae's right of approval on both casting and script. Still, rumors of the West-Timony split became so widespread that Mae granted an interview to deny the story. "Mr. Timony is my manager, he always has been my manager, he always will be my manager," she told the reporter. She claimed that people heard them arguing business procedures and concluded they were quarreling. "We don't fight," she said. "Mr. Timony is a very fine manager and I don't want to lose him."

Told of her response, Timony replied, "Miss West is a very fine client and I don't want to lose *her*."

But coping with their relationship became increasingly difficult for Mae as her popularity zoomed. Curiosity about her personal life made her acutely uncomfortable about being seen with Timony. Always secretive about her romances, she saw any romantic connection with him as destructive to her image as a sex symbol. To be linked with a corpulent, red-faced old gentleman with a limp—even a colorful limp caused when a gangster shot him through the foot—humiliated her.

Timony, fully aware of her feelings, placed himself on a stringent diet to lose twenty pounds, exercised to tone up his muscles and even sacrificed his beloved bat-wing collars because he knew that Mae had always hated them. Paradoxically the better the deal he negotiated for her, the further in jeopardy he placed himself. When he succeeded in nudging the William Morris office into obtaining a flat $300,000 per picture plus $100,000 per screenplay, he made her financially independent. She set up an annuity and began to indulge a long-held interest in real estate. On Sunday afternoons—when not occupied with one of her stable of studs—she went driving with Timony through the San Fernando Valley, which was still undeveloped countryside.

Mae foresaw its possibilities, while Timony remained oblivious to his surroundings. He took the drives only to have her to himself. Her interest in real estate was a mystery to him. His indifference was so deep that when his father, who had been a developer of executive homes on the North Shore of Long Island

and of churches and office buildings in Brooklyn, died and left him his holdings, Timony sold what he could and allowed the rest to be seized for back taxes. "He couldn't be bothered, see. Why, he could have made millions!" Mae said disdainfully.

During their excursions she would spot a pretty site and tell Timony to buy it. He would grumble but do as she instructed. Luckily he did. One of the many pretty sites turned into several city blocks in the center of Van Nuys. She paid $16,000 for the land. Later she sold a small parcel of it to Mary Pickford for $180,000. In 1979 Mae estimated she had parlayed the original $16,000 into $5 million.

She also acquired, in 1934, a sixteen-acre orange ranch, near Van Nuys, which included a ten-room house, two small guest-houses and a private racetrack. Gradually she bought trotters and made money even from them. "Those jockeys were always turning out winners for me," she said.

By design or instinct, her purchase of the ranch marked Mae's assumption of Matilda's role in the West family. The ranch provided a haven for her father, her brother, her sister and, temporarily, even her sister's current husband. To John and John II, Mae extended food, shelter and small extravagances that would have been beyond their reach.

Her attempts to establish John with Paramount were less than successful. To keep her happy, the studio hired him as foreman of a labor gang, but shortly after he took over, there was a severe drop in the amount of work accomplished. Investigation revealed that John habitually slept on the job, leaving the men unsuper-vised. Called before his superiors, he indignantly defended himself by saying, "Just because I sleep don't mean my men aren't working." End of job.

Her largess toward Beverly was on a different plane. Theirs was a complex relationship whose roots extended back to the time when they had been unconscious rivals for their parents' approval. It was further complicated by Matilda's early attempts to place Mae in a surrogate mother role when first she convinced her to put Beverly in the sister act and later when she persuaded her to cast Beverly in *Diamond Lil*. Although for a time Mae seemed able to reject any such maternalistic feelings, by 1934 she took on responsibilities toward her sister in a way that would have pleased Matilda.

Certainly Mae and Beverly held ambivalent feelings about their roles. Mae had the controlled personality's mixture of amusement, anger and pity when she discussed her erratic, childlike sister; Beverly was simultaneously grateful and resentful of Mae, on whom she increasingly depended. Rage at and about each other as they might, there was an underlying, deeply felt bond between them.

When Mae's father, suffering from heart disease, took a turn for the worse in November 1934, she rented an apartment for him in the Ravenswood. Timony, of whom he had always been fond, provided companionship for him. It was not for long. On January 7, 1935, seventy-three-year-old Battlin' Jack West died from a cerebral embolism and chronic myocarditis. Mae, who couldn't take time out from filming to accompany the body east, sent Beverly, John and Timony to inter him in the Cypress Hills crypt which she had purchased upon her mother's death.

Timony's devotion to her father touched Mae deeply, even though she made it clear that nothing could rekindle their romantic involvement.

II

Louella Parsons greeted the announcement of Mae's next picture, *Goin' to Town,* as if stifling a yawn:

> Some way there doesn't seem to be quite the excitement over choosing a leading man to play opposite Mae West as there was immediately after her success in *She Done Him Wrong.* Maybe it's because the censors have tamed our Mae and her lines aren't allowed to be as naughty as they were then. . . .

Louella's negative appraisal of Mae and her career was shared by others among the popular press, but serious people were still analyzing her individuality. F. Scott Fitzgerald said she was "the only Hollywood actress with an ironic edge and a comic spark." Novelist Hugh Walpole was impressed by her parody of "the fraying morals of a dreary world."

George Jean Nathan, wittiest of the American drama critics, wrote:

> What the "movie" audiences had uniformly been privileged to see before, over the years, had been nothing but an endless succession of imported lesbians, spindle-shanked, flat-chested flappers, forty-year-old Baby Dolls, beauty parlor imitations of women and

Sylvia-massaged stringbeans, in not one of whom there was any real, genuine, honest-to-God female quality to interest even a vegetarian cannibal. In the midst of this dearth the Mlle. West came like a rainfall, a veritable torrent, upon a dry desert. Here, unmistakably, whatever one might think of her art, was a woman, a female. No little dried-up cutie, no pretty little narrow-shouldered skeleton of a chicken, no parched and skinny pseudo-vamp, no trumped-up, artificial siren, but a good, large, full, round, old-time 1890 woman, with "woman" up and down and sidewise written plainly on her every feature—and all other places.

It remained for Colette to discern the essence of Mae's screen personality:

She alone, out of an enormous and dull catalogue of heroines, does not get married at the end of the film, does not gaze sadly at her declining youth in a silver-framed mirror in the worst possible taste; and she alone does not experience the bitterness of the abandoned "older woman." She alone has no parents, no children, no husband. This impudent woman is, in her style, as solitary as Charlie Chaplin used to be. . . .

. . . Can you honestly name another artist, male or female, in the cinema whose comic acting equals that of this ample blonde who undulates in little waves, who is ornamental with her real diamonds, whose eye is pale and hard, whose throat swells with the coos of a professional dove?

Naturally anyone so original as Mae was perceived to be found it difficult to fit into Hollywood's assembly line.

Paramount, after announcing her for *Goin' to Town,* wavered on that project and began to develop a "modified version" of evangelist Aimee Semple McPherson's life—whatever that may have been. Next, word was sent out that the studio had acquired rights from MGM to *The Unsinkable Mrs. Brown* (a chapter from Gene Fowler's *Timberline*), which had been intended for, of all people, Marie Dressler.

Paramount finally put into production the original choice, *Goin' to Town.* The story, or perhaps the script, depending on who told of the development of the project, was the work of Marion Morgan and George B. Dowell, although Mae limited their contributions and took screenplay and dialogue credits for herself.

The plot tells of Cleo Borden, won in a crap game by a rancher, who finds herself a rich widow after he is gunned down. Inspecting an oil field, part of her inheritance, Cleo spots a polished English geological engineer whom she lassoes and draws to her. He is infuriated, but Cleo is intrigued. When he's sent to Buenos Aires ("Bonus Heiress" in her rendition), she follows, ostensibly to enter her horse in the sweepstakes. There she encounters a society woman who has Cleo's horse drugged, gets involved with the woman's gigolo and enters a marriage of convenience to the socialite's ne'er-do-well nephew, who is contemplating suicide. They move to Southampton and Newport, where Cleo tries to crash society. One of her ploys is a performance of a scene from the opera *Samson and Delilah* in which she sings the aria "My Heart at Thy Sweet Voice."

Meanwhile, the society matron schemes to have the gigolo discredit Cleo. He is more interested in rifling her safe. Cleo's husband discovers the robbery and is accidentally shot. In a mechanical way the socialite is exposed, her nephew is conveniently dispatched to the hereafter by the gigolo, who is captured by the law, making it possible for Cleo to end in the attractive arms of the English engineer, who turns out to be—the Earl of Stratton!!

In addition to the aria, Mae sings "He's a Bad Man," "Love Is Love in Any Woman's Heart" and "Now I'm a Lady," whose tag is "Come up 'n' see me sometime."

Allotted a smaller budget than *Belle of the Nineties, Goin' to Town*, with its scenes of life among the rich and social, attempted to comment on high society, a milieu about which the authors offered no sense of firsthand observation. Difficulty developed in casting the dowager. Janet Beecher refused the role on grounds that no other actress ever showed to advantage in a Mae West film. When other contract players turned down the part, Paramount brought Marjorie Gateson out from New York. Alexander Hall, the film editor on *She Done Him Wrong*, directed.

Shooting began on December 18 and finished on schedule in February 1935. When the picture opened in May, critical response was mixed. Regina Crewe of Hearst's New York *American* tore into it as "trite stuff . . . straining after the flip retort." Howard Barnes of the *Herald Tribune* found it "rowdier, more satirical and generally more amusing stuff than her last starring engagement." After identifying himself as one of Mae's "most abject idolators," Andre Senwald of *The New York Times* lamented that "the great lady is revealing intimations of mortality" and concluded that despite many diverting moments, *Goin' to Town* "is the least successful of the Mae West pictures."

What many critics failed to take into consideration was that unlike most movies, Mae's vehicles operated on the assumption that nothing—the story, the director, the other actors—mattered so long as the opportunity was presented for Mae to exert her spell. In her next film Mae would abandon this premise and attempt something more ambitious.

Mae occupied a paradoxical position at the beginning of 1935. Her salary that year would increase to $480,000 compared to $334,160 for 1934. Overtures to her from MGM, Warners' and Columbia attested to her popularity, and even though she made only one film, she ranked eleventh among box-office stars. But the resignation of Emanuel Cohen as vice-president in charge of creative production at the studio shortly before she finished *Goin' to Town* caused internal problems which affected her. His successors, Ernst Lubitsch and Harry Herzbrun, immediately cut back from an output of five to eight productions a month to one for March. Stories were postponed, and projects shelved. There was nothing penciled in for Mae. She and Lubitsch had differences which made him less than enthusiastic about her. In a discussion of a script, he remonstrated with her for taking all the good lines and giving none to her fellow actors. "I'm writin' the story and I'm the star," she told him. Lubitsch reminded her, "But in every story there must be two characters. Look at *Romeo and Juliet*." Mae sniffed. "Let Shakespeare do it his way. I'll do it mine. We'll see who comes out better."

In search of the right story Mae spent countless hours sitting with William Le Baron, listening to writers outline plots. "Forget it. That's not Mae West. She wouldn't do that," she would interrupt when her screen personality was violated. For instance, *she* never took another woman's husband or even borrowed him for a few hours. *She* never chased a man, *Goin' to Town* notwithstanding. *She* might indicate her interest, but he had to take it from there. On the one hand, *she* never played anyone's mother. On the other, no one except herself could imply either by attitude or dialogue that *she* was "tough 'n' hard-boiled." *She* seldom showed her "limbs," explaining that exposing her body detracted from her face.

Mae was always interested in developing scenes that would broaden "Mae West's" appeal. "I always try to include somethin' for the kiddies, yuh know what I mean? Like lassoing the Englishman in *Goin' to Town*. Or puttin' my head in the lion's mouth."

For the females, she offered opulent costumes and fresh faces—Cary Grant, Kent Taylor and Johnny Mack Brown. "If I play opposite some timeworn leading man, the women in the audience might feel like they were watchin' an ex-husband with another woman. It's old stuff. I like to give 'em somethin' fresh."

During these discussions Mae never deviated from the position that she knew the Mae West character—as she called her—better than anyone else did. Nor did she attempt to put writers who were talking their stories at ease. "She'll listen, agree or argue as long as she's interested in the story. Once she starts humming under her breath, I know it's useless to pursue the discussion," Le Baron told a reporter.

The search for Mae's next film ended when Marion Morgan and George Dowell came up with a treatment of a female evangelist's adventures in saving a mission located in a rough Alaskan mining settlement. This time there was no humming. Prior to Mae's film debut, she had planned to appear on Broadway in *Frisco Kate*, virtually a rewrite of *Diamond Lil*. Now she proposed combining elements from the play with the Morgan-Dowell *Soul Savin' Annie* story to create a script that pitted sex against religion. After various title changes it became known as *Klondike Annie*.

The opening scenes, taken from the play, present the Frisco Doll as mistress of Chan Lo, at whose Oriental entertainment palace she is the cosseted and zealously protected star attraction. Yearning for a man of her "own race," the Doll plots her escape, but Chan Lo discovers the plan and attempts to thwart it. In the struggle that ensues, he is accidentally stabbed to death with his own dagger (shades of Russian Rita in *Diamond Lil*). The Doll boards a tramp steamer bound for Alaska. Captain Bull Brackett immediately becomes enamored of her, but she rebuffs his advances until, during a stop in Seattle, Bull learns the Doll is wanted for murder, a bit of information which changes her response to him. In Vancouver Sister Annie Alden comes aboard. She is headed for the Nome settlement house. During the voyage she and the Doll share a cabin and spar about the satisfaction of the hedonistic versus the spiritual life-style. Annie suddenly becomes ill and dies just before the ship docks at Nome, where the police are awaiting the Doll. In desperation she dons Sister Annie's garb and decks out the dead missionary in her drag, painting Annie's face like that of a prostitute.

The Doll's impersonation of Annie gradually changes her outlook. Because of her respect for the dead woman, she sets out to rescue the floundering settlement house. She jazzes up the services, twists the arms of the dance hall girls, the gamblers and prospectors to attend and pay off the settlement house's $876 debt. Privately she juggles her relationship with Bull and her new lover, law officer Jack Forrest, who refuses to give her up even after he discovers her sordid past. But she renounces him to protect his career. Then, donning her Frisco finery, she sets sail with Bull for the Barbary Coast to clear her name. Aboard ship in her cabin, she pulls Bull toward her, closing the film with "Bull, yuh ain't no oil paintin', but you're a fascinatin' monster."

Klondike Annie was beset with problems from the beginning. The budget skyrocketed because of Mae's demands that seven models of each gown be executed so she could choose the most flattering. She was disenchanted with Raoul Walsh, whom she specifically had requested, because he refused to fight Lubitsch to obtain the services of her favorite cameraman, Karl Struss, who was busy on *Anything Goes.* Victor Milner and Teddy Tetzlaff, two of Paramount's top cameramen, were successively assigned, but eleven days into production only four pages of script had been filmed at a cost of $200,000 because of Mae's insistence on retakes after viewing the dailies. Walsh was ready to quit when George Clemens, Struss's assistant, took over to photograph Mae, deemphasizing as much as possible that she had grown unusually plump.

Mae habitually was a half hour late in reporting for filming each morning—spending two hours on her wardrobe and makeup. Finally, Lubitsch stormed into her dressing room on the sound stage to demand an explanation. Without answering, Mae turned, whacked him with a hand mirror and chased him off the set to the accompaniment of her curses and the extras' cheers. It was a humiliating experience for a man who was in a power struggle with Le Baron for control of the studio.

Walsh recalled in his autobiography that Mae had threatened,

"If that Dutch clown comes near me again, I'll wreck him." She continued being a half hour tardy every day, causing Walsh to suspect her of trying to bait Lubitsch into reappearing, giving her an excuse to beat the studio head to a pulp.

About the same time Mae's softer side came into focus when she hired a punch-drunk fighter called Kid Moreno. His single line of dialogue was: "There's a boatload of guns in the harbor." What made Moreno memorable to the cast was that practical joker Walter Catlett coached the Kid to read his line in a way Catlett said would earn him an Oscar. The scene was set in Mae's living room. The Kid rushed in, cleared his throat and said, "There's a boatload of cunts in the harbor." Without batting an eye, Mae ad-libbed, "Bring them ashore. We'll open a sporting house and you can be piano player."

With the high jinks and occasional temperament, the picture ran twenty-seven days behind schedule and $250,000 over budget. By January 1936 rumors that Paramount had failed to exercise its option on Mae's contract promptly were denied. During the last week in February she declared the studio in default and announced she was signing to do a film for the deposed Emanuel Cohen. Paramount insisted it had exercised its option, but finally, on March 11 it admitted that during the upheaval in which Lubitsch was replaced by Le Baron the studio had failed to renew her contract.

Mae promptly signed a two-picture agreement with Emanuel Cohen at $300,000 per picture. A delighted Timony granted an interview in which he gloated, "Lubitsch thought, in his Hitler way, he'd push Miss West around. He wouldn't even give her the cameraman she wanted. Well, in the end she pushed him around."

In the wake of this feuding *Klondike Annie,* with Victor McLaglen, newcomer Philip Reed, Helen Jerome Eddy, Conway Tearle and singer-organist-songwriter Gene Austin, opened to less enthusiastic reviews than in retrospect it seems to have deserved.

One of Mae's most effective scenes is her rendition of "I'm an Occidental Woman in an Oriental Mood for Love," delivered to the accompaniment of authentic Oriental musical instruments. For some of her other nine numbers the accompanist was Gene Austin, who, with Jimmy Johnson, had written all but one. The musical interludes alone provided a reason for West fans to see the film.

"I'm a spinster, see?" the world's leading sex symbol was fond of saying at the peak of her career. "Marriage? I ain't got time for a husband or child. All my life I've looked after myself as if I was my own child." It was a wonderful, space-grabbing technique. Sometimes she varied it by saying she'd never met a man whom she wanted to father her child. "Isn't that why women have children?" she asked. For her part, she said, "I like a man who's good, but not too good. The good die young and I hate a dead one." But she added, "The man I don't like doesn't exist. I've got 'em all divided into groups. Not measurements like low, medium and high. Just good, very good and better. I don't go around lookin' for a dream man. They have a habit of fadin' at the wrong time. But I've always taken men just as I found 'em, and thank heavens I've been able to find 'em."

Mae relished that kind of attention in the press and was never shy about fueling it. One widely published revelation she wanted no part of was printed April 21, 1935, after a WPA worker in Milwaukee stumbled across a long-forgotten marriage license issued to Frank Wallace and Mae West.

Mae denied everything. "Frank Wallace? Why, I never heard of the guy. I've had lots of rabbits given me for Easter—but never a husband before." With her typical chutzpah she reiterated, "I'm a spinster. And I'm not forty-two. I was practically a child in 1911. Say, just how old do you think I am anyway? Let this alleged Mr. Mae West come up 'n' see my lawyer and prove it."

Witnesses surfaced for each side. Mae's sister, Beverly, airily suggested it was a case of mistaken identity. "There were two or three other Mae Wests," she said. Timony, who many had assumed was Mae's secret husband, insisted that in all the years he had known Mae he had neither met nor heard of any spouse of hers. Trixie Friganza thought the Milwaukee Mae must have been a burlesque queen of that name who hailed from Illinois or Oregon and was a brunette—or was it a redhead? But none of Mae's apologists could explain away the information on the application stating that Mae had been born in Brooklyn eighteen years earlier and was the daughter of John and Matilda Dilker West.

As newspapermen questioned Broadway veterans, they turned up some who supported Wallace. Sign painter Jay Kay claimed to have known Mae and Wallace for twenty years. He believed the story but refused to elaborate on grounds of violating the friendship. Jack Shea, editor of the *Vaudeville Guide,* recalled Wallace often claimed Mae was his wife. Wallace's mother, Mrs. Anthony Szatkus of Albany, New York, confirmed her son recently had visited home for the first time in eight years looking for his wedding picture and had thrown a tantrum when she confessed to having destroyed it. "My son married a girl we knew as Mamie West," Mrs. Szatkus told a reporter. "She was about fifteen and he was a year older. She was a good girl. They separated later. . . . I don't know much about the movies and I don't know who the famous Mae West is. The only one I know was Mamie West, the girl my son married twenty-four years ago."

Upon being shown a theatrical photo that an enterprising newsman had unearthed of a saucy brunette seated in a quarter moon in front of a rather gaunt, balding young man, Mae acknowledged, "Yes, I know his face." But she dismissed him along with a circus midget, press agents, sheepherders and eight other guys who called long distance to ask if she were the wife they had mislaid during the Spanish-American War.

On May 10, 1935, attorney Lee Beilin petitioned the New York Supreme Court to grant Wallace permission to determine his and Mae's marital status by publication, an obscure procedure in which the plaintiff claims he or she was not notified of a previous court action in time to put up a legal defense. Again shown the photo, Mae quipped, "He may be the man in the moon to that gal, but that doesn't happen to be me. She's got black hair, and I don't concede that. I've always been a blonde."

On June 30 Wallace's attorneys asked the courts to make a declaratory judgment based on the evidence he would produce. Meanwhile, Wallace did his credibility little good by appearing at Club Richman billed:

WE'RE GOIN' TO TOWN
WITH FRANK WALLACE, HUSBAND OF MAE WEST,
AND IT AIN'T NO SIN TO BE HERE!

As the case dragged on, Wallace, desperately in need of money, accepted an engagement at the Eltinge burlesque theater billed as

"Mr. Mae West" and "Mae West's First Husband." Because of such exploitation of Mae's name, the general public remained skeptical of his claims. Typical of the reaction was the response of Matilda Schnapp. At ten years of age Matilda had been introduced to Mae through her uncle Robert Sterling, who had written the song "Diamond Lil." Miss Schnapp always regarded Mae as the epitome of glamour.

By 1935 the Depression had forced Matilda to accept $5-a-night jobs as a club date singer. One Saturday she was booked, along with a magician and a dance team, into a Nyack, New York, tavern. "The male member of the dance team doubled as emcee," she said. "The girl had a name out of cheap literature—Trixie LeMay—and badly bleached, dark-at-the-roots hair. She was a vulnerable, skinny little thing who looked at her partner worshipfully. They had small-time written all over them, and their rag-doll dance was a horror from start to finish.

"We did two shows, and before the second they gave us midnight lunch. We sat down for coffee and sandwiches, and this emcee sat beside me. He said his name was Frank Wallace. For some reason, he took his teeth out and placed them in a napkin while he ate. And somehow, he happened to mention he was Mae West's husband.

"Well, my reaction was panic. Remember, I was seventeen. Here was Mae West, a big, glamorous star, and he claimed to be married to her. The only thing I could think was that he was insane. Why else would this emaciated, balding, toothless wreck claim this very sexy, dynamic lady as his wife? He might have lied about almost anyone else—but MAE WEST!"

Whatever anyone's reaction, Wallace persisted. On February 28, 1936, he obtained an emendation to allow a sheriff to serve papers on Mae at the cost of $5, even though he was without further funds to retrieve a trunk held for nonpayment of room rent. He claimed the trunk contained Mae's love letters.

Apprized of his move and his mention of the trunk, Mae laughed about both as attempts to secure attention. "The guy's tryin' to cash in again," she said. "I got a new picture out now, and he's pullin' the same stunt he pulled the last time one was released. I don't know the man. I'm not married to him. I never was."

Wallace thought his case was moving slowly because his lawyer was not convinced of the legitimacy of his claims. He sought out attorney Samuel Siegel, who not only believed him but worked out a plan to prove his case.

Through legal maneuvering Louis Nizer, Mae's lawyer, succeeded on June 10, 1936, in getting the suit dismissed on grounds that she had not been properly served and that the New York Supreme Court had no jurisdiction in the case. Justice Salvatore Cotillo ruled that if Wallace was determined to be "Mr. Mae West," he must file new proceedings.

Next day the West forces moved to strike the case from the calendar on grounds that New York courts had no jurisdiction over Mae since she had been a California resident for over three years. On December 14, 1936, Mae received an early Christmas present—the ruling ending attempts to have the New York courts declare Wallace her legal husband.

The present proved a booby trap set by Siegel. He had hoped to goad Nizer into just such a declaration. "Because in California we had the community property law with us," he later explained. "So we immediately brought action to have her examined. On May 8, 1937, she appeared but on advice from her California attorney refused to answer questions beyond identifying herself as Mae West. That was our first hopeful development—having her threatened with a contempt citation."

Mae's reaction? "I'm not worried." She was wrong not to be. On July 8, 1937, in the limousine that was transporting her to court, she continued to deny all allegations, but once *under oath,* she admitted the ceremony had been performed twenty-six years earlier. However, she also swore the marriage had never been consummated, thus opening the question of whether California's community property law applied. The next day the presiding judge ruled she need not answer additional questions related to the marriage but further ruled this did not nullify the right of Wallace forces to subpoena her to answer such questions later. Additionally, Siegel succeeded in getting the court to order Mae to pay Wallace's legal costs.

For once Mae had no flip comment. The woman who previously had been able to brazen out any situation went into seclusion and was unavailable for interviews.

The years dragged by, punctuated by court skirmishes, until Mae finally filed for divorce seven years after the accidental discovery of the marriage. Wallace then withdrew his separate maintenance suit, and warned by the judge that he could never reinstate it, he replied, "I don't want to now. All I ever wanted was to do my work." In her autobiography Mae airily refers to a few blue-chip stocks that she settled on him.

12

More receptive to guidance in terms of material than at any time since becoming an international star, Mae went along with Emanuel Cohen's decision to acquire the film rights to *Personal Appearance* under his Major Pictures banner. This highly successful Broadway comedy, in which Gladys George had etched a honey-and-vitriol portrait of an affected, lecherous Hollywood star, was considered a risky movie project. MGM had investigated it for their platinum blond Jean Harlow until the Hays Office reacted negatively.

Cohen and his staff floundered in their attempts to adapt the story line, which deals with the havoc a movie queen creates in the lives of some small-town Americans when her limousine breaks down during a promotional tour. Not until Henry Hathaway was approached to direct did anyone present a reasonable solution.

Hathaway came to the project as a favor to Cohen. He had directed *Lives of a Bengal Lancer,* Cohen's biggest grossing picture during his tenure at Paramount, *Trail of the Lonesome Pine* and other successes. Originally he had been scheduled to handle

Pennies from Heaven with Bing Crosby, but he agreed to direct Mae when Cohen had difficulty finding a first-rate director.

The pragmatic Hathaway told Cohen, "Look, none of her pictures are very good—unless you like Mae West. If you do, they're wonderful. Mae is the picture, and we focus it around her. Hell, any director who works with her is working with a woman who is completely special."

Cohen and Hathaway assembled an impressive cast that included Randolph Scott, Alice Brady, Lyle Talbot, Isabel Jewell, Jack LaRue, Elizabeth Patterson and Warren William plus Xavier Cugat and his Orchestra. They hired Johnny Burke and Arthur Johnson to write three songs, "On a Tropical Night," "I Was Saying to the Moon" and "Go West, Young Man," which became the title of the film.

"In spite of what I'd said to Cohen, I was quite excited before starting the picture, but by the end of the first day I was completely disillusioned," said Hathaway. "She came on the set in a skintight satin dress. I took one look and asked our cameraman, Karl Struss, if her belly would show. He assured me it indeed would. So I took Mae aside and suggested maybe she should put on a girdle. She was outraged. 'You're a very sexy woman,' I said, trying to soothe her, 'but in the camera it looks as if you have a potbelly. We don't know how to drape it.' With the patience of a great teacher she took my hand and placed it on the bulge. She proceeded to wiggle it sideways, up and down, crosswise. 'Don't worry about me,' she said. 'It took me a long time to develop that. You just worry about yourself.'"

Mae again asserted herself later that same day. Hathaway remembered, "I started the camera on a beautiful Rolls-Royce. I had it drive up. A footman and a chauffeur in livery jumped out, went around and opened the door. Then I cut to a bulldog getting out. It had a diamond collar and was on a diamond leash. As it emerged, I cut behind, and its ass was wiggling just like Mae's as they walked away from the camera. Well, when she saw that, she nearly went crazy. Out it went. 'Nobody gets laughs in my pictures but me, see?'"

Mae resisted every directorial touch Hathaway attempted to introduce. He set up a scene in which Randolph Scott, her leading man, took her past a willow tree to the barn to show her the invention he hoped would revolutionize motion pictures. Just as Mae and Scott passed the willow, Hathaway had a little whirlwind start, causing the leaves to seem to whistle at Mae. She killed the effect. In another scene during an argument with Warren William, who played the press agent, Mae paced up and down, up and down. As she did, Hathaway cut to an old light shade whose fringe wiggled suggestively. "Out!" she cried.

"She called the shots—all of them. In many ways she was one of the smartest women I ever met, but she used her intelligence only to protect herself, her creation of this fabulous character, Mae West. In one scene, she was singing with a band, and we hired Xavier Cugat, who was brand-new at the time. We started to shoot, and she asked, 'Who's that guy with the bald head?' I told her he was Cugat, the rage of the day. She didn't acknowledge the existence of any other rage. 'Put a wig on him!' she ordered. Well, I had a hell of a time because Cugat objected, but Mae retreated to her dressing room and refused to return to the set. 'I'm not gonna stand up in front of that band with a bald-headed leader,' she insisted. 'I don't have bald-headed men in my life.' Cugat had to be fitted with a wig."

Hathaway soon concluded Mae's pictures could be directed by a traffic cop. "Any direction I might give she regarded as demeaning. That is the reason she always gave exactly the same performance," he said. "The only way I could direct her was to take her aside and explain that by moving her arm in a certain way, she created the *illusion* that it wasn't firm or that her armpit showed. Then *maybe* she'd listen. But if I said, 'Mae, don't move your arm there,' in front of anyone, she would give me two hours on why it was necessary.

"Still, she wanted to be protected. She had an obsession against having a leading man tower over her. She wore platform shoes, but she wouldn't stand on a box as some stars did because it was uncomfortable. Randy Scott was tall. So I filmed them separately as often as possible. When she and Randy did a close two-shot, he had to stand in a hole."

Lyle Talbot, who had turned down a role in the Chicago company of *Sex* years before, gladly accepted the part of a senator with whom Mae is having an affair. It was a character who had not existed in the play, but Mae added it to the film to reinforce her reputation for always having multiple men in her professional as well as her personal life.

Talbot was surprised at the conciliatory way in which Hathaway dealt with Mae, considering his reputation for despotically controlling his actors. On the set of *Go West, Young Man,* the director seemed intentionally to close his eyes to the crosscurrent between Mae and Alice Brady. Miss Brady, who had been a preeminent dramatic actress on Broadway before coming to Hollywood, made it apparent that she thought Mae was an artist of no importance. Mae retaliated by insisting that the once-beautiful star be made up to look her dowdiest. Nor did Mae waste any consideration on the highly talented but erratic newcomer Isabel Jewell.

To Mae's leading men—Scott, Warren William and Talbot—the star was invariably friendly and intimate. "We had a scene on the balcony outside her suite that she reworked without even telling Hathaway," Talbot said. "She and I were leaning over the rail. The reporters and photographers were below. 'Talbot, forget about the lines. This is a love scene. Now we can't go too far because of the censors, but you look pretty good to me,' she murmured, staring down at my fly with her 'come-up-'n'-see-me-sometime' bit.

"Hathaway called out that it was a dolly shot. The camera moved in for a close-up with Mae giving me the business under her breath and me, of course, going along with it. Then the sound man objected he couldn't hear. 'Yeah,' Mae called out, 'that's how I want it, and that's the way it's goin' to be'—which it was. In the picture audiences never really hear what we're saying so each person can fantasize about what we're telling one another.

"I doubt that technique had been used since silent pictures. But Mae came up with it just before the shot. I don't know whether Hathaway was sold on the idea or not. Luckily it turned out to be a lot better than the way it was written—a very funny and original scene."

Since Mae would accept little in the way of direction, Hathaway amused himself by observing her leading men's responses to her. "For certain types, Mae had great fascination. Warren William was completely—uh—amused is a bad word. Fascinated is too much the other thing—but in between fascination and amusement—*intrigued,* he was intrigued by her. Lyle Talbot was bemused. Randolph Scott was always courteous, but she was not his kind of woman.

"Timony was completely dominated by her at this time. So was this trainer Johnny Indrisano, her lover. The physical attraction was still alive there. You know they lived together for a long time. Johnny and she jogged. He exercised her like a promising young pug."

In Hathaway's opinion, neither lovers nor money represented the peak of Mae's aspirations. "Power. That's what interested her," he observed. "The power she got from making a picture was more important even than money. Her requirements demanded that she have authority, not material things. She never needed a Rolls-Royce. She never bought an elaborate estate or a Beverly Hills mansion. She had a modest house in the Valley and a fairly big place at the beach—in Santa Monica, not Malibu Colony. But think about where she spent most of her time—in that little apartment on Rossmore. And she liked it there because that was a place where she could create the illusion of being in complete control."

After filming was finished in September, Talbot, Scott and William were scheduled for some publicity stills with Mae. "She came out wearing this sheer thing that didn't leave much to the imagination," Talbot recalled. "Real sexy stuff, you know. I still have some shots I got at the time. They were just unpublishable in those days."

Mae was prepared to make personal appearances with the film, taking along Talbot and Jack LaRue, who appeared in the prologue, as well as Gene Austin and a maid. But when she learned Paramount would pay only $10,500 a week for the unit instead of the $25,000 she demanded, she retreated to the desert to "regain her health."

The genesis of the next West-Cohen collaboration is, as usual, cloaked in mystery. Mae had her heart set on Catherine the Great, but Cohen rejected the project as too costly. On August 10 he announced her new motion picture would be based on *Sapphire Sal.* Jo Swerling had written the screenplay, and Eddie Sutherland would direct. Sets were under construction, and production was scheduled to begin in two weeks. As Mae told it, neither she nor Cohen had faith in Swerling's script, but they had to proceed with it since the sets were built. Sutherland, Mae and Cohen listened to some songs Sam Coslow wanted to demonstrate. They hoped they could use a couple to jazz up the picture. Only one, "Mademoiselle Fifi from Gay Paree," impressed Mae.

In *Goodness Had Nothing to Do with It,* she wrote that after

Coslow left, she told Cohen and Sutherland that she must have that song. She needed it as the basis for the film that would be known as *Every Day's a Holiday*. She claimed she spent the next hour and a half dictating "the story line."

"It didn't occur to me that I had experienced ESP until later when I asked, 'How can I think up a complete story for a full-length movie in fifty seconds?' All the characters, the dialogue—I saw and heard everything in my psychic eye. You see, with ESP you can—because you're using the part of your mind that dreams and the longest dream lasts a minute or so."

What no one has ever mentioned, after Swerling's script was rejected, is the contribution of Allan Rivkin, who during the research for this book volunteered in conversation one evening that he had written the screenplay for *Every Day's a Holiday*. "The Screen Writers Guild at that time had no position on writers' credits," Rivkin explained. "Cohen needed someone to do a script. Mae West had an idea about a New Year's Eve thing, and I built a script for her."

What Mae had was the idea of a Tenth Avenue slum girl who went to Paris from New York to learn French and returned to the United States masquerading as a French singer. Rivkin added to the character, making her an adventuress named Peaches O'Day, whose specialty was selling the Brooklyn Bridge to gullible rich men. After a term in jail she dons a brunette wig and becomes the rage as a Parisian chanteuse. The story told of Mademoiselle Fifi's romantic entanglements with a butler whom she mistakes for his employer and assorted other characters, including an honest police captain whom she nominates for mayor. She then has to kidnap him to keep him from being murdered by a crooked rival for the job. Plans backfire. The honest captain is held prisoner, and Peaches campaigns for him, organizing a street parade headed by Louis Armstrong and His Orchestra. The captain is elected, freed and welcomed into Peaches's arms.

Rivkin turned in his script, Mae read it and summoned him to her Rossmore apartment to discuss it. When he rang the bell, a muscleman met him and ushered him into her bedroom. "She's in bed, propped up, and she's got a writing table in front of her," Rivkin related. "On it is the manuscript. After we'd said good afternoon, she announced she'd like to talk about the script. 'I got some questions to ask you.' Then she started, 'In the first scene what am I up to?' and I explained to her what I thought she was supposed to be doing. 'Mmmmmmm,' she said. 'That's right.' So we went on to the second scene, and we continued like that for an hour and a half as she put a series of questions to me. When she finished, she said, 'Thank you very much, Mr. Rivkin. Very nice. Now I'll make it good.'"

Shortly after, Sutherland complained to Rivkin that Mae had to move around a lot. "You've got her walking down steps, things like that. On those stilts she wears for shoes, she'll look as if her knee is in her thigh. So here's how I'm going to shoot it. She'll start down the steps; then I'll cut to her admirer, and then pick her up at the bottom of the staircase. Her whole impact is predicated on a series of close shots. If you have her moving around in a long shot, you've got to be very careful."

Rivkin was then called to Cohen's office and told his name could not appear in the credits. Cohen went on to explain, "My deal with Miss West is that she has to be given solo screen credit." Cohen paused, then offered, "Let me give you a five-thousand-dollar bonus and a three-month vacation with pay." At the time Rivkin was eager to return to his farm in Vermont and, since there were no rules against it, accepted the compromise. Speaking of the project in 1979, Rivkin said, "The picture was made, came out as a Paramount release. Her name was on the screen, and my name was nowhere."

Concerned that the plot was weak, Mae and Sutherland sought especially strong musical material. For the Louis Armstrong street rally they called Hoagy Carmichael to the studio. He played every unpublished composition in his repertoire without gaining their approval.

After he finished, Sutherland took Carmichael home with him and told him to stay at the piano until he came up with a suitable number. All night Carmichael kept the butler serving drinks as he wrestled with his problem. Next morning he demonstrated the result to Mae and Sutherland. They were not pleased. Sleepy and desperate, Carmichael recalled a song he and Stanley Adams had written and forgotten. As it filled the room, the listeners perked up. "Yes, yes, darling," Mae said. Sutherland boasted he could always spot a hit number and announced this was a hit if he ever heard one.

Armstrong and his orchestra performed the number, "Jubilee," with gusto. In his autobiography *Sometimes I Wonder,* Carmichael wrote: "Louis played and sang it and it was a complete bust. This songwriting isn't easy."

The completed film, starring Mae and featuring Edmund Lowe, Charles Butterworth, Charles Winninger, Walter Catlett, Lloyd Nolan, Herman Bing, Chester Conklin and Louis Armstrong, was given a B rating by the Legion of Decency on the basis of two lines: "I wouldn't even lift my veil for that guy," and "I wouldn't let him touch me with a ten-foot pole." Mae deleted the lines, earning an acceptable rating. Editing was finished in December 1937, but meanwhile, a brouhaha developed which postponed, and for a time threatened to block, the release of the film altogether.

13

Mae had fought too long and hard developing her showman-
ship to allow her career to peter out in a series of weak vehicles.
Though the Benevolent Order of Santa Clauses might vote her
and Shirley Temple their favorite film actresses, she was finding
it difficult to operate within the constricted area allowed by the
Hays Office.

Mae sought some outlandish stunt to thrust her into the
headlines. She found it in radio. Her previous guest spots with
Rudy Vallee and Louella Parsons promoted her pictures. But she
had something else in mind when she signed for the December
12, 1937 *Chase and Sanborn Hour,* a program starring Edgar
Bergen and Charlie McCarthy which recently had been voted the
most popular on the air.

Mae's first scene in the show contained some mildly risqué
repartee. She admitted to Bergen that Charlie had accepted her
invitation to come up and see her. She'd shown him her etchings
and he'd shown her his stamp collection. When Bergen complacently concluded, "Oh, that's all that happened," Charlie
chortled, "Oh, he's so naïve!"

After some additional byplay Mae invited Charlie to visit her again. He equivocated and Mae sneered, "So good-time Charlie is gonna play hard to get. . . . Your Casanova stuff is just a front, all a false front." Charlie implored Mae to remember his girl friends, who were listening. "Oh, yeah, all wood and a yard long," she came back. "You weren't so nervous and backward at my apartment. In fact, you didn't need any encouragement to kiss me."

"Did I do that?"

"You certainly did. I got the marks to prove it. 'N' the splinters, too."

This was followed by the "disgraceful" Adam and Eve sketch by Arch Oboler. Certainly the producers realized the casting was off-beat, but all that was intended was some good-natured levity. Mae played Eve; Don Ameche, Adam; and Charlie, the snake. In the playlet, introduced as "what might have taken place in the Garden of Eden," Eve is bored with the Garden and husband Adam,' whom she describes as "long, lazy and lukewarm." She implores him to take her away.

Horrified, he tells her that is impossible unless, of course, he eats an apple from the forbidden tree—to him, an unthinkable act. While he goes fishing, she cons the serpent into picking an apple for her. "Now get me a big one," she says. "I feel like doin' a big apple." When she feeds the fruit to Adam in the guise of applesauce, God throws them out of Eden. Then, for the first time seeing each other as physically attractive, they kiss. Innocuous as it all sounds, Mae managed to load it with innuendo.

To some in the studio audience that evening, the program was surprising in tone but hardly shocking. Doris Stein, wife of Jules Stein, then head of the Music Corporation of America, attended the broadcast and regarded it as mildly risqué and funny. Upon returning home, she was puzzled to receive a phone call from her husband in New York, who announced that Mae had finished herself in radio. Doris was mystified at her husband's prediction of a "terrible furor and outcry."

If anything, he understated the reaction. Two congressmen grabbed headlines by reprimanding the Federal Communications Commission, the network, the advertising agency, the sponsor and the individual stations that had carried the program. Newspapers cited a flood of letters protesting the broadcast as "profane," "indecent," "obscene," "filthy," "sexy," "vulgar" and generally insulting to the American public. Chase and Sanborn

PHOTOGRAPH COURTESY OF RICHARD LAMPARSKI

(Above) Baby Mae was a charmer even before she began performing. (TIM MAL-OCHOSKY)

(Above) Unlikely as it might seem in of her career as a vamp, in 1916 appeared on vaudeville circuits as a impersonator. (HOBLITZELLE THE ARTS LIBRARY, UNIVERSITY OF TEXA AUSTIN)

(Left) Frank Wallace, shown with hi partner, Trixie LeMay, secretly ma Mae in 1911. A quarter of a century he turned up in nightclubs and burle as "Mr. Mae West" and "Mae West's band." (HOBLITZELLE THEATRE ART BRARY, UNIVERSITY OF TEXAS AT AU

(Facing page) Mae's Broadway c. reached a peak with *Diamond Lil* in In the 1948 revival she glittered more brightly. (DR. JULES STEIN)

the peak of Mae-mania, everyone from
ry Pickford to Helen Hayes was photo-
phed with her. *(Above)* she hams it up
h the two Johns—Carradine *(left)* and
rymore.

squelch rumors of a feud, the publicity
artment had Mae and Marlene Die-
h pose together. The actresses comple-
nted one another since Dietrich
oyed cooking as much as Mae did
ing. (TIM MALOCHOSKY)

cing page) Mae played a cooch dancer-
trainer who marries into society in *I'm
Angel* ('33). Once again she chose Grant
appear with her, explaining, "I liked
so much the first time I had him, I
ted to have him again." (TIM MAL-
HOSKY)

(Left) After Mae was robbed of jewel[
a large amount of cash, chauffeur C
Wright drove police officers Jack S
who lay on the floor, and Harry
who got into Mae West drag to re
her purse—and possibly snag the rol
(MOTION PICTURE ACADEMY OF ARTS
SCIENCES)

(Below) Mae's relationship with Wrig[
the subject of much speculation
pecially after she hired his broth
drive and returned Chalky to boxin
his manager, she promoted him int
title of Featherweight Champ in
(RON'S NOW AND THEN)

le of the Nineties ('34) teamed Mae with
nny Mack Brown *(center, above),* Roger
vor and John Milijan. (TIM MAL-
HOSKY) *Below,* she wears one of the
ected costumes from the "American
auty" musical tableau. Her Statue of
erty costume inspired one critic to
gest she looked more like the Statue of
bido. (SPECIAL COLLECTIONS, DOHENY
BRARY, UNIVERSITY OF SOUTHERN CAL-
ORNIA)

(Above) Mae's longtime manager and ex-lover, James Timony, and her sister, Beverly, often accompanied her to the races at Santa Anita, as well as to boxing and wrestling matches. (TIM MALOCHOSKY)

(Right) Her brother, John, was a permanent part of her Hollywood entourage. Her attempts to secure studio employment for him were doomed by his sleeping on the job. (TIM MALOCHOSKY)

(Far right) Beverly was more ambitious. In the early '30s, she attempted to capitalize on Mae's popularity by donning Gay Nineties garb and taking an all-girl act out in what was left of vaudeville. (HOBLITZELLE THEATRE ARTS LIBRARY, UNIVERSITY OF TEXAS AT AUSTIN)

Li
W
f
OV
IO
RS
)

(Above) George Eiferman (left) and Paul Novak made the cover of the May 1955 issue of *Strength and Health*. Both were in Mae's nightclub act, which for Paul was the beginning of a twenty-seven-year relationship with her. (STRENGTH AND HEALTH)

(Left) Wrestler Vincent Lopez, one of Mae's serious romances, also managed her nightclub muscleman act during the early part of its two-season run. (TIM MALOCHOSKY)

Everyone came to see Mae and her act, including Liberace at Lou Walter's Latin Quarter and two show-biz greats, Ethel Merman and Judy Garland, in Las Vegas. (TIM MALOCHOSKY) Sometimes Mae herself went visiting, too. On the set of Robert Wise's *Star*, a curious Julie Andrews seems more intent upon checking out Mae than Mae, Julie. (SPECIAL COLLECTIONS, DOHENY LIBRARY, UNIVERSITY OF SOUTHERN CALIFORNIA)

(Right) After a long absence from films, Mae returned in *Myra Breckenridge* in 1970. When costar Raquel Welch presented her with roses and suggested a photo, Mae seized and held them so the bouquet hid their waistlines. (TIM MALOCHOSKY)

(Below left) Rock Hudson and Mae rehearse for the 1958 Academy Awards telecast in which they were a national sensation performing "Baby, It's Cold Outside." (ROCK HUDSON)

(Below right) Nepotism stirred slightly when Mae secured a small part in *Myra* for nephew John, the son of her brother. (SPECIAL COLLECTIONS, DOHENY LIBRARY, UNIVERSITY OF SOUTHERN CALIFORNIA)

products were threatened with organized boycotts. *Variety* reported: "Clergymen, many of whom certainly did not hear the broadcast, are raising a truly fearsome uproar."

In the face of growing criticism the president of the J. Walter Thompson advertising agency apologized to the president of NBC. He pointed out the purpose of the broadcasts—"to afford wholesome entertainment." He cited eight years of programming as evidence of this goal, then admitted, "The script of this feature of the broadcast is our responsibility," and concluded, "It was a mistake and we can assure the public at large that the same mistake will not be made again."

NBC's president issued a statement sharing "the regret." Six days later the general manager of the NBC station group banned any mention of Mae's name or of the incident on the network. It was acknowledged as the biggest scandal to hit radio until then.

On December 27 columnist Hedda Hopper joined the attack. After admitting that Mae had attracted a larger crowd at the NBC studio than Clark Gable had, Hedda expressed surprise that a Sunday show, catering to children, would ignore the rules regarding right of privacy and impropriety and would air such salacious material. She reported:

> At 5 P.M. Mae was wearing a black evening gown, a long silver-fox cape, orchids and lillies of the valley, black eyelashes, the longest I've ever seen. . . . She wore a pair of lorgnettes on a diamond-studded chain around her neck, but like a man who wears both suspenders and a belt, she had a pair of glasses which she wore while broadcasting. . . .
>
> I've never seen anyone as embarrassed as Don Ameche. And I understand, when they first showed him the sketch, he absolutely refused to do it. They assured him Mae would play it straight and not indulge in any of her Westian nuances and if he refused to go on they would keep him off the air. . . .

Looking back in 1978, Edgar Bergen spoke of what he called the Mae West incident. "We had to have a star every week, and she seemed a logical choice. She was a sex star. We were fully aware of that.

"*Adam and Eve,* as you probably know, had been performed before without any untoward incidents. Possibly our program being on Sunday and our having a little fun with the Bible was dangerous. But we worried more about the opening exchange between Mae and Charlie.

"Anyway, we always had two rehearsals. One on Saturday evening, after which we would rewrite and tighten. Then we would do a Sunday afternoon read-through. At that read-through Mae read her lines straight. It was obvious she knew what she was doing—how to lay out lines—but she didn't give things that Mae West twist till the broadcast. I've always said, we had far more permissive material on a previous show. We did a program with Fred Allen. Allen supposedly hadn't been working, and Charlie advertised for a ventriloquist because he was leaving me. Fred answered the ad and said, 'I came to see about the job.'

"Charlie told him, 'Well, you haven't been working much lately, have you?'

"'Wellll—no. I did work for a long time and I saved my money so I'd have something to fall back on.'

"Charlie said, 'And so you've decided to get up off it. Well, I'll try you out.'

"'Will I ever get a joke? A little titter? Or a laugh?'

"'Maybe.'

"'Oh, Mr. McCarthy, I kiss the hem of your tuxedo.'

"'It's a tailcoat.'

"There was a pause. Then Allen said, 'I'll throw you a kiss.'"

Bergen chuckled recalling the moment and continued. "But to get back to Mae. Everybody else apologized. I just ran and hid. The net result was that our rating went up to the highest we ever had. Our only mistake was that we were twenty-five years ahead of our time." (On February 2, 1938, *Variety* reported the *Chase and Sanborn Hour* had leaped seven points to 44.9 in the Cooperative Analysis of Broadcasting, a copyrighted trade barometer, thanks to Mae's appearance. "Looks like the public is not much concerned with the moral aspects of the much vaunted case. . . . By these standards, and on the mathematical logic of C.A.B., a figure of 44.9 means that half the radio sets in the United States tuned in on the Edgar Bergen-Charlie McCarthy gala," the paper stated.)

Cohen and Paramount assessed Mae's rating and decided to capitalize on the furor, regarding it as the kind of promotion for *Every Day's a Holiday* that no amount of money could buy. To supplement the free publicity, between $35,000 and $40,000 was budgeted for advertising.

As usual with Mae's films, this one opened to mixed reviews, ranging from "Sex ain't what it used to be, or maybe Mae West isn't," to *Every Day's a Holiday* is a better picture than *She Done Him Wrong*—and clean which should make it a hit all around." Amazingly, despite the clamor from the broadcast, it was Mae's first box-office failure.

With her name fresh from the headlines, Mae launched a personal appearance tour with an engagement at the Los Angeles Paramount and hyped the box office for *Every Day's a Holiday* there and wherever she appeared, demonstrating that when she could do what she did the way she wanted to do it, she remained box-office dynamite. For the act, she carried Milton Watson, orchestra leader Lionel Newman and her Six Leading Men, all over six feet tall, wearing top hats and tailcoats.

The presentation opened with the Leading Men singing snatches of songs from her films as a prelude to her entrance. When she rolled into view, she was resplendent in a figure-hugging black bugle-beaded floor-length gown with a white monkey-fur bolero, and she wore an extravagant ostrich head-dress, 500 carats of diamonds and star sapphires plus false eyelashes long enough to be curled twice. After a special number laced with innuendo, she went into a sketch with Milton Watson and her six male sex symbols. Watson then sang "I Kiss Your Hand, Madame," which served as a stimulant for Mae's sighs, waggles, moans and wisecracks. The twenty-two-minute stint was brought to a sizzling, sensuous climax with Mae, Watson and the Leading Men performing a song-and-dance rendition of "Slow Motion."

In 1978 Newman recalled his audition for the job. "I was a tall, skinny young guy, and when I went to her apartment for the interview, I was scared to death. I was still a virgin, and I thought she was going to rape me. She received me in her bedroom. She didn't look young, or old either. She showed no sexual interest in me whatever. I was such a kid she never called me Lionel or Mr. Newman. It was always, 'Hey, Newman!' On those tours we didn't carry an orchestra. We'd go into a town and hire musicians. But whatever they wore, she demanded I wear tails."

Newman remembered that after his first appearance with her she summoned him to her dressing room and instructed him to keep his hands to his sides while leading the orchestra. No explanation that the first rule of conducting calls for the conductor to keep his hands in front of him persuaded her. She wanted his hands as inconspicuous as possible. "They ain't comin' to see you or hear the orchestra," she announced. "They're comin' to see *me*."

What made working with Mae worthwhile to Newman was that she was a perfectionist. "She did six and eight shows a day, and after the first show she'd call a rehearsal," he said. "She gave it her all. Always trying to make it a little better, a little more exciting."

To what extremes she carried discipline is illustrated during their Brooklyn stand when Newman's father, whom he hadn't seen since he was a child, turned up at the stage door one morning. Newman asked to be excused from rehearsal. "He's gonna have to wait," Mae said. "We got work to do." So the elder Newman waited outside for two hours before seeing his son. "She never apologized," Newman said. "As far as she was concerned, 'We got work to do' said it all. But I forgave her because she was as good at the nine A.M. show as she was at the big show at eight that night."

Each afternoon Mae took a break to go for a drive. "We had six guys in the show, strapping, good-looking kids. Before she went for her ride, she'd pick one of those boys to go along. My best friend was among them. I asked what the hell went on. 'She doesn't say a damn word. She just hums to herself,' he told me. But she must have said something. Because if a guy got called to take a ride, he was the one for the night, which upset Timony. If he saw she was physically attracted to somebody, he automatically called the guy 'a syphilitic son of a bitch.'"

Mae became increasingly annoyed at her manager's interference and at one point during the tour sent Timony back to Hollywood, ostensibly to set up a production of *Catherine the Great* and to look over the Hollytown Theater, located on New Hampshire Avenue. It was a converted church and, she said, offered a perfect place to try out new plays. Although she didn't want Timony to suspect it, she would later acquire the theater and the bungalow behind to provide him with a place to work and live. In this way she removed him from the Ravenswood without hurting his feelings.

Mae's attempt to rid herself of Timony painlessly didn't succeed. He was soon back on the tour, sitting outside her dressing room, guarding her more zealously than ever. "He'd sit there with a gun in his pocket," Newman remembered. "It got more difficult to see her. Harder than getting into the White

House, because he was still in love with her and was jealous of everybody, including me.

"By the time I went to work for her you couldn't get to know Jim except as it related to her. He was a man who'd given up everything—including an office with a staff of nine—for her. He was still a power when the first tour opened in the winter of 1938 but became senile during our second tour beginning around March 1939. He got to be ridiculous. He'd be sitting in a chair and his gun would fall on the floor.

"We traveled by rail, and once the train made an unscheduled stop in the middle of the night," Newman recollected. "I stuck my head out and saw our road manager, Lew Epstein. I asked what was up. I don't know whether he was putting me on or not. It's hard to believe, but he said the rocking and rolling of the train was causing Our Star to have orgasms so they had to get her some pills to prevent that."

If there was a time when Mae was not preoccupied with herself as a sex object, Newman among others seldom observed it. She managed to interpret any incident as a tribute to her allure. During the early show she attracted the "Overcoat Brigade." Newman was unaware of their presence until she called his attention to them. "She told me to watch the first couple of rows," he said. "I did. And you'd see these guys scattered around masturbating under their coats. And that, to her, was the greatest compliment you could give her." In one Connecticut town she had a dressing room on a courtyard. Local youths kept trying to peek in to catch her undressed. Was she upset? "Not at all," Newman maintained. "The more they peeked, the more excited she got."

All stars receive a certain amount of lewd fan mail. Mae's was the kinkiest Newman ever saw. "Sometimes there was not even a note. There would just be naked bodies with the heads cut off. And the larger the prick, the more it tickled her. 'Look at that fucker!' she'd say. She talked turkey, and she adored getting letters, the dirtier the better. She gave me a book at the end of the tour. It was some leather-bound porno cartoons someone had done starring her and various celebrities—Jimmy Durante, Groucho Marx, Popeye. She just loved it. There weren't many like her."

Newman's only complaint was that when Mae was onstage, she demanded he be a part of the audience as well as the orchestra leader. "You had to do your bit—laughing. And after the first couple of months my jaws were killing me from forcing phony laughs at the same damned jokes I'd been hearing eight times a day." He grimaced.

"But there are two points I want to make about Mae," he said. "She was into the sexual revolution long before it was popular. And in the old days Hollywood was thought to be filled with sirens and gigolos and Mae represented the epitome of what the layman thought Hollywood was. She was that way on and off screen. She was *always* 'Mae West, World's Greatest Movie Siren!'"

Although in 1938 a publicity-seeking theater chain owner had branded Mae along with Marlene Dietrich, Katharine Hepburn, Greta Garbo, Joan Crawford, Fred Astaire and Edward Arnold as "Box Office Poison," her 1938 and 1939 personal appearance tours proved he was off the mark where she was concerned. Arriving in New York on March 1, 1939, she once again was front-page news. Reporters told their readers that she had dismissed the suggestion that she might be presenting what they called "Sally Randish" entertainment with "I don't have to do that. If you've got It, you don't need fans. If you haven't got It, fans don't do any good, do they?"—which suggested either Mae, her press agent or the reporter had been reading playwright J. M. Barrie on the subject of charm. She cut a dashing figure in her floor-length black crepe gown, cerise scarf and sable wrap with 500 carats of diamond bracelets, rings and necklaces glittering in the sunlight. Startling newspaper readers, she came out in favor of censorship. "It upholds the dignity of the profession, know what I mean? Otherwise, not the big studios but the independents would try to outdo each other in dirt. Yeah, dirt."

In her spare time she offered encouragement to Timony, who was producing a play called *Clean Beds* for Broadway. This had been the most promising project to come out of the Hollytown, with then-neophyte actors Tom Drake, Michael Whalen and Gertrude Walker. Miss Walker, who went on to become a screenwriter, claims that *Clean Beds* was Russian refugee George Sitosky's rewrite of *The Lower Depths* with added jokes by Mae. "It'd been quite a success in Los Angeles," she said. "Lady Mendl came to see it, Cole Porter, Anita Loos and what Louella Parsons called 'dozens of our distinguished intelligentsia.' We opened in New Haven, where the Yale kids hooted, yelled and hollered.

The notices were terrible. And I got a postopening wire from Queenie Smith, the musical comedy star, which read: 'Gert, dear, I hope it runs long enough to change the sheets.'"

It didn't. The production opened in Manhattan May 30, 1939, and collapsed after three performances which the *World-Telegram*'s man equated with "the death of the 1938–1939 season." The play's quick closing destroyed any vestigial influence Timony might have had on Mae.

"It was pathetic," Miss Walker said. "I feel she wanted to be rid of him but didn't want to dump him. She used to come around to the Hollytown fairly often, but it was obviously out of loyalty. She wasn't deeply involved. He was probably hurt more than he showed. You couldn't really tell. He had the con man's inexhaustible optimism."

The depths to which Timony had sunk is illustrated in a story related by former actors' agent Richard Segel. One day Segel's younger brother Don arrived home from the Hollytown, where he worked backstage after school. He excitedly told Richard the plot of a play Timony was developing for Mae. He described it vividly and quoted some hilarious gag lines. It was, situation by situation, character by character, a synopsis of *Diamond Lil*. Richard restrained himself from revealing that the once-wily old fox had been reduced to conning teenagers. "His plight," Richard said, "struck me as inexpressibly sad."

In one of Mae's visits to the Hollytown she met Anthony Quinn, who was rehearsing in a play there. In his autobiography Quinn says she talked to him and told him that when he was a little older to come up and see her sometime. Later she heard the callow youth auditioning for a part written with John Barrymore in mind and advised the director not to pass over a good thing as she had. Quinn never accepted her invitation, and if the doorman at the Ravenswood was to be believed, it may have been fortunate since the in-and-out traffic was heavy.

This is not to imply that every encounter was sexually motivated. Often, as in the case of Joe Louis, Mae seemed set upon doing a good deed whether or not things worked out in the bedroom. In 1937 she heard of a proposed match between Louis and Slapsie Maxie Rosenbloom. Mae became concerned when she learned Louis's manager had agreed to the match on the condition that Maxie refrain from the slap blows that cut his opponents. Rosenbloom's promise wasn't good enough for Mae.

She telephoned her old friend Owney Madden in Hot Springs, Arkansas, and persuaded him to give Louis a shot at champion James J. Braddock. The result: Madden canceled the Louis-Rosenbloom match and the Brown Bomber flattened Braddock to become one of the most memorable heavyweight champions ever to hold the title.

Mae's two main romantic attachments in the late 1930's were Johnny Indrisano and Chalky Wright, a fighter turned chauffeur. (Even though Mae and Wright won a 1950's retraction from *Confidential* magazine for alleging they once had been lovers, intimates insisted there could be no question that their relationship was a passionate one.)

Mae also took an interest in reactivating Wright's boxing career after hearing he had been mismanaged. When he cited financial obligations to his family, she countered by hiring his brother to replace him as her chauffeur and took over his management. Through promoter Morrie Cohen she set up a series of matches leading to Wright's knockout of Joey Archibald on September 11, 1941, making him featherweight champion of the world.

In the spring of 1939 Mae was approached by Universal Pictures, the company that had resuscitated Marlene Dietrich's faltering career by casting her as a western heroine in *Destry Rides Again* to costar with W. C. Fields. Because hardly anyone could figure out how to use Mae at her best and still meet censorship restrictions, she was no longer in a position to impose her wishes on any motion picture company and was, in fact, lucky to be offered a film job. Universal was willing to gamble a modest budget that the combination of two such preposterous personalities as Mae and Fields might provide distraction from the war jitters that were sweeping the country.

Early in June 1939 columnist Louella Parsons sought out Mae to get the lowdown, and Mae assured her that she would sign no contract until she had read a script "with intestinal fortitude, but which at the same time is acceptable to the Hays Office." Receiving no other offers, Mae finally signed for $40,000, one-tenth of what she had received in her heyday.

A month later Louella reported that:

> if Bill Fields ever had a booster, it's his new movie partner. She says she and Bill will be starred side by side in that new picture

Grover James [note: actually Jones] is writing for them at Universal. Mae says there will be no trouble over whose name comes first on the marquee and that Bill will have a chance to do all the things he alone can do. "There is only one Fields," says Mae, "and why should I or anyone else try to change his style?" Her signature has just been put on a ticket which calls for three Universal comedies starring her.

The contract actually was for one film with options for two more.

Universal's publicity department, remembering all the attention Mae and Billy Sunday had reaped from their meeting, persuaded a famous but naïve religious leader to come up and see her. Even a bemused B. R. Crisler of *The New York Times* devoted considerable space to this manipulation, commenting, "As startling in its way as the Nazi-Soviet pact was the unexpected interview between Mae West and Dr. Frank Buchman, the English theologue, who is the leader of the so-called Moral-Rearmament Movement on the Pacific Coast."

Maneuvering Dr. Buchman onto a sofa beneath a nude painting of herself for the benefit of photographers, Mae, effulgent in a sheer pink negligee, assured him that she owed all her success to the kind of Moral Rearmament he represented. The guileless Buchman replied: "You are a splendid character, Miss West. You have done wonderful work, too, in pleasing and entertaining millions with your charming personality." Dr. Buchman apologized that he was an amateur at this kind of thing, but Mae told him he was doing fine and inquired whether he had met W. C. Fields. Buchman hadn't, and Mae regretted this, telling him, "Moral Rearmament is just what Bill needs. Give it to him in a bottle and he'll go for it." Having scored all her points, Mae allowed the press agents to escort Dr. Buchman back to a world in which he was more experienced.

After the first day's shooting on what eventually was known as *My Little Chickadee,* Louella, on October 31, told her readers there were "no casualties." A month later she claimed, "Diamond Mae and Bill Fields—were acting like buddies on the set this week and agreeing on every scene. For the first time in the history of a West picture, they have a complete script which is actually being followed except when Bill tears off a particularly hilarious ad-lib."

In light of Mae's subsequent statements, one might be tempted to dismiss Louella's items as movie column twaddle. While Fields was still alive, Mae restricted herself to claims that she had secured a clause in her contract that if he drank, she could refuse to work until he was sober or was sent home. He slipped only once, and as he was being hustled out, he ceremoniously tipped his hat to her. Or she might claim she was the star and Fields was featured.

But after Fields's death Mae added details to make herself come off better. "He was sneaky," she charged. "He knew a cutter, and they'd go into the cutting room 'n' take out my best lines. When the studio found out about it, they said he'd never make another picture after his contract ran out." Or she'd say, "I never talked to Fields. We never had time." Or, "I didn't want people thinkin' of us as a team. Fields was a sharpie—a crooked one!"

When Fields's cultists rose to reprimand Mae for her distortions of fact, she began saying he was "all right"—which was West shorthand for unprincipled, untalented and unlikable. If a reporter persisted that she wasn't sincere in saying Fields was "all right," Mae would release a barrage of resentment, beginning with the claim "He was envious of me.

"Everyone told him *My Little Chickadee* was his best thing. I wrote it, and he put in eight pages of a bar scene. Then he wouldn't shoot the rest of his stuff until they gave in and agreed to say he was coauthor." To another interviewer, she confessed, "I sorta stepped off my pedestal when I made that movie."

The consensus of those connected with the picture is that jealousy lay behind many of Mae's charges against Fields. As Dick Foran, one of her leading men in the film, observed, she was for the first time working with a performer whose legend was the equal of her own. Foran also said she probably was fearful that "Uncle Claude" knew as many scene-stealing tricks as she. Each was wary of the other, and Foran saw a great deal of jockeying for position by two consummate professionals. This slowed the shooting schedule, much to the delight of the other actors, but no one reported seeing Mae display open rancor toward Fields (except when he drank) until she viewed the finished picture. Then she realized that he had come off better, which may have been inevitable since director Edward Cline had been a former

Keystone Kop and was an inveterate admirer of Fields's brand of comedy.

"But Mae was a pip," Foran said. "A pip before the camera and off. When they were making a setup, I said to her, 'Honey, you got a beautiful pair of gams. Everybody thinks of you with the boobs. You ought to surprise them with the gams.' She beamed and gave me this big flash all the way to Christmas. But she wouldn't show her legs on the screen.

"On camera she would try to switch material around. In one scene she was locked in her room with me. Joseph Calleia was outside the window and Uncle Claude was knocking on the door trying to get in.

"'Who's theah?' she called.

"'A little messenger boy, dear, a little messenger boy,' said Fields, disguising his voice. Which was a pretty neat trick.

"So she says, 'Whatta ya got?'

"And he says, 'Oh, a telegram for Miss Flower Belle.'

"And here's the way she read a perfectly innocuous line. 'Well, shove it'—pause—'under the door.'

"I fell out of bed. Calleia fell from his perch on the trellis. Cline lost his temper. Uncle Claude walked away in disgust, and Mae inquired, 'What'd I do wrong? It's right here in the script. Right in black and white!' It was. She could take any line and switch it."

As executive producer of *My Little Chickadee*, Lester Cowan, more than anyone else, knew the facts about the production. Having worked with Fields in *You Can't Cheat an Honest Man*, he was the one who came up with the idea of costarring Fields and Mae. "She says she sold the story to Universal, but you'll notice no one is credited with the original story," Cowan said. "And for good reason. I'll now confess for the first time that I took the plot from Ferenc Molnar's *The Guardsman* and made it into a Fields-West western. The masked bandit whose kiss is his signature is the key. Read Molnar's play. I didn't take the writing credit because I'd fought to stop producers from grabbing such credit. But I swiped the idea and helped Grover Jones write the screenplay. In the script Jones turned out, there was a bird puppet that sat on Fields's shoulder and talked to him. Brilliant showwoman that she was, Mae immediately spotted this as an original, scene-stealing gimmick that would turn her into Fields's leading lady instead of his costar."

Unhappy with the Cowan-Jones material, Mae began writing her version. Eventually she arrived at Cowan's office to ask that he listen to her script. Cowan reached into his desk and removed eighteen pages Fields had submitted which he handed her. "'What is this?' she asked. I said, 'Bill thinks it's a script.' I read her Fields's pages—which naturally she didn't like. I certainly didn't think much of her efforts either, although I must admit she came up with some funny lines. Irritating as she could be," Cowan conceded, "she was one of the smartest women I've ever tackled, if not *the* smartest."

Cowan agreed to her request that she be allowed to read her script to her costar, confident that a man who had starred for Ziegfeld and D. W. Griffith would be capable of dispatching Mae's literary efforts. But Cowan misjudged Mae's persuasive powers.

"She cleverly got herself into a sexy blue negligee, invited him to her boudoir for the reading and began fussing with his hair, fixing it as it should be for the picture. She vamped him, flirted with him and won his approval of her script. He was smitten with her."

In *W. C. Fields by Himself,* there is a letter to Mae suggesting the infatuation Cowan mentions. Fields wrote, "I want you to be assured that I will do nothing on the story without first mulling it over with you and I also want you to know I have great admiration for you as a writer, an actress and for yourself."

In 1978 Cowan recollected that before he was aware of Mae's seductive tactics, he asked Fields his reaction to her script and was astounded to hear him describe it as "fine." "She understands muh charactah," he intoned. Nothing Cowan could do or say would shake that judgment. So Mae had a free hand adding jokes for herself and introducing another leading man, Dick Foran, to join Fields and Joseph Calleia. "I have to have one for comedy, one for drama and one for romance," she explained. The bird puppet, needless to say, had disappeared, diminishing the focus of attention on Fields without drawing any complaint from him.

Only after shooting was well under way did Fields realize what had happened and begin to resent it. He muttered and complained to Cowan. He stalled, but he never went directly to Mae. "He was a gentleman and he realized he'd been had," Cowan remarked. He added that in his opinion Mae succeeded in her career because she enjoyed nothing more than plotting moves so she'd come out in the best position. Cowan cited her first visit to his office when she pointed to a spot on his desk and announced, "The telephone goes there." Cowan was mystified. Mae said she wanted him to install a private line because she didn't trust switchboard operators. They might be paid to spy for the opposition.

Cowan credits the two stars with teaching him how to work with big names. "The way to deal with them is to be more temperamental than they are," he confided. "It's the only way. All of them are glad to get a job when a film is offered. But once production is under way, they revert to their true selves. These two even wanted screenplay credit."

Years later Humphrey Bogart further confused the issue of who wrote *My Little Chickadee*. Bogie, who had been offered the role Calleia played, told columnist Jim Bacon, "I went to the producer's office and was handed a script. I had a few lines, then the next thirty pages would be blank except for the notation: 'Material to be supplied by Miss West.' Another few lines for me and then thirty more blank pages. 'Material to be supplied by Mr. Fields.' The whole damn script was like that. I left quietly through an open window."

The preview of *My Little Chickadee* was held at the Hollywood Pantages on February 6, 1940, and went into general release in March. *Life* chose to cover the event rather than review the film. It used the movie as an excuse to run photos of Mae's apartment and to quote some of the better lines from the script. To a suitor who wants to know what kind of woman she is, Mae responds, "Too bad I can't give out samples." To another who observes that spring is the time for love, she asks, "What's wrong with the rest of the year?" After being kissed by the masked bandit, she observes, "A man's kiss is his signature." And, perhaps best of all: "I was in a tight spot, but I managed to wriggle out of it."

Metropolitan critics displayed a distinct sense of disappointment. *Variety* was more optimistic and in the long run more prescient in predicting that the film would benefit and earn a profit by drawing from both Mae's and Fields's fans, but even so, the paper complained that the results would have been better if the plot had brought the stars together more often.

Most reviewers frankly admitted the story was difficult to capsulize. It deals with Flower Belle's involvement with a masked bandit which results in her being run out of town. She meets con man Cuthbert J. Twillie, who sets up a fake marriage. He is appointed sheriff to clean up a western town while Flower Belle carries on several liaisons simultaneously and does more to bring about law and order through distributing what were then called her "favors" than Twillie does officially.

But whatever the escapades, partisans of both Mae and Fields claimed victory for their favorite. Each star is sometimes shown to advantage, but Fields's unconventional behavior was less likely to offend the sex-obsessed censors than Mae's freewheeling libido. For this reason alone—and there are others—it was inevitable that he should dominate the picture. Producer Cowan, admittedly a Fields partisan, certainly played some part in giving Fields the edge during editing. The unfortunate circumstance, from Mae's point of view, is that *My Little Chickadee* is the most frequently shown of her films. Seeing Mae only as Flower Belle is tantamount to seeing a sailing ship on a day when strong gusts of wind only occasionally arise to reveal its full beauty and power. Still, in 1940, Mae could capture the public's imagination. With war already under way in Europe, Royal Air Force pilots named their bulky life jackets Mae Wests in honor of that part of her anatomy which Dick Foran had suggested she deemphasize. The term is still included in most dictionaries, and she came up with a crack that showed how severely the Hays code, the Legion of Decency and women's clubs were inhibiting her on the screen. Said she: "Mmmmm. Sorta makes me feel like I started muh own second front. I've been in *Who's Who*, 'n' I know what's what, but it's the first time I ever made a dictionary."

The final film of Mae's first Hollywood career came in 1943. Director Gregory Ratoff, who was a relative of one of Beverly's husbands, approached Mae to star in the film version of the Broadway musical *Tropicana*. He forthrightly admitted he needed her name to get the project off the ground. She committed herself only if the story line made sense. "Dollink," she quoted Ratoff as saying, "only sense and passion." For once Mae encountered someone trickier than she. Ratoff craftily persuaded her to appear in a couple of expensive musical numbers before showing her the script. When she read it, she was appalled to find she was not the pivotal character, but she couldn't withdraw without putting Ratoff behind the financial eight ball and risking industry charges of irresponsibility.

The plot concerns a musical comedy star (Mae) who leaves the producer (William Gaxton) of a show she feels is destined to flop to join a revue a rival producer (Alan Dinehart) is putting on. Then Gaxton persuades the addlepated brother (Victor Moore) of the head of the League of Purity (Almira Sessions) to swindle money from the league. By investing in Dinehart's revue, Gaxton can take over the show and give Moore's niece (Mary Roche) a crack at Broadway stardom. In the end Mae gets Broadway success and Mary Roche gets the fiancé (Lloyd Bridges) she's wanted all along. The two plots receive equal time, so it is almost impossible to tell, amidst the interruption by vaudeville turns, which is the major and which the subplot. One thing is certain: the slimmed-down Mae, who bears a startling resemblance to Betty Grable, is off screen too often. Lloyd Bridges later lamented having no scenes with her. "It's curious, but I never saw her," he said. "I was kind of looking forward to it, too."

Four writers preceded Fitzroy Davis, author of the 1940's best-selling novel *Quicksilver*, but even he could do little to punch up the story line. If he achieved nothing else, Davis received a crash course in Mae's view of the Mae West character. *She*, he learned, could never be made to look ridiculous or undignified. *She* must never be pushed around by another character but must handle every situation with queenly grace. By her edict, *she* must emerge totally triumphant from every encounter. "Above all," Davis observed with grim humor, "*she* had to make the audience laugh every time she opened her mouth."

"They don't look at the screen and see the character," Mae explained. "They see MAE WEST. And they'll hold it against her if she does or says something they don't like."

Filming went at a breakneck pace. Scenes barely out of the typewriter at noon were shot later in the day. Mae and Ratoff quarreled violently the day before Davis was to leave for New York. During the exchange she accused Ratoff of trying to destroy her career. Next morning, going on the set to bid Mae good-bye, Davis found her and Ratoff amiably discussing the best possible title. They proposed a contest, giving a war bond to the person who came up with the most provocative name. "Feetz," Ratoff said to Davis, "you should be the one to win. Write one."

/   199

Mae nodded and chimed in, "Somethin' like *The Heat's On.*"

The Heat's On opened in November 1943 with *The New York Times* announcing, "The heat is off, but definitely." *Time* magazine was closer to the mark, writing:

> Cinemactress West is not on the screen half enough. But she is still one of the most entertaining and original personalities in pictures. She can still make something unmailable out of the twitch of a feather or a polysyllable. She is still capable of the low-minded grand manner which made *She Done Him Wrong* (1933) a minor masterpiece that might have panicked William Congreve.

When *The Heat's On* was revived at the Vagabond Theater in Los Angeles thirty-five years later, Mae *was* the show. Whether she was doing "I'm a Stranger in Town," a tongue-in-cheek Gay Nineties number with a chorus of adoring gentlemen or drawling her one-liners, it was Mae who received what she always called yells from the audience. (To Victor Moore, whose toupee got shoved over one eye during an arduous amorous scene, she murmured, "Don't look now, honey, but your hair's skiddin'.") She far overshadowed everyone else, including such expert variety artists as Hazel Scott and Xavier Cugat.

It was a terrible, yet glorious exit from films.

14

To head off threats of federal government censorship, the motion picture companies had hired Will Hays to devise and administer an industry-developed code of ethics. This ploy worked satisfactorily for a while. Then a spate of films such as *The Story of Temple Drake, Hoopla, Girl Without a Room, Gambling Ship, All of Me, She Made Her Bed* and *She Done Him Wrong* drew the ire of various religious and civic groups. Mae, with her flair for innuendo, insinuation and shameless flirtation with the camera, was accused of creating moral erosion.

The response of the Hays Office was to sharpen the teeth of its code to safeguard "against any situation, action or line capable of corrupting the mind and morals of a child." Hays, who was based in New York, set policy and gave final approval, while Joseph I. Breen and his staff in Hollywood functioned on a day-to-day basis with the studios.

Hays and Breen, in counseling the film companies, attempted to set down concrete examples of material that would be found offensive to such organizations as the PTA, the Legion of Decency, the American Citizenship Council, the Federation of Women's Clubs, the American Association of University Women, the YMCA, the YWCA, the WCTU, the National Council of Catholic Women, the National Council of Jewish Women, the Seamen's Institute, the Council of the Methodist Episcopal Church, the Young Ladies' Institute, the Boy Scouts of America and the Campfire Girls of America. The Hays Office was in a no-win situation, considering the contradictory judgments of what was wholesome or salacious, decent or indecent and, in the end, acceptable or unacceptable to such a diverse group of moral guardians.

Hays's task was further complicated by attempts of the Hollywood executives to withhold information about their production plans from those in charge at the home office in New York. Hollywood, anxious to be creatively innovative, sometimes would mislead New York about the theme and content of movies being contemplated, and Hays would find himself enmeshed in a bewildering web of double talk.

In the Production Code files at the Association of Motion Picture and Television Producers, Breen's memo to Hays about the Hollywood schism is on record. After both Louis B. Mayer and Emanuel Cohen had asked him not to send them letters (carbons of which would go to the New York offices of MGM and Paramount) regarding censorship problems on screenplays being planned for production, Breen wrote to Hays:

> The suggestion that we refrain from writing letters is, in our judgment, an attempt on the part of the studio executives to keep from their company heads in New York knowledge of the true situation with regard to pictures and scripts within the studios. . . . I think you will readily see the danger to our entire machinery if such a plan is followed in all studios. . . . There has been much undercover work going on that smacks to me of the desire of the studios definitely to outsmart and outwit the machinery of the Code, to fly a lone kite in the matter of production, without any counsel or guidance from the New York offices.
>
> The general attitude we have found here with regard to public criticism, which has become so widespread, is to belittle it all, sneer at our critics and to continue to make pictures to suit themselves.

Hollywood's wish to "fly a lone kite" was certainly demonstrated in the filming of *She Done Him Wrong*. When Harry Warner heard Paramount had scheduled this movie version of *Diamond Lil* for Mae, he sent off a sarcastic wire to Hays, demanding an explanation:

PLEASE WIRE IMMEDIATELY WHETHER I CAN BELIEVE MY EARS
THAT PARAMOUNT HAS ARRANGED TO MAKE <u>DIAMOND LIL</u> WITH
MAE WEST AND METRO <u>THE PAINTED VEIL</u>. RECOLLECT THAT IT
WAS ABSOLUTELY DEFINITE <u>DIAMOND LIL</u> AND <u>PAINTED VEIL</u> WERE
NOT TO BE PRODUCED. AM NOT SENDING THIS WIRE AS A PROTEST,
BUT I WANT TO KNOW HOW TO RUN OUR BUSINESS IN THE
FUTURE.

Hays replied to Warner that Paramount had indeed been considering the *Diamond Lil* project but that production plans had been abandoned. In fact, *Diamond Lil* had not been jettisoned but had been assigned to John Bright for adaptation to the screen under the title *Ruby Red,* with the central character's name changed to Lady Lou. Paramount submitted Bright's treatment to Breen, and, after considerable negotiation, the Hays Office granted the studio permission to use the basic *Diamond Lil* story, subject to several provisions. One of them was to have a salutary effect on what the world came to know as the Mae West personality: *"In view of the low tone of backgrounds and characters, comedy should be emphasized."*

In November 1932 the script, retitled *She Done Him Wrong,* was judged acceptable under the code. The Hays Office believed that with proper restraint in execution the finished picture would be eligible for its seal of approval. Proper restraint was not in Mae's repertory. When Breen and his staff saw the film, they were irate at how Mae had interpreted seemingly innocuous material and dispatched a demand for twenty-five changes—major and minor.

Some were as simple as the deletion of the lines "Day or night work, Rita?," "It takes two to get one in trouble," "Oh, I don't know. Hands ain't everything" and even such a lame crack as "I remember when he came right into my room and had pups."

Breen also called for the cutting of such visually titillating scenes—to him, at least—as Lou's changing her dress behind the screen, Rita's "unduly exposed" breasts and, after Cummings (Cary Grant) says good night, Lou's "action of approaching him, then pushing him away while both stand at the door." Also out was Lou's exchange with prisoners, all of whom she seems to know from somewhere else, during her visit to Sing Sing.

Breen was satisfied that the implication Lou had been kept by several men, an aspect of the play which had worried the Hays organization, was deleted. To soften the inference that the heroine could commit homicide and connive to conceal the body,

Breen decreed that Cummings's last speech to Lou be reshot to read: "You are still my prisoner and as soon as you clear the law I'm going to be your jailer a long, long time." Breen backed his decision by saying, "This will at least supply a point to argue from should the question of legal ethics be raised."

The Hays Office compromised on one issue. The song "A Guy What Takes His Time," which it had ordered totally removed, was allowed to remain for a single verse and chorus.

In spite of all the precautions taken, *She Done Him Wrong* was rejected totally in Java, Latvia, Australia and New Zealand and was subjected to a variety of deletions by local censorship boards the world over. In Sweden, where sexually explicit films first would be legalized, the only scenes excised were the ones in which Rita throws herself on the dagger and dies and Flynn is shot.

I'm No Angel was subjected to the same line-by-line scrutiny that *She Done Him Wrong* had undergone. Because of the difficulties this created in writing for the Mae West character, it is surprising that her films ever went before the camera. In spite of the popularity of *She Done Him Wrong* and *I'm No Angel*, censorship groups registered such vociferous protests with the Hays Office that by 1935 both films had been reclassified and placed in a category prohibiting any further showings unless Paramount agreed to make specific changes.

The Hays Office totally rejected the *Belle of the Nineties* script, saying:

It is a yarn which is quite patently a glorification of prostitution and violent crime. From the outset, the leading character is established as a person with a long and violent criminal record who displays all the habits and practices of a prostitute and aids in the operation of a dishonest gambling house, drugs a prizefighter, robs her employer and deliberately sets fire to his premises and in the end goes off scot-free in the company of her illicit lover who is a self-confessed criminal, thief and murderer.

This script suggests the kind of picture that is certain to violate the provisions of our production code for any one or all of the following reasons:

(a) vulgarity and obscenity
(b) glorification of crime and criminals
(c) glorification of a prostitute
(d) general theme of the story which is definitely on the side of evil and crime.

Paramount ordered a new script, written with the Hays Office's objections as a guideline. When the studio finally received a seal of approval, Breen wrote a congratulatory letter to Emanuel Cohen and expressed pleasure that he had effected these five thematic changes:

1. Ruby is no longer a prostitute or ex-prostitute.
2. There is no suggestion that the Tiger Kid is an ex-convict; he is only an ambitious prizefighter.
3. Much of the sexually suggestive offensiveness has been removed, specifically that Ruby and the Kid have had an affair in her apartment that lasted five days.
4. The action of Ruby stealing money from her employer has been removed.
5. Ruby's relation with Brooks, the wholesome young man, has been cleaned up. Lustful kissing, in which he fondles her body and she fondles his, has been removed.

After all of the trouble—and the high cost of retakes—with *Belle of the Nineties,* Paramount decided to treat the script of Mae's next film, *Goin' to Town,* with meticulous care. The studio was so successful that the Hays Office raised no major objections. Breen specified, as usual, that Mae was not to be presented as an ex-prostitute. Otherwise, he fretted that Argentina might be offended if the gigolo was depicted as a resident of Buenos Aires. "They are very sensitive about this," he admonished, suggesting the gigolo be from somewhere outside Latin America. Paramount turned him into a Russian.

The Hays Office did receive some protests against *Goin' to Town.* One was from a minister in New Albany, Indiana, representing the Conference of the Methodist Episcopal Church. He wrote:

Re Goin' To Town, starred in by May [*sic*] West. I have not seen the screening nor will I. The New York Times pronounces it a vulgar, demoralizing exhibition. So all my friends report it is the same old May [*sic*] with no effort at cleaning up. The play was produced after a blare of reform. I agree that must [*sic*] good has been done—thanks to the leadership of the Roman Catholic Church but what I cannot understand is how this particular actor who stands for a particular phase of morals should have been permitted to put another over on American youth.

Breen thanked the man for his interest but quoted a recommendation of the film by the Motion Picture Bureau of the International Federation of Catholic Alumni.

The Indiana preacher's condemnation of a film he had not seen pointed up a dilemma that faced Mae and her producers. She was, in effect, a prisoner of her own notoriety, and this would cause her many problems in her most ambitious screen role, Frisco Doll, the nightclub singer who poses as a settlement worker in *Klondike Annie*.

Upon receiving the first draft of the script, the Hays Office immediately spelled out two danger points:

1. It must be made clear that Miss West is not masquerading as a preacher, revivalist or any other character known and accepted as a minister, ordained or otherwise. Rather, her assumed character is to be that of a social worker, rescuing poor unfortunate girls, etc., along the lines of numerous rescue missions which are basically philanthropic and not specifically identified with, promoted by or financed by religious bodies.
2. There should be no feeling of burlesque of this social service work or no tongue-in-cheek portrayal of scenes or dialogue. Although Miss West will not be shown as entering this work in order to escape the law her activities should be shown as genuine to the point where she herself eventually becomes a changed woman.

Though script revisions were made to avoid these "danger points," the Hays Office skittishly demanded that Mae neither wear religious garb nor carry a Bible and, further, that she never utter the word "religion" but substitute "livin' good." Such Westian one-liners as "She may sing hymns, but I bet she knows a lot of other kinds of songs, too," were deleted; and actual quotes from the Bible were prohibited, as if Mae's delivery would taint them.

The Hays Office then made some creative suggestions to "improve" the moral tone, if not the artistry, of the script:

Under the heading of *Good and Welfare* we would like to suggest the possibility of your working into the script as part of the activities of the settlement workers, shots of Doll playing games, possibly with rough miners, teaching them Mother Goose rhymes, etc. Settlement workers make it a practice to gather children around the settlement house to cut out paper dolls or play charades. Why not have Doll giving the rough miners a bit of the same instruction? Why not inject into the picture a few Eskimos

206   /

and Chinook Indians? And how about Doll as a sort of Carry Nation, cleaning up the saloon and building up the settlement house as a rendezvous for the workers? Why not plant early in the picture that Doll has in her possession a large sum of money, $3,000, which she is determined never to let out of her hands and later show that she is spending her money freely for some good purpose, say the hiring of an airplane [circa 1900?] to get serum for a dying child?

For all of Mae's efforts to present her version of a morality play on film, the picture was weakened by local censorship boards' demands for removal of the accidental stabbing of the Doll's Chinese boss and the scene where she dresses and paints Annie Alden's face to look like a whore. Deletion of the stabbing footage in particular left a vacuum in the development of the story. In later years Mae, blessed with the ability to banish any setback from her consciousness, could not remember if the excised scenes had ever been shot.

Klondike Annie's problems were increased by a two-pronged attack by the Paul Block and William Randolph Hearst newspaper chains. Block's thrust primarily was a criticism of the Hays Office's severity against cartoons and features which poked fun at the New Deal and fascism in Germany and Italy while "being soft on" the kind of "salacious" material Mae dealt in.

Hearst, who, according to *Time* magazine, was inflamed because Mae supposedly had made a slighting remark about his mistress Marion Davies, sent the following memo to all his managing editors:

The Mae West picture *Klondike Annie* is a filthy picture.

I think we should have editorials roasting the picture and Mae West and the Paramount Company for producing such a picture—the producer, director, everyone concerned with it.

We should say it is an affront to the decency of the public and to the interests of the motion picture profession.

Will Hays must be asleep to allow such a thing to come out, but it is to be hoped the churches of the community are awake to the necessity of boycotting such a picture and demanding its prompt withdrawal. After you have had a couple of good editorials regarding the indecency of this picture then DO NOT MENTION MAE WEST IN OUR PAPERS AGAIN WHILE SHE IS ON THE SCREEN AND DO NOT ACCEPT ANY ADVERTISING FOR THIS PICTURE.

It is astounding that apparently the Paramount people should have had the stupidity to produce such a picture when it has been demonstrated to what degree the screen has benefitted by clean pictures that have been made since the public uproar against screen filth. It goes to show that screen producers are not influenced by any of the moral considerations but only by public indignation.

And the only way of influencing such producers is by the community saying that pandering to the lewd element in the community is not profitable.

The beleaguered Breen sent the following memo to the members of his staff:

Just so long as we have Mae West on our hands, with the particular kind of story she goes in for, we are going to have trouble.

Difficulty is inherent with a Mae West picture. Lines and pieces of business, which in the script seem to be thoroughly innocuous, turn out when shown on the screen to be questionable at best, when they are not definitely offensive. A special memorandum should be prepared on this matter for presentation to Mr. Hays.

Molly Haskell later observed in an essay that there is irony in that moment in *Klondike Annie* when Mae rolls her eyes heavenward and addresses Sister Annie: "You were right about the wages of sin, Annie. I never thought I'd get caught."

After discouraging tentative plans of various studios to adapt *Personal Appearance* to the screen, the Hays Office failed to dissuade Emanuel Cohen, who wanted to produce it under the title of *Go West, Young Man,* starring Mae. Cohen guaranteed he would change the story materially to meet censorship requirements. The bottom line turned out to be that the leading character should not be portrayed as a nymphomaniac, that no aspersions be cast against Hollywood, that the U.S. Senate not be defamed in the portrayal of Senator Francis X. Harrigan and that all nudity and flagrant sexuality be eliminated.

There was even less trouble in store for Mae with *Every Day's a Holiday.* In submitting an early draft of the script to Breen, Emanuel Cohen said he felt that Mae had censored herself to the point of marring the entertainment value but that he hoped to ascertain whether the basic story of this musical comedy was acceptable to the Hays Office. Breen replied that in addition to some double entendres, he found altogether too much drinking.

These elements would have to be kept to a minimum, he advised.

Cohen, in submitting a revised version of the screenplay, wrote Breen: "I would like to call your attention to the fact the basic characterization of Miss West in this picture is completely different from anything she has ever done before. There are no sex contacts, no sex situations that could possibly arouse criticism that her pictures previously received."

Still, Breen requested a few changes, including deletion of the lines "Yeah, I always carry it with me and put down anything that comes up" and "I don't know a lot about politics, but I know a good party man when I see one." Mae was adamant about keeping in the latter. She wired Postmaster General James Farley, who was so amused he interceded with Will Hays and saved the gag.

By the time Mae made *My Little Chickadee* and *The Heat's On,* her final two pictures in her early film career, producers had become so intimidated by censors that they had given up trying to inject any of her lustier contributions. Still, it was a tribute to Mae's unflagging inventiveness that she managed to project the audacity and humor of her personality. When she returned to pictures, the production code had been replaced by a rating system that made permissible the raunchiest lines Mae or anyone else could come up with. Looking back on her censorship battles, Mae went Shakespearean and dismissed them as "much ado about nothing."

15

The lull in her film career following *The Heat's On* caused Mae to examine how fragile success and even life itself could be. She sought reassurance beyond the material wealth and pervasive fame she had acquired. Over the years she had rejected organized Christianity's puritanical prohibition of sexual freedom. While agreeing with H. L. Mencken's definition of Puritanism as "the haunting fear that someone, somewhere may be happy," she hungered for spiritual sustenance and decided seriously to investigate mysticism.

Her first encounter with what would turn into a consuming interest had occurred in 1928, when she met Sri Deva Ram Sukul, a holy man from India. After becoming a movie star, she grew too busy to devote time to the study of mysticism, but in 1941 she sought out the *sri* and enlisted his aid in helping her to open her consciousness to the Forces. She had become convinced she could either lead a very wicked life or develop spiritually.

She confided to a friend that even after becoming a famous star, she found herself irresistibly attracted to the underworld and its power to conduct all kinds of illegal enterprises and go unpunished. She fantasized about the most lurid escapades as the queen of vice. Through George Raft she mixed with Bugsy Siegel, Mickey Cohen and other mobsters. She was fascinated by their accounts of crime and how, at that time, it was paying them royally. Their adventures and brushes with death excited her.

Death. The thought of it always ended her fantasies and brought her back to reality. She was unprepared to face anything so final, and, obsessed, she began looking for proof there was life after death.

The *sri*'s guidance in her quest only partially satisfied her, and she began to look elsewhere. In the fall of 1941 Timony pointed out a newspaper announcement about a spiritualists' convention in Los Angeles, but her vaudeville experiences with mentalists and spook workers had persuaded her that what was not trickery was, as she put it, "for the squirrels." She sent Timony and a boxer friend to survey the group. They were intrigued by the Reverend Thomas Jack Kelly, minister of the Spiritualist Church of Life in Buffalo, who, they were told, had been tested by the parapsychology department at Duke University.

When Mae heard that Kelly had demonstrated some remarkable feats of extrasensory perception, including accurately telling the boxer that his father had been murdered, she instructed Timony to arrange a séance at the Ravenswood. After their meeting, Kelly predicted a surprise attack against America by the Japanese, President Roosevelt's election to a fourth term which he would not live to fulfill and that America and England would win the war. The bombing of Pearl Harbor a few weeks later made a firm believer of Mae.

Kelly reinforced his position shortly afterward, when the police department contacted Beverly about a Brooklyn acquaintance who had visited her. He was suspected of having murdered his wife before coming to California. Fearing a scandal, Mae summoned Kelly, who informed her that the wanted man had been taken into custody twenty minutes earlier. A telephone call to police headquarters verified that the arrest had been made in San Diego at the time Kelly claimed. Under Kelly's guidance, Mae began to learn to meditate and to recognize the messages from her inner voice. As she developed what Kelly told her was a natural gift, she grew to rely more and more on the supernatural, and she actually believed she once made contact with her mother.

Eager to repay Kelly for the peace of mind he had helped her find, she arranged a press conference to publicize his claims of success in solving murder cases which, she hoped, would persuade law enforcement officers to use his services more often. Aware of the *sri*'s jealousy, she didn't invite him. "But Big Mouth Timony let the cat out of the bag and the *sri* showed up," she recalled later. "So I put him on the defensive by pretendin' to be mad because he hadn't left word where I could get hold of him." Mae said the *sri* accepted her excuse but annoyed her by writing a question for Kelly in Sanskrit. "What're you tryin' to pull?" she asked. "Yuh tryin' to make a fool of him?"

The *sri* assured her he was only testing Kelly to make sure he was legitimate. If he was, he would be able to read the query with the aid of the Forces. Shortly after, Kelly read the question and accurately told the *sri* he would decide against returning to India and remain at Miss West's side. Mae now had two trusted advisers. The *sri* was with her constantly while she was preparing for her next major project for which both he and Kelly had prophesied great success.

Ever since her rise to stardom in Hollywood, Mae had harbored the urge to bring Catherine the Great to the screen. But suspicion about the appeal of foreign costume drama, escalating production costs and loss of the European market had blocked consummation of a deal for the film. Finally, in July 1943, flamboyant Broadway showman Mike Todd announced that in addition to a play by Gypsy Rose Lee and a musical by Cole Porter, he would present Mae as Catherine during the upcoming season.

Their first conflict came with Mae's tantrum over his title, *The Men in Her Life*. Later, explaining her confrontation with Todd, Mae said, "Lee Shubert called me up and said, 'I'm sendin' out a guy to produce your play. He's not too smart, but he'll run his legs off for you.' So I just set him straight." What Todd intended was a rowdy comedy. What Mae had in mind was a demonstration that in dramatic power she was the peer of Katharine Cornell and Helen Hayes. After all, the *sri* had just given her a direct message from Catherine the Great—who had died in 1796—that she wanted the approach to be serious.

Arriving in New York, Mae boasted to reporters she had read twelve biographies as preparation for writing the script. "I'll say Catherine was great," she enthused. "Why, she was the Diamond Lil of her day." Todd immediately appropriated Mae's praise for the leading character as the title, called the play *Catherine Was Great,* and pushed ahead, devising what one writer called "a typical Mike Todd production. Two of everything—and twice as big."

What Todd had initially envisioned as bawdy comedy had blossomed into a full-blown historical drama by the time casting got under way. Early auditions were a shambles. Swashbuckling actors were a necessity, but the mumblers and shufflers who showed up for what they thought was a typical Mae West production could deliver neither the style nor élan required to bring the cardboard characters and hackneyed scenes to life.

Finally, director Roy Hargrave sent out for some belts and sabers, and groups of actors were asked to put them on and walk across the stage. He said, "Every son of a bitch who doesn't trip gets a chance to read." Other casting methods were equally unorthodox. Mae spied Lester Towne's red hair and hired him, believing redheads were lucky omens. One of Towne's duties would be to stand in the wings so she could touch his flaming locks for good luck as she made her first entrance.

Female impersonator Ray Bourbon's camping, which had always amused Mae, inspired her to write in the part of a French dressmaker for him, giving him two assistants, one of whom, Dick Ellis, was to earn fame as "Mr. Blackwell," couturier and originator of the "10 Worst Dressed Women" list, which Mae made in the 1970's.

Mae's two principal leading men could not have been more disparate in backgrounds or in their attitudes toward the star. Todd was determined to have Philip Huston as Gregory Orloff. At the time Huston was appearing with Uta Hagen, Paul Robeson and Jose Ferrer in *Othello* and was reluctant to leave Shakespeare for such a lugubrious script. But after Todd offered a huge salary plus a clause that allowed him to leave the cast a couple of months after opening, Huston signed.

Out of curiosity, Mae attended a performance of *Othello.* When she came back to congratulate Huston, he asked whether she had any criticism of the performance. "Yeah," she said, "Paul should've worn makeup." Huston laughed but later concluded he was dealing with a canny theatrical intelligence. He realized all other actors had worn rich-colored, almost balletlike makeup. What Mae had discerned was a need for highlights to make Robeson fit in with his fellow players.

"I have played opposite every leading lady from Judith Anderson to Vera Zorina," Huston said years later. "And Miss West was one of the treats of my life. She was extraordinary. She had great composure, the famed bravado—all that is synonymous with Mae West. In addition, she was blessed with a wonderful sort of—not so much vulnerability—but shyness before an audience. I enjoyed the rehearsals and performances terrifically because of her. The play, as you know, wasn't exactly Pulitzer Prize material."

The other actor who played opposite Mae was Joel Ashley, ex-construction worker, ex-boxer, stage and film leading man. He hesitated about going to the audition, but a pregnant wife and a dwindling bank account persuaded him. When he came onstage and was introduced to Mae, she opened the conversation by asking him, "Mr. Ashley, how tall are you?"

"Six feet, three and a quarter."

"How much do you weigh?"

"I weigh two hundred three pounds. Stripped."

"And how big are you around the waist?"

Now she had him worried. "Twenty-nine inches."

There was a long pause, then: "Oh, king-size, huh?"

He was asked to read and was chagrined to be assigned the part of Bunin, *a* lead but not *the* lead. On the fourth day of rehearsals the actor playing Potemkin left, and Mae and Todd asked Ashley whether he could handle this pivotal role. His answer: "For more money? Of course."

When casting was completed and rehearsals began at the Adelphi Theater, it soon became apparent to Mae and Todd that the director, who previously had handled small-cast, one-set shows, was floundering. When Todd expressed reservations, Hargrave blamed the preposterousness of the script. Two days later Todd brought an authority on Russian history to the theater. The astonished historian informed the producer that events in the play had been scrambled, chronology ignored and the script could only be described as a canard.

Irate, Todd faced Mae, who coolly responded that of course, the professor was right. "Didn'tcha read the prologue?" The prologue? Mae flew into a tantrum. Could she be blamed if he ignored the opening of the script which put everything into perspective? A messenger was sent to the producer's office to fetch the scene, but none could be found. Mae walked out in feigned anger and rushed back to the hotel where she and her secretary-writer, Larry Lee, stayed up all night devising a scene in which World War II soldiers spoke of Catherine—planting the idea that what was about to transpire was the dream of one of them.

The *sri* was in the center of things, supposedly looking after Mae's spiritual and physical well-being. Attending all rehearsals, he amused cast members by sleeping through every session. But he always was at the ready to supervise Mae's diet and to give her a daily "lesson." According to Don de Leo, who played Ambassador Murad Pasha, the "lesson" consisted of yoga exercises which ended with the *sri*, fully clothed, lying on top of Mae while she experienced an orgasm.

Early on in rehearsals Mae, rolling her eyes, suggested to Joel Ashley he ought to study with the *sri*. When he challenged her to give one good reason, she said, "Oh, it's so mah-velous. You can reach an orgasm in thirty seconds."

"Christ," Ashley replied, "I don't want to turn into a damned rabbit."

"Not you, dear," she corrected. "The woman. *Me!*"

There was much speculation about who actually had written the play. Dayton Lummis, who played Chechkovski, concluded Larry Lee was the author on the grounds that like any playwright, Lee knew every line while Mae was slow learning her own. As rehearsals deteriorated, Todd grew increasingly alarmed. Finally, he told his star, "Look, Mae, forget the heavy drama. The audience knows you as a comedienne. Don't go highbrow on them. They won't take it."

"Why, you son of a bitch, take your cigar and get out of my sight," several members of the company recalled her saying. "I was a star when you were a bricklayer." Todd retreated.

"Sometimes there was mild absurdity in her seriousness," Huston recalled. "She said to me one day, 'Yoo read Shakespeare. Why doncha teach these fellas diction?' Then we made our entrance and one of her first lines was: 'Greggoroff'—as she called me—'I apperent you Lord of the Admiralty.' She was a puzzling contradiction. She wouldn't use gags, but neither would she give up her strange Brooklynese. She had marvelous strength, great voice projection, she could have acted a straight part, but she wasn't secure enough or adventurous enough—whatever—to discard the mannerisms she'd made her own. She said, 'Entah!' She could have said 'enter' like everyone else, but 'entah' was part and parcel of the public image she'd developed."

The July premiere in Philadelphia brought enthusiasm for the sets and costumes, mild praise for the star and a bitter attack on the play. In the Philadelphia *News*, reviewer Jerry Gahagan began his notice: "*Catherine Was Great*—but Gahagan was miserable." The audience was confused by what they saw. And it was Huston's impression that Mae was stunned by the meager audience reaction and the mild applause at curtain calls. As she left the stage, she saw the director and said, "Hargrave, ya threw my play right down the tur-let."

As a solution to a weakness at the end of the second act, Ashley remembered an old dirty joke (with the tag line "The least you can do is take your shoes off!") which he thought offered a solution. He wrote it up as a pantomime in which Potemkin opens the portieres of Catherine's raised bed, embraces her and gets on top of her. He snuffs out the candles, leaving only a pool of moonlight onstage. He tosses one jackboot, then the other, into the pool of moonlight. Curtain.

"I immediately mailed the original material to myself in a sealed envelope and gave her a copy. She never said, 'Thank you,' or anything. The next morning she announced to Hargrave she had a marvelous idea for a second-act curtain. Mine. I went directly to Mike Todd and told him that if she persisted, I'd either get an injunction to close the show or I'd sue him for plagiarism. He said, 'Oh, for Christ's sake, she can't get away with that kind of crap. What do you want for it?' I named a figure, and he paid it. He was damned generous that way as long as he had it."

Todd did not interfere until the conclusion of the second performance in Philadelphia. Only Mae and Ashley remained on stage when Todd appeared. "He got on her really deep," Ashley recalled. "Using gutter language, he yelled, 'Who the fuck do you think you are? Helen Hayes?' Now that's a direct quote. He said, 'God damn it, you can't act. What I want you to do is be funny. And if you don't snap out of your shit and play what you're supposed to play, you're not going to be able to get a booking in an outhouse.' He had a cigar flopping up and down in the corner of his mouth.

"She didn't attempt to defend herself. And all I wanted was to get out of there without witnessing anything more."

The next evening when Ashley arrived at the theater, the company manager informed him that he was wanted onstage. "I didn't have my makeup on, but he told me to go at once. There were only three people there, Miss West, Todd and Lee Shubert. I told them I didn't want any part of this, but Shubert said since I'd been present the night before and heard what Todd had said to Miss West, he wanted me to hear what he was going to tell Mr. Todd. God spoke and I stayed. He turned and asked Mike how much money he had in the play. Todd said something like sixty-five grand of his own money. And Shubert said, 'Tomorrow morning you'll have a certified check for sixty-five thousand dollars. From now on you'll be the nominal producer and you'll receive fifteen percent of the profits—if any.' Then he said, 'If I ever hear of you talking to Miss West like that again, you'll be very fortunate to book a play of yours into a phone booth.' She hadn't bothered to reply directly to Todd. She had just gone to a phone, called Lee Shubert for help and he backed her up."

Having bested Todd in one-upmanship, Mae nevertheless heeded his advice. That night, as she and Huston passed by the twelve magnificently attired guards positioned to line her way to the throne—handsome men recruited off beaches and out of prizefight rings for their appearance rather than their acting ability—Mae looked over each appreciatively. Suddenly she stopped, looked at a tall blond's crotch and murmured, "You're new around here, aren't ya?"

Later, when Joel Ashley entered, she commented that his boots were dirty. He ad-libbed that the courtyard was muddy, and Mae brought down the house with "Thanks for the weather report."

"The ad lib got a big solid laugh," Huston said, recalling it. "That's why I say playing with her was one of the honors of my life. She *was* Americana. There was W. C. Fields, Chaplin, Keaton and maybe five or six others in all of show business who kicked the bell the way she did."

As the days passed, Mae continued to incorporate wisecracks—Potemkin: "I'm yours to command." Catherine: "I command you to attack." She adapted old gags to new situations. For example, when Gene Barry, who played Bunin, approached her with his sword swinging and the hilt poked her in the pelvis, Mae quipped, "Oh, honey, is that your sword? Or are you just glad to see me?" (Remember? "Is that a gun in your pocket or are you just glad to see me?") She also agreed to add a song, "Strong,

Solid and Sensational." But perhaps her happiest inspiration was a curtain speech in which she confided, "I'm glad you liked my Catherine. I like her, too. She ruled thirty million people and had three thousand lovers. I do the best I can in two hours." It got the heartiest laugh of the evening.

While in Philadelphia, the cast soon began observing Mae's libidinous nature. Red Towne learned to keep an eye on the husky men playing members of the Russian Army. "First one guy and then another would turn up with a new suit," he said. "When someone's wardrobe began to improve, you could guess he was *the* one. Temporarily. And those suits had a certain easily identifiable something you could always spot.

"There were always several men in her life," Towne continued. "But she was as harmless as Sister Kenny compared to the things people do today. She didn't dissipate, but she had to have sex at least once a day."

Don de Leo was taken aback by Mae's lack of inhibition. "Miss West was a very unusual person," he said. "When she met somebody she liked, she went. If it was a cabdriver, a wrestler, a Park Avenue playboy or an actor. Black or white, it didn't make any difference. In *Catherine,* she finally picked one guy. It could have been me. After I knew her twenty minutes, she had me in the dressing room kissing me and running her hands all over me. It was wild, but a man likes to be the aggressor. Or did at that time. But she had no qualms about it."

Her number one favorite turned out to be Jerry Lucas, who began as one of the guards and eventually was elevated to the role of Captain Danilov. Lucas, big-boned, tall, almost an ax handle wide, carried his 240 pounds gracefully. Together, the petite star and the powerfully built Lucas made a striking pair. According to one observer, Lucas would have been ideally cast in a Warner Brothers gangster movie of the thirties. "He had a great deal of influence with Miss West," said a source who requested anonymity. "The problem—if there was a problem—was that Jerry had goals and ambitions of his own and Miss West didn't like that."

The premiere at the Shubert Theater in Manhattan on August 2, 1944, prompted *PM*'s Louis Kronenberger to pun, "Mae West Slips on the Steppes." Joseph Wood Krutch in the *Nation* regretted:

I am very much afraid we highbrows are going to have to give up the attempt to find something really significant in Mae. One of us—it may even have been I—once said she was a vamp to end all vamps and that the evolution of Theda Bara to *Diamond Lil* showed how we were growing up. Miss West did not, I now fear, mean to end all vamps. She merely wanted to be a new and more outspoken kind.

John Chapman of the New York *Daily News* drew a laugh at Mae's expense, writing, "I am afraid it will be a bust, which will give Miss West one more than she needs."

Despite the reviews and a $4.80 top, the price then commanded by lavish musical comedies, Mae attracted standees for the second performance. But by the third week Todd and the Shuberts had to drop twenty actors to pare operating expenses, and by the fifth week Sunday performances were instituted to shore up declining attendance. Then business improved enough so that at the end of the second month the show was moved from the Shubert to the Royale, a theater from which Mae professed to receive good vibrations since it was there she had scored in *Diamond Lil*. Miraculously box-office grosses continued to increase until by the twelfth week *Variety* felt safe in predicting the "heavy production outlay will be earned back during the Broadway engagement." This proved overly optimistic. The show closed in January 1945, after completing thirty-four weeks on Broadway, but it failed to recoup its investment.

Mae, who shared in profits, had refused to pay high salaries or grant run-of-the-play contracts on the grounds that such actions would "give actors ideas." In late October, Joel Ashley turned in his notice to accept a film assignment. Although Mae had stopped speaking to him during the Philadelphia tryout, she was distraught. She summoned him and turned on the charm. "It was the only time in my experience she showed any humility," the actor later said. "She claimed she couldn't find and rehearse a replacement in two weeks. I finally agreed to let them have four weeks at a lot of money."

In that final month Ashley's feelings toward Mae mellowed, and he began to see the humorous side of her shenanigans and to recognize her as a trouper who wore heavy costumes during the summer heat wave without complaint, who was tireless in attempting to improve the performance long after the opening and who gave her all to the audience. "Those were qualities I could admire," he said. "I almost began to feel I'd been humorless about her after I left for Hollywood. She made good dinner conversation."

Ashley's replacement, Charles G. Martin, established a much better professional and social rapport with Mae than his predecessor had and would work with her not only in *Catherine* but also for a national tour of *Come On Up* and for the revival of *Diamond Lil. Catherine Was Great*'s road tour opened in Baltimore. In Boston the company manager came backstage smoking a cigar. Mae asked him not to smoke in her presence. The following night he appeared with a cigar in his mouth again. The next day she arranged for him to disappear permanently, and Mae for all practical purposes assumed managerial duties. During the Boston stand *Variety* filed a report that applied to most cities—Pittsburgh, Cleveland, Chicago, Detroit, St. Louis, Kansas City—that Mae played. It read: "Critics cold but b.o. hot."

"On tour Jerry Lucas's importance increased," a cast member noted. "Mae seemed so much under his spell, he could almost be forgiven for forgetting that *she*, not he, was the star. He began acting as if he were the show." Attached to him as she was, that ended their relationship. Once again she chose public success over private ecstasy—and was seemingly able to do so without regret.

In Chicago, of the six daily reviewers, only Ashton Stevens found the performance entertaining. Astute showwoman that she was, Mae suggested to the press agent that she send Stevens a letter in hopes he would publish it, earning the company free promotion. "You know, Ashton," she said, regarding the other critics, "the way the boys wrote up the show I'm surprised they weren't raided. Those kids should really be writing stuff for me instead of about me. The way they described certain scenes made me wonder how I ever got past the Boston censors. And to think I purposely took out a few of the stronger lines and situations for Chicago on account of Lent."

In spite of 90 to 100 percent capacity business, the production ultimately failed to pay off because of both the large initial investment and an unorthodox agreement giving Mae not only royalties but also 50 percent of the weekly operating profit, with additional percentages going to the Shuberts and Todd. In fact, Mae's personal deal was so good that she agreed to undertake a series of one-night stands, hopscotching from Des Moines to

Wichita, Tulsa, Little Rock and Memphis, to name only a few of the cities.

At the time a critical platitude had it that Alfred Lunt and Lynn Fontanne could provide an amusing evening reading the telephone book. Large sections of the theatergoing public seemed willing to endorse Mae's talents just as enthusiastically, refusing to be warned away from *Catherine Was Great*. Nonetheless, from an objective point of view, the project that had for so long represented the highest peak of her dramatic ambition was a critical and financial failure.

Even so, her personal earnings were large enough that on July 2, 1945, George S. George and Vadim Uraneff, who had worked at the Hollytown, brought suit against Mae and Mike Todd, claiming they had originated the play, ignoring historical fact to tailor it to Mae's well-defined talents. In response, Mae denied using any of their material, denied entering into any profit-sharing agreement with them and concluded by observing that if any agreement was made, it had been done in Hollywood in 1938, which meant that the California statute of limitations had run out.

In August 1948 two screenwriters, Edwin K. O'Brien and Michael Kane, also sued Mae, claiming that Timony had hired them to do a script for her and that after considering Joan of Arc and the Queen of Sheba, they settled on Catherine of Russia. Timony insisted the men had only been hired for two months as researchers at a meager $15 a week—which may account for O'Brien's explanation for the lack of a copy of a third act: "We ran out of carbon paper."

Mae testified she had first toyed with the idea of playing Catherine in 1933 and, to prove it, brought out a tattered vaudeville sketch entitled *One Hour of Love*. Producer Albert Kaufman swore that they had discussed the project that year, and director Edward Sutherland then took the stand to confirm that Mae had submitted a polished screenplay about Catherine to Emanuel Cohen in 1936, but it had been rejected as too expensive. After a six-week trial the case went to the jury, which deliberated for three days before declaring itself deadlocked, seven to five for acquittal.

There was no litigation over *Ring Twice Tonight*, a comedy by Miles Mander, Fred Schiller and Thomas Dunphy, which Mae opened for a projected nine-month tour, beginning in Long

Beach, California, on May 16, 1946. The show crisscrossed the country, playing split weeks, one-night stands and a sprinkling of longer engagements.

Most minor-league critics, unaware that audience laughter has little to do with the standards by which New York reviewers judge plays, predicted Mae had a hit in the making. The wispy plot sets her up as an FBI agent posing as a nightclub singer. She hides out in her fiancé's apartment to escape involvement in a killing. To provide divertisement, one of Mae's maids releases balloons, inviting the finders to come up and see her mistress. The novelty lies in having Mae fight off, rather than seduce, sailors, a cabdriver, a gangster, a Mexican murderer, a U.S. senator, her fiancé and his father.

As the two-week stand in Los Angeles hit a $40,000-plus gross, J. J. Shubert penciled in the production for the Cort Theater, but after sitting through a performance during its second week, he canceled the booking. Unemployable in Hollywood and now deserted by the Shuberts, Mae saw her career reach its nadir. What she needed was a boost to put her into orbit again. When it came, it was from a totally unexpected source.

16

On September 11, 1947, Mae boarded the *Queen Mary* to sail to England for a provincial tour to be followed by a West End presentation of *Diamond Lil.*

Auditions, which were held in London, were no better organized than they had been for *Catherine*. Bruno Barnabe, who played the villainous Juarez, recalled, "I was the Latin Lover. For this part she interviewed some eighty actors. I was the fifty-seventh, and when she first saw me, she said I was too old. About a week before the show was due to open in Manchester, she decided to have me audition again, and I went to her hotel. She explained the highlight in my part of the bedroom scene where I was to approach her from behind and place my hands on her breasts. Would I rehearse that? I did so and rotating my hands on that famous bosom, I asked, 'Now what?' She answered, 'You're in,' and that was that."

On the pre-London tour the breast-fondling business was played everywhere except in Blackpool, which drew a family audience. After ten weeks of strenuous changes and adjustments by producers Val Parnell and Tom Arnold, *Lil* opened January 24 in London on a twice-nightly basis at the Prince of Wales. The audience had never seen anyone quite like Mae—although she faintly suggested Marie Lloyd, a music hall favorite. Theatrical historians Raymond Mander and Joe Mitchenson recalled the play for two reasons: "We would say that *Diamond Lil* was the first *obviously* (obvious to us) miked production in London. It was directed so the miking all seemed part of the show as Miss West moved from one hidden microphone to another. As to the lighting, it was generally so subdued that when the spot moved about following her it was noticeable. It was a mixture of blue and pink."

Each night Mae stopped the show with her third-act song-alog—"Come Up and See Me Sometime," "My Man Friday," "A Good Man Is Hard to Find," "You Made Me Love You" and "Frankie and Johnny." At the conclusion of the third act she made a speech and usually took five or more curtain calls.

Once again critical enthusiasm was unbounded for Mae and *Lil*. "Mae West is triumphant—she came to London last night—and conquered it!" was the opinion of Hannen Swaffer, dean of the then current drama critics. The *Daily Express*'s reviewer wrote: "Mae West is entertainment. She herself is a restoration comedy rolled into one body—earthy and outspoken. Shock me? No, I just liked her." But Mae did shock some theatergoers. For the first few weeks Bruno Barnabe played the breast-fondling scene as rehearsed. "Then so many letters of objection were sent the management and the censor that some cuts had to be made. Almost overnight business dropped," Barnabe recalled. "Mae told me to put the fondling back. I told her I couldn't. They could send me to prison for contempt of the law. 'That would be great publicity, Bruno.' But I refused to risk it."

Barnabe said he commented on her wonderfully firm breasts. She told him she kept them in tone through special exercises. " 'If your wife or girl friend's bosom needs firming up, tell her to do this,' she said. And she clasped her hands together with the fingers between each other, the arms shoulder high and parallel to the floor; then she quickly brought her palms together."

If Mae's association with Barnabe was frank and amiable, her relationship with Noele Gordon, who appeared as Russian Rita, was rocky, as was always the case with any potential rival for male admiration. Thirty years later, when asked to discuss the experience, Miss Gordon declined, saying it was a period of her life she would prefer to forget since working with Mae had not been easy for her.

If Mae's behavior with fellow professionals was direct and sometimes difficult, her demeanor with Peter Glenville, a director who introduced her to what Hedda Hopper called British swells, was almost demure. "I didn't know her *that* well. But I thought she had a sweetness of disposition and great shyness," Glenville said. "Although she dealt with very raunchy subjects in her jokes and was a sex symbol, in her private conversations there was a certain innocence about her."

Earlier Glenville and Mae had met backstage somewhere. When she came to England, he called her after seeing the play and went around to the Savoy to have supper. "She had one of the old-fashioned suites with lots of gilt and silk damask in the panels of the walls. The only decoration she had in this rococo room, apart from flowers, was a very tiny, very ordinary picture of her mother. Bang. Right in the middle of the silk damask," he said.

Glenville decided to give a party for her—mostly the theater crowd, but a few from other walks of life. "That night Mae met a great many people—one hundred or more—many of whom she probably would have met in the course of events," he said. "Not all. Certainly not Nancy Cunard and other members of the frivolous social set."

Word got around about Glenville's friendship with the American actress. One of the literary Sitwells rang him and said they were giving a big, totally nontheatrical party and they thought it would be "great fun to have a sort of fairy atop the Christmas tree—suddenly to have Mae West there."

Glenville telephoned Mae to ask if she'd care to go to the Sitwells' to a party at which the Duchess of Kent would be the guest of honor. "What's that, dear?" she asked. Glenville repeated the information, and suddenly his line went dead. Three minutes later Mae called. He said they'd been disconnected, but she corrected him. "We weren't cut off, dear. I just wanted to make sure somebody wasn't pullin' somethin' on me."

"Very cautious, she was," he said. "And showing horse sense in a way." The night he went to pick her up for the party, Glenville found a mob of fans outside her stage door. As he escorted her to his car, people were pushing, shoving, trying to get close to her.

"I don't think it happens as much now, but even in those days she had it more than most. Anyway, that night she was absolutely besieged. One man nearly broke the side window. He was a huge, great man with a sort of cap. And she had the window down just a bit and said, 'Hello, honey. Hello, rough trade.' Then she put the window up tight and off we went."

Mae wore a Grecian white classical gown with a white hood thrown over her yellow hair and a single stone—"No bigger than a man's fist," she said—at her cleavage. Edith Sitwell complimented her, saying, "You look like a vestal virgin." Mae replied, "Baby, you don't know what you're sayin'."

"But for the most part she was self-contained, a bit shy," according to Glenville. "She said a few funny things, very quietly. Watched everything. People were charmed by her."

What had Glenville thought of *Diamond Lil*? As a director, he found a lot to be desired. "But I liked the way she put the numbers across—not a big voice—but one that had a marvelous lilt and a purity of quality and, of course, a lot of humor. She also did a shrewd thing in London. It was obviously put in for the occasion. She was told there were a lot of moderately rich immigrants who spoke Yiddish. Anyway, in came a gangster type and for the next four minutes the play was entirely in Yiddish and getting screams of laughter from some sixty percent of the audience."

Glenville's overall assessment: "You went to see the outrageous, astonishing Mae West, not the direction, decor, lighting or supporting cast. From my point of view, in her own funny little province she was an artist, in that she invented her style, invented her personality and, indeed, invented her appearance. That, in a sense, is artistry. Now I think, for instance, the greatest film comedian was Charlie Chaplin. He totally invented *that* personality—the look, the style, the angle—and it had nothing to do with *his* personality. Those people who determine what they want and create for themselves an image—or indeed, an actor who can create a whole series of characters—those are the artists as opposed to many of the folk heroes of the pop world today."

Diamond Lil ran for three months, twice nightly, closing the first week in May. On the fifteenth of that month, Mae sailed on the *Queen Mary* for New York, telling ship's reporters she hoped to return to the West End soon in a new play. The Forces must have been vacationing. For Mae had no inkling of what lay in store for her.

Variety's report of her London success had intrigued a friend from vaudeville, Albert H. Rosen, who, with Albert H. Lewis and Charles K. Freeman, was attempting to convert their stock company in Montclair, New Jersey, into a year-round operation. Sometime late in October of 1948 Rosen suggested booking *Lil* for a week. If it proved to be the success he envisioned, they would send it on the road. Lewis and Freeman feared their staid New Jersey following might be affronted. Rosen, unfazed by their timidity, approached Mae on his own and found she had no definite commitments.

Said Freeman: "Hell, I didn't know her or the play except by reputation. So Al got us a script. I read it, but I couldn't make head or tail of it."

Said Mae: "Some of my plays don't read too good. I know what I'm doin' and when to do it. So I don't write out long descriptions."

Rosen told Mae that Freeman was eager to get her ideas on a production. The meeting was set, and for Freeman it turned out to be an occasion. "When I first met her, I immediately had a good reaction," Freeman recollected. "And when she read a few lines, I realized this gal wasn't a faded Hollywood star trading on her name. She still really had something. I knew the play would be fun to do and audiences would have a good time. I got so excited over the possibilities I began urging Rosen and Lewis to give it a first-class production, but they prudently stuck to the regular stock budget."

In many ways this cutting of monetary corners contributed exactly the right sleazy atmosphere for the play's rendering of the Gay Nineties. Mae's wardrobe was the exception. She wore brilliantly designed and executed costumes by Paul Dupont, who was adept at adding flattering period touches to her gowns. Wherever possible, Freeman hired actors who had pleased Mae in some other production. Charles G. Martin of *Catherine Was Great* and *Ring Twice Tonight* was engaged. Jack Howard and Billy Van, members of the 1928 production, were hired again. Also cast was Patsy Perroni, an ex-fighter and the anonymous sexual athlete who, she says, once climaxed twenty-six times in the twenty-four hours they spent together. (Mae claimed she could keep count because she had "that many protectors" in a drawer beside her bed.) Ray Bourbon joined, too. "We got everybody she liked who was at liberty. Everyone who would work for our kind of money," Freeman said, "because Rosen was determined to have a cheap tryout."

Rosen secured the all-important bed from a nearby warehouse. It was Grand Rapids style, and there was no way the resident scene designer could transform it into a replica of the famous swan bed that had graced the original production. When Mae caught sight of the dreary prop, she announced she was canceling her engagement. A swan bed was pivotal to the success of the play. A bold, coldly professional manner replaced her comradely relationship with Freeman. He had betrayed her. She refused to rehearse.

By this time Freeman was in her thrall, convinced the production on which he would collect a weekly royalty would go far beyond the initial booking. So he persuaded Rosen to hire Ben Edwards to design a swan bed and touch up the set enough to lure the sulking star onstage. Edwards also drew up plans for more elaborate settings for the projected tour.

What began as a one-week tryout stretched to a three-week stand in Montclair as word of mouth sent theater people and socialites to New Jersey to supplement the local audience. "Lil's the sort of show, of course, that serves as a greater amusement today than it did on Broadway 20 years ago," Nat Kahn reported in *Variety,* as the production headed for a $23,000 week at capacity. So strong was *Lil*'s attraction that for perhaps the only time on record New York scalpers handled tickets to a stock-company production. In Mae's view, that was only as it should have been since her satisfaction in life came from breaking records.

Following the third week, the company closed while a new set was built and the actors re-rehearsed in preparation for the December 27 opening of a two-week stand at Philadelphia's Forest Theater. Some recasting was necessary. One unsuccessful auditioner was Norman Stuart, who was surprised that the audition required no reading. As she had with Bruno Barnabe, Mae requested that Stuart stand behind her and caress her breasts. When he had finished, she gave him a typical Mae West look and announced, "I think you better go out and live a little."

(A few years later in Hollywood, Mae visited the set of a film Alexander Hall was directing. Stuart was working in a scene, and Hall introduced him to Mae. Stuart said, "It's nice to see you again. I auditioned for you a couple of years ago." Mae flashed him a smile and replied, "Yeah, I remember. Ya look like you've lived a little.")

On opening in Philadelphia, Mae began a run that, with interruptions, lasted until November 1951. Under the new setup Al Rosen intended to function as sole producer and the only general partner, but because of various problems, a shrewd businessman named Herbert J. Freezer was elevated to co-producer of the $35,000 production. Mae's guarantee was $1,500 per week plus 10 percent of the gross over $20,000—which invariably was exceeded.

In addition to those already mentioned, the cast included Steve Cochran and Richard Coogan as leading men; Miriam Goldina, a protégée of Stanislavsky's; Sheila Trent, a brilliant but alcoholic actress; Sylvia Syms, a jazz singer making her acting debut; and David Lapin, a pianist with whom Al Rosen had worked at Loew's State.

Mae looked over the actors and focused her interest on Steve Cochran, a dark, handsome, randy young man-about-Broadway, who talked seriously of founding a harem. He planned to import six late-teen live-in (in every sense of the word) foreign domestics. "They couldn't leave me for two years and I'd always have six girls around the house," he fantasized.

Although assistant stage manager Lester Laurence noticed that during rehearsal breaks Mae and Cochran "rehearsed" in her dressing room, Cochran was then too seriously involved with the French actress Denise Darcel to offer anything more than physical gratification—which was all Mae demanded.

One of Cochran's traits that annoyed her was his humor. If there were any laughs, she wanted to get them. At one out-of-town rehearsal in Baltimore, Mae and Cochran arrived to find Laurence reading the star's lines. When the scene finished, Mae told Laurence how impressed she was with the way he did her part. And Cochran added, "So am I. Why don't ya come down to my dressing room and see me sometime?" Everyone roared but Mae. That joke, according to Laurence, put the final strain on Mae's and Cochran's tenuous sex play.

After a few brief forays with other company members Mae

settled her attentions on David Lapin. "I remember Steve saying, 'Well, Charlie, I guess she's found herself a boyfriend,'" Charles Martin recalled. There seems to be general agreement that Lapin exerted a powerful influence over Mae, although their relationship remained unpublicized until January 15, 1949, when newspapers reported he accompanied her as she was rushed to a hospital at 4:00 A.M. from her suite at the Lord Baltimore Hotel. Her physician described her condition as "only fair" to the press.

Doctors disagreed whether she was suffering from appendicitis or an abdominal blockage, but all concurred that exploratory surgery was prudent. Mae again refused to allow her body to be marred. The argument continued even as she was being prepared for the operating room. Finally, she hysterically demanded that Lapin and Rosen get her out of there. Rosen urged that she follow conventional medical advice, but at 11:00 A.M. her will prevailed. She signed herself out of the hospital, was bundled into a wheelchair and, with Lapin solicitously dancing attendance, returned to the Lord Baltimore.

By siding with Mae against the doctors and Rosen, Lapin exploited the minor breach that had already developed between the star and the producer. Thereafter Mae and Lapin surprised members of the company by making no attempt to hide their romance, though Lapin had a wife and child, ordinarily a situation that was anathema to Mae. As an indication of how drawn to him she was, where other lovers had been presented new suits, Lapin eventually received a Rolls-Royce. No one except Mae could doubt that he had real influence, which he used to almost everyone else's disadvantage, including the star's.

Immediately after her release from the hospital Rosen and Freezer canceled two engagements. Mae, having summoned the *sri* and Reverend Kelly, recovered in time to play Syracuse and Buffalo. It was in Buffalo that Sylvia Syms fell into Mae's disfavor. Sylvia, a stocky, unglamorous youngster, was the kind of woman Mae never regarded as competition. Admiring Sylvia's talent, she treated her as something of a protégée. But when a photographer casually picked Sylvia to appear with a local supernumerary for a newspaper picture, all of Mae's competitive instinct was aroused. Lapin convinced her to stop speaking to Sylvia.

Mae's objection was based on the assumption that every photo and column item had to be focused on her since she correctly believed she was what the audience paid to see. True though this may have been, it made it difficult for press agents Dick Williams and Michael Sean O'Shea. "Unfortunately Mae just went crazy over Lapin," Williams said. "He moved in and for several years there came as near to running her life as was possible with a strong woman."

The general consensus is that having always delighted in intrigue, Mae allowed Lapin to do things she might have hesitated doing herself. Fanning Mae's smoldering resentment against Rosen for opposing her wishes during the medical crisis, Lapin soon had her refusing to communicate with his former mentor. "You tell Al I said . . ." she would instruct Williams. When he countered that it would be more appropriate coming from her, she threatened to have Lapin take care of it. "And he was willing," Williams said. "It was incredible."

In spite of out-of-town critics' praise of Mae's truly spectacular performance, Rosen and Freezer were unsure how harshly the script would be treated by the New York press. They cautiously dismissed several bit players, deleted one song and negotiated to reduce the required number of stagehands and musicians. Their object was to establish a $20,000-a-week break-even point at the Coronet Theater in New York. Mae was outraged at their lack of confidence in her "classic." Once again she was proved correct. Usually blasé first-nighters greeted her initial entrance with five minutes of sustained applause and huzzahs. And daily reviewers, reeling from such theatrical ineptitudes as *Mr. Meadowlark* and *Don't Listen, Ladies,* embraced not only Mae but also the play and the production.

Critical gadfly George Jean Nathan announced it prudent first to protect "the purity of your critical judgment" by assuming a lofty tone. "Very well," he wrote, "Mae West is not much of an actress by tony critical standards and *Diamond Lil* by any such standard is trash. But—let the tumbril come if it must—they are disgracefully good sport."

Wolcott Gibbs of the *New Yorker* reprinted sections from Charles Brackett's 1928 review of the play and announced that this "expresses almost precisely my own feeling," concluding, "I guess that Miss West's charm both as a playwright and as an actress is unique and perennial."

Life's man saluted her as handsomer than ever, adding,

"Despite her unswerving loyalty to sex, Mae is not exactly a Love Goddess. She is a razzle dazzle priestess of sexy, barroom humor whose sayings have become a part of the nation's folklore."

John Mason Brown of the *Saturday Review* commented that Mae had never asked to be taken seriously (an arguable assumption). But Brown made a valid point, writing:

> Sex itself is for her a cartoon which she delights in animating. If she is a high priestess of desire she is also its most unabashed and hilarious parodist. When she gets through with the Tenderloin, it is ham—sheer, unadulterated Smithfield.
>
> As an archetype of the predatory female, Miss West is about as sinister as a retrieved copy of *The Police Gazette*. Her choice has always been to be an anachronism. For all her contour, and in spite of a dromedary dip with which she walks, the incessant pelvic rotations that punctuate her sentences, and the steaming sultriness of her voice, her chief invitation is now, as it was in the beginning, to laughter. Had she been only a siren, Puritan America could never have been "had" by her. But she is also a farceur and a comedienne. And it is these endowments which originally saved her and which continue to endear her.

Harold Clurman, one of America's best stage directors and probably its most perceptive theater critic, accepted Mae on her own terms. He wrote:

> Mae West is complete. Her *Diamond Lil* is a genuine creation, and we need not hesitate, because her art is comically low and her aim is mercenary, to treat it seriously. Mae West is a consummate technician: she has high visibility, rhythm and a remarkable mimic sense and great guile in self-display. All of this is at the service of an image based on the memory of another epoch (that of Lillian Russell) for which most of us harbor an abiding nostalgia, as if it represented a time of less constriction. Mae West's *Diamond Lil* is not at all of that era, it is only her model. Her art stems from the taste of the twenties, when, because of prosperity and prohibition, the raffish was glorified as the idol of atheists, and the quasi-obscene was venerated as a tribute to license.
>
> Mae West is worth study, above all, as an expression of our attitude toward sex; in the words of Sophie Tucker, "Gentlemen don't like love, they just like to kick it around."*
>
> A Mae West is unthinkable in France, where sex is l'amour and has a good reputation—on both lower and higher levels.

*Cole Porter's "Most Gentlemen Don't Like Love."

Brooks Atkinson and others are right in pointing out that *Diamond Lil* has very little sex. That is just the point; Mae West will have no truck with such dirt. She knows America's preoccupation with sex and the embarrassment that covers their fear of it. She gives her public what it wants: a glittering facsimile of what it craves and, through laughter, a means of keeping itself free of what it fears. She horses around with sex so that we can have our cake and not eat it.

With all this, Mae West is a true theater artist: almost every detail of her show—including the vulgar sleaziness of its scenery—is right. Look at the stage when she is delivering her songs: the ensemble is wonderfully chosen to evoke the feeling of the Bowery with all it connotes of drab gaiety, a depressed, beat-up glamorousness. It is *The Iceman Cometh* turned to farce.

With such acclaim, it would seem everyone was entitled to sit back and to enjoy great applause and profits. Not so. On February 26, three weeks after the opening, Mae was to make a guest appearance on John Chapman's TV show between the Saturday matinee and evening performance. Rushing, she tripped over a rug on her bathroom floor and twisted her ankle.

Chapman, who was waiting to escort her to the studio, hurried back to WPIX to report the accident and alert ticket holders that the Saturday night performance of *Lil* would be canceled. X rays showed that Mae had suffered a multiple fracture of her left ankle. She entered Doctors Hospital and was released on March 6. At her side constantly was Lapin, kowtowing to her every whim. Eager to keep the momentum the show had been building, Rosen announced that Mae would return to Broadway on March 21. That day came and went without the return of Mae. Fortunately the producers had insured the production with Lloyd's of London so that salaries would be paid and key performers kept available.

On June 8 Mae granted an interview to a *New York Times* reporter. Her physician, Dr. Lester Breidenbach, said that the ankle had completely healed, she revealed, but he was unwilling to hazard a guess as to when she might resume work. Although she no longer suffered severe pain, according to the reporter, Mae limped noticeably and used a cane. She said that until she regained freedom of movement, she would be unable to perform since an essential ingredient of her characterization lay in her undulations.

The producers became increasingly annoyed as the production, which had earned back production costs before the accident, slipped back into the red as they paid out unreimbursed costs incurred during the long-delayed reopening. Rosen accused Lapin of persuading the attending physician of prohibiting Mae to work, saying, "You know it doesn't require five months to heal a fractured ankle."

During that time, Lapin took control of Mae's life as few other men ever had. She needed someone to lean on, both literally and metaphorically. She was becoming increasingly paranoid, believing that everyone was out to steal from her—her material, her personality, her possessions. The toll taken by fighting her way up from a rough-and-tumble background and maintaining her position left her feeling perpetually vulnerable. Like most narcissists, she needed constant outside reassurance that she was as good as she claimed to be. Ironically she chose to trust the type of person who would tell her anything she wanted to hear while using her to his advantage.

By midsummer Rosen finally found a way to lure her back to work. When he reported he'd arranged for *Diamond Lil* to be invited—in preference to Arthur Miller's *Death of a Salesman* and Robinson Jeffers's *Medea*—as the climax of the 14th Annual Play Festival at Central City, Colorado, Mae agreed to go.

The company opened July 30 for two weeks at the famed Opera House, but Mae's drawing power was so strong a third week was added. Then the scenery was rushed back to Broadway, where on September 7 *Diamond Lil* resumed its run. This time the play was housed at the Plymouth instead of the Coronet. Through Mae's cooperation with the press, she managed to rekindle enough excitement for the production to remain on Broadway until January 21, 1950.

She enjoyed the last performance as much as the first and looked forward to touring. She found it inconceivable that anyone could tire of *Lil*. When Lucius Beebe of the *Herald Tribune* inquired how long she thought any actress could continue to portray heroines with "bounce and seductiveness," Mae told him: "Just as long as she has her health and feels the part, and I may say that in my case that may be almost forever. Look at Bernhardt; she went on carrying on like a mad thing for many years with only one leg. I'm one up on her right there. Then again I have very little competition. There's hardly anybody as bold and brazen and hussyish available on the stage today. . . . I'm practically indestructible.

"*Diamond Lil* is all mine. I'm she. She's I, and in my modest way I consider her a classic. Like *Hamlet,* sort of, but funnier. I'm permanently typecast and I love every minute of it."

Although Beebe may have tidied up Mae's grammar, she meant what she said. Later, during the national tour, some members of the company rehearsed scenes from other plays to alleviate the boredom and loneliness that were part of spending months in a series of strange towns. When Mae discovered the rehearsals, she was outraged and only with greatest difficulty was dissuaded from firing the actors for what she regarded as their disloyalty to *Lil.*

Much as Mae loved *Lil,* she treated most real women with such undisguised contempt that Sylvia Syms said a quarter of a century later, "Mae West was the first male chauvinist pig." Let the neophyte Sylvia and the experienced artist Miriam Goldina speak for the women who worked with Mae during her post-film-acting career.

Casting a Stanislavsky-trained Russian actress in a Mae West production is the stuff of which farces are made. Yet through a set of complicated circumstances Miriam Goldina, a leading lady of the Hebrew-speaking Soviet-based Habimah Theater, joined the cast of *Diamond Lil* during the first part of its run. Goldina, a fiery brunette with flashing eyes and great dramatic intensity, had left Russia on a world tour in 1925. Before Goldina and her husband, a director of the company, departed from Russia, he had signed an assurance that all members of the group would return. After several defected, he sent a coded letter to a Soviet friend inquiring whether he and his wife might return safely. The friend's reply: "If you pass by and see a fire, would you pour oil on it?" Reluctantly the Goldinas decided to remain in the United States.

Employment was scarce because of language difficulties. Miriam eventually appeared in *The Dybbuk* at the Pasadena Playhouse. Although she had to learn the role phonetically, she received brilliant notices. On Broadway she was seen in many distinguished plays, most notably in Sean O'Casey's *Within the*

Gates. But by 1948 her husband had died and she was forced to accept almost any role offered to support herself and their child. After reading nine times for Mae, Goldina was hired to play Russian Rita.

Conceding Mae was a clever performer and a shrewd businesswoman, Goldina not surprisingly was appalled at Mae's approach to theater. "Always it had been a joy just to be in a play," Goldina said thirty years later, her diction retaining charming traces of her origin. "But Mae West? I'm in the theater fifty years, but never such an experience before or after. In one scene we sat at a table looking at pictures. She looks at a picture and under her breath she mutters, 'You tell that son of a bitch there's no light on me.' In other words, she is only concerned about herself. Not the production. Everything else does not matter. Only her. She had a rounded figure. I was slender then. So she sends her maid with a blanket to put around my waist under my costume!"

Russian Rita has one highly emotional encounter with Lil in the bedroom over the saloon. In the scene Rita is stabbed to death. Lil conceals the murder by pretending to brush Rita's long black tresses and flipping the hair over Rita's face and bosom to hide the dagger.

Stanislavsky's former protégée used techniques he'd taught her to infuse the hokey confrontation with true emotional impact. "And can you imagine what she does?" Goldina asked dramatically. Then she began swaying her hips and launched into a remarkable impression of Mae—edged in vitriol—'Ooooooh, what're ya gettin' yourself so worked up for? Why ya gettin' all excited? They didn't come tuh see you. They're here tuh see me, see? 'N' don't you forget it!' Well, the first time she did that with her back to the audience, talking to me, I almost forgot my lines."

After several fiery exchanges Mae told director Charles Freeman, "She must be a communist. She always talks back!" Eventually tension caused Goldina to turn in her notice. Shortly after, when Mae became disenchanted with her replacement, she had Freeman call Goldina to suggest she return. "Not for a thousand a week," she said. "It's that bad?" he asked. "Worse," she told him, then added, "When you work for Mae West, it is not for art, but from hunger."

In contrast with the trained artist that Goldina represented,

Sylvia Syms found working with Mae both an opportunity and a frustration. Before the schism in Buffalo, Sylvia had come to Mae's attention when the star visited the Cinderella Club in Greenwich Village to see Ray Bourbon. Mae listened to Sylvia's voice, called her to the table and asked whether she'd like to read for the show.

"'Would I!' Here I was, a big, fat kid who didn't look much different in 1948 than in 1978 except that I like to think I've acquired style—at least a little bit," she said thirty years later. She was eager to accept the opportunity not only because of her personal ambition but also to prove something to her husband, Bret Morrison, the Shadow on radio, who scoffed at the idea of her becoming an actress.

Next day Sylvia went to Mae's suite at the Warwick Hotel. Mae gave her a script and instructed her to read. "I was so green I read everybody's part," she recalled. "But everything was fine. I played the shoplifter and sang a song. One funny thing, I'm a pretty chesty chick, but she had me padded with kapok. First you met my bosom; then you met me."

Very quickly Sylvia learned that Mae had spies in the company, that she loved intrigue and enjoyed knowing who was doing what to whom. "That should have warned me to keep out of her territory," she said. "Then after the Buffalo incident she wanted me to quit. I wouldn't. I knew I could learn from her. She had such style. And I picked up some incredible things from her about timing. I learned to hear a line for the first time night after night and how to deliver one as if it were an ad lib. For example, Steve Cochran would say, 'Oh, Lil, I'd go through fire and flood for you.' And she'd say, 'You better make it fire. I'd rather have you hot than wet.' Corny? Not the way she delivered it."

By studying Mae, Sylvia also observed the obligations, as well as the joys, of stardom. To this day, she maintains, "I've never seen a more beautiful woman. In her mid-fifties Mae's skin was alabaster; her teeth were her own and absolutely beautiful. And contrary to what most people thought, her legs were great. She sold glamour, and she had the most incredible discipline and sense of dedication in achieving it.

"Every night all these people lined up to get a glimpse of her as she came out of the stage door. There were cops on horseback to control the crowds. She would emerge in a full-length fur—

/   237

ermine, whatever—laden with jewels, and get into that limousine. She'd roll down the window and greet her subjects. After she'd satisfied their urge to *see* a real, live star, the driver would pull slowly away. He'd drive around the city until the crowd had dispersed. Then she'd go back to her dressing room, have the maid put away her glamour costume, get into her slacks and babushka and go home."

Having given Mae full credit for her professionalism and talent, Sylvia still felt that Mae's lack of compassion for other human beings was unforgivable. Some of Mae's associates attributed her insensitivity to the counsel of her spiritual advisers. They thought these men persuaded her that giving in to emotion upset the blood chemistry, but possibly it was Mae's narcissism that made her unable to empathize.

Once when stage manager Lester Laurence wavered in delivering one of her harsher reprimands to a member of the company, Mae commanded him to do so, assuring him the message would change nothing. "I'm a firm believer in predestination," she informed him. "See that cleanin' woman over there? There's nothing could change her lot. Because she was destined to be a cleanin' woman. Me, I was always destined to be a star."

Diamond Lil opened its road tour in Boston, where it sold out against competition from William Inge's Critics Prize play *Come Back, Little Sheba* and Giraudoux's *Madwoman of Chaillot.* Most engagements did capacity business. As the final attraction at Pittsburgh's forty-three-year-old Nixon Theater, which was being torn down to make way for a skyscraper, Mae, plus the sentimental occasion, drew such crowds that the usually vacant 800-seat upper balcony sold out.

In her first appearance in Chicago in five years, newspapers reported she was receiving an ovation at the Blackstone unequaled in memory. At the end of her songalog, the opening-night audience "stomped and yelled and gave her two encores and then good-naturedly booed when actors attempted to go on with the threads of the hokey melodrama." She remained at the Blackstone for sixteen weeks.

Fans besieged her new stage manager, Herbert Kenwith, with requests for private meetings with their idol. Kenwith, who had quickly developed a close relationship with the star, turned most of them away. But one day a charming young girl who worked at a bakery arrived with a carton of macaroons. Knowing of Mae's sweet tooth, he ushered the girl into Mae's dressing room, which quickly filled with the aroma of the freshly baked cookies. Mae gave her a signed picture, and as soon as the girl left, Mae seized the carton and ripped it open. She was about to pop one of the macaroons into her mouth when her suspicious nature caused her to have second thoughts. She thrust the carton toward Kenwith, saying, "Here, dear, you first." Realizing what she was up to, he took a macaroon, broke it in two and said, "Let's split one." She agreed and put her half in her mouth. But she waited to chew until he had consumed his. Reassured when he did not keel over, she ate hers plus all the rest in the carton.

During the tour David Lapin aroused increasingly widespread resentment for his dictatorial behavior toward members of the company. He was widely regarded by the actors as a snitch. Kenwith soon became aware that one of Lapin's eyes peered out from the crack in Mae's dressing-room door, and he finally told him, "If you'd open the door wide enough for both your eyes, you'd be able to see better."

Lapin retaliated next day by roughly shoving Kenwith out of the star's path and into a piece of scenery, injuring his shoulder. Kenwith threatened to bring a $1 million suit for damages. When Mae attempted to talk him out of it, he frankly told her of the dissension the man was creating. She realized then the relationship with Lapin had to be brought to a close. When she tried to end the affair and send him on his way, Lapin proclaimed his love for her and apologized for his behavior. Seemingly there was no way she could drop him without a nerve-shattering fracas.

As 1951 began, Mae played St. Louis a second time, cut through the Midwest and veered south. Banned in Atlanta, she told an Atlanta *Journal* reporter, "Atlanta's ban will mean more dollars to me than if I played Peachtree a month. . . . Publicity is worth something too." The tour continued, ending in California in April.

By now Mae was completely disenchanted with Lapin. He was not only alienating co-workers but also creating scenes in public. She confronted the problem and set about solving it. After arranging for a New York agent to ask her to come east to discuss an offer, she booked flights for Lapin and herself. With their bags packed, she began complaining of a toothache. She would have to see her dentist, she said, but insisted he go ahead and make ready her suite at the Sherry Netherland. She promised to join him in two or three days. Lapin left. Mae never followed. Nor would she ever again respond to his wires, letters or phone calls. A few years later when Charles Martin asked her what had happened to him, she vaguely said, "Oh, he served his time."

Surprisingly, in September 1951, Mae was appearing in another revival of *Lil*, unexpectedly rescuing Montreal's Gaiety from strippers and baggy pants comedians for eleven days, although lack of preopening publicity or advertising limited attendance. Even so, the poor gross did not deter Mae's new producer, George Brandt, from taking *Lil* into the Broadway Theater for a "limited engagement."

By now the critics were bored with the play, impatient with the shoddiness of the production and derisive about the quality of acting—and small wonder. Writer Allen Arthur Lewis was a twenty-one-year-old newcomer to the city in 1951. He knew he wanted to be associated with the arts but wasn't sure exactly how. As he was passing the Astor Pharmacy one day, a man asked Lewis how tall he was. He replied six feet two. Asked if he wanted to work nights, Lewis said it depended on what kind of work the stranger had in mind. "Don't worry, don't worry," he was told. As Lewis and the stranger entered a theater and the stranger led Lewis into the lounge, he found himself face-to-face with Mae. Auditions were in progress. Someone handed him a script and asked him to read. He did, and after looking him over from toes to head, Mae murmured, "He'll do. Send him over to Eaves for a costume."

"And that's how I ended up playing in *Diamond Lil*. Apparently Miss West felt that as long as she knew what she was doing—and she did—it didn't make a whit of difference how inept the rest of the cast might be," Lewis recalled. But Mae had exposed herself once too often. In its follow-up notice *Variety*, which had had reservations about the first revival, turned savage: ". . . a freak show can stand just so much seeing and this time around both *Lil* and Miss West seem tiresome." The engagement lasted sixty-four performances.

Mae again needed an outrageous novelty to capture the public's attention. Although it would take a couple of years, she eventually would devise a presentation so unusual that a quarter of a century would pass before other showmen adapted it.

17

On April 5, 1954, while preparing breakfast in his bungalow, Timony was felled by a massive heart attack and died almost instantly. Though his professional influence on Mae ended with the failure of *Clean Beds,* he had continued to submit scripts to her and make vague plans for trying them out at the Hollytown.

If she had been working, undoubtedly she could better have coped with Timony's death. As it was, she went into seclusion at the Ravenswood, leaving it to Larry Lee to meet with reporters and tell them she was inconsolable over the loss of the man she always had credited for establishing her as a star. Timony's spinster sister and a nephew took charge of the funeral arrangements and accompanied the body to New York for interment at Holy Cross Cemetery. Mae was kept very much an outsider.

Reporter Irene Kuhn recalled, "His family resented the way Timony had given up his law practice for Mae. They were very straitlaced Irish Catholics, and if a member of the family went off and got a gal like Mae, then they'd have divided feelings. Partly proud that he'd got her, partly shamed. It was a strange, complex thing."

Most painful to Mae was the realization that while lovers and business associates might come and go, waxing enthusiastic and eventually becoming disillusioned, she always could count on Timony's unwavering conviction of her superiority. The Betty Grables, Rita Hayworths and Marilyn Monroes in his eyes were only shooting stars. Mae alone remained perennially worthy.

In response to her despair, she plunged into a flurry of activity that left her little time to dwell on the past. Within a month she was singing and dancing on the Dean Martin television variety show. More important, her imagination was at work on an amorphous plan for an unprecedented nightclub revue. Over the years she had refused all offers. "I always had the idea women weren't too crazy about their men ogling the chorus girls every nightclub carried," she said. "And I thought addin' me to them would be like addin' frostin' to the cake."

The inspiration for her new approach came from Richard DuBois, the new twenty-one-year-old Mr. America. He admitted his overwhelming ambition always had been to meet Mae West. She cast several approving glances over his hairless, strongly muscled frame and a million-dollar idea crystallized. Why not build a nightclub act around herself, Mr. America and a half dozen more top body builders, providing something for the girls? Thus, by a quarter of a century, Mae foresaw the market for male striptease clubs that would burgeon in the 1970's.

Bill Miller of the Sahara Hotel in Las Vegas responded to her idea, and by the time the act was ready to go into rehearsal she had chosen eight musclemen she would like to have come up and see her sometime. In addition, she selected young Steve Rossi as her leading man, Louise Beavers as her maid and added two dancers and three singers. As producer-director-choreographer, she hired Charles O'Curran.

To stimulate interest in the new revue, she granted an interview to Hedda Hopper. At the opportune moment Mr. America arrived. He, to quote Hedda, "got into his acting costume in nothing flat. . . . 'Flex your muscles,' Mae instructed.

"'What do you do in the act?' I [Hedda] asked.

"'I don't know,' said the bewildered young man.

"'And what would you like to do?' I wanted to know.

"'I haven't the faintest idea,' he said. That statement alone should get him the nomination as the most unimaginative male in these parts," she concluded.

Privately Mae was experiencing none of the élan she projected for Hedda. She realized that the musclemen, attractive as they might be, were awkward performers. She told O'Curran to rehearse the athletes first. He choreographed routines that substituted exercising for dancing. "I used all kinds of Mickey Mouse things," O'Curran recalled. "I'd underscore muscle movements with music and have one guy keep looking down at his crotch as if *that* was supposed to move, too. I had another guy perform the old falling-off-the-ball trick. The idea was for all the guys to perform in unison. This one fellow was always a little late on everything. The psychology behind it was to get the audience asking themselves, 'Why does she keep that rotten dancer?' Then they come to the conclusion, 'Oh, he must have a big prick.' And the audience always howled."

On the morning of the first scheduled rehearsal involving Mae at Nico Charisse's studios, she called to say she would not be in until the following day. One call followed another until only a little over a week remained before the opening. O'Curran informed Bill Miller that unless Mae started rehearsing immediately, there would be no show. Miller was reluctant to issue any ultimatum to her, so O'Curran volunteered to handle the situation. When she began making excuses for not being able to appear that day, he bluntly told her, "You aren't going to have a show unless you get your ass down here immediately."

O'Curran's strategy worked—to a point. A couple of hours later two husky fellows carried her in and set her down in the rehearsal area, where she stood swaying on her high platform Wedgies. "I don't like you," was her greeting to O'Curran. He recalled snarling in his best 1930's Warner Brothers musical tradition, "I don't give a damn whether you like me or not. We've got a show to put on. That's all I'm interested in."

Getting to work, he was distressed to discover she had not mastered her special numbers. He sensed she was deeply troubled and unable to concentrate on projecting her familiar image as long as she remained uncertain of the words. In desperation, he arranged for a clever mimic singer to record the songs with Mae's inflections. The next day he gave the recordings to Mae, who learned the lyrics by listening to them. What impressed O'Curran was how she eventually modified her imitator's readings and found a dozen or more extra laughs in the material.

One afternoon during rehearsals O'Curran worked with Mae at the Ravenswood. He found her without a wig and was impressed with her baby-fine hair. "It was bleached the color of cornsilk," he remembered. "Much more attractive than her lacquered wigs. She wore this sheer negligee, and her body was surprisingly thin, the figure terrific. The negligee was so tight you could see the whole bush. They say when you stop having sex, you lose your pubic hair. But believe me, she really had a bush. And absolutely beatiful."

The West-O'Curran détente was short-lived. One afternoon she saw a particularly attractive photo of Marilyn Monroe in a newspaper. Seeking assurance, she seriously inquired whether O'Curran thought she looked as old as Marilyn. Evading the question, he told her he had never thought about either's age, adding he hadn't seen Marilyn for a long time. His failure to tell Mae she outshone Marilyn revived her antagonism. But the final rift occurred upon their arrival in Las Vegas. "Bill Miller was so appreciative of what I'd done with the staging, he surprised me with a marquee reading, 'CHARLES O'CURRAN presents THE MAE WEST SHOW,'" O'Curran said. "Needless to say, that billing was soon out, and so was I. By the time the show played New York Mae told Dorothy Kilgallen, the columnist, that I hadn't staged the act and she didn't even know me."

Mae opened in the Congo Room at the Sahara, Las Vegas, on July 27, 1954. Beginning with the first show of the evening through the final time she performed it in 1959, the concept never varied, yet no performance was ever the same. For instance, the opening number might be performed by five, six or seven singing and tap dancing males, clad in top hats and tails, but however many men there were, they always described the allure and the triumphs of that star of stars Mae West. At the climax the spotlight picked up Mae reclining on a chaise longue carried by eight body builders, who wore only the briefest loincloths.

For Las Vegas Mae wore a black-sequined gown with a net midriff—somewhat conservative for a room in which nine months earlier Marlene Dietrich had appeared in a diaphanous top—an ermine stole and a black plumed headdress specially designed to create the illusion of height. (Partly because she was reluctant to spend the money and partly because she genuinely regarded the dress as a good-luck token, Mae wore it at every performance for two seasons. Slimmed down for her Las Vegas opening, she gained several pounds over the months, which required inserting new material at her waistline a number of times, but she steadfastly refused to replace the costume.)

She opened the show with "I'd Like to Do All Day What I Do All Night" and closed with "What a Night," in which she passed out keys for her hotel suite to the panting musclemen, announcing, "Don't crowd me, boys. There's enough for everybody."

In the forty-five-minute act, she danced with Steve Rossi, who later was replaced by Anthony Dexter, to "It Takes Two to Bango" [sic]. She listened to Mr. America sing "Everything I Have Is Yours" and assured him, "Yes, and I'll know what to do with it." She introduced the musclemen to the audience with "I've Got Something for the Girls—Boys, Boys, Boys," performed "Everyone Knows It's a Man's World," did her *Latin Lover* sketch, which she had performed with Georges Metaxa as early as 1933. Louise Beavers was on hand to introduce and set the scene for Mae's *Diamond Lil* recitation, which the star ended with a belting rendition of "Frankie and Johnny."

Years later spectators recalled the gasps when the cape-shrouded (and presumably nude) body builders marched onstage, faced Mae with their backs to the audience, and opened their capes for review. Mae looked each up and down, her eyes lingering at every crotch as she delivered punch lines:

"I feel like a million tonight. But—one at a time."

"I'm glad to meet you—face-to-face."

"This muscle boy is an all-around man. He won the broad jump, too."

"Take it easy, boys, and last a long time."

"Mr. America has my special warranty. If there are any defective parts, send them back to me. Because he's got my ninety-day factory guarantee."

Without actually mentioning Marilyn Monroe, who had recently married Joe DiMaggio, she got in a subtle dig by asking, "Why marry a ballplayer when you can have the whole team?"

During her two and a half weeks at the Sahara, she sensibly held the show to forty-five minutes or less, insuring plenty of time for gambling. Yet she drew such crowds of high rollers that she was immediately rebooked for another stint during the Christmas holidays.

Everywhere she played she did turnaway business. At the Latin

Quarter in New York she averaged $92,000 weekly during her six-week stay, easily outdrawing such attractions as Frank Sinatra and Sophie Tucker and dethroning the previous top grosser, Milton Berle. The lone exception to this string of successes was at Copa City in Miami, where she was booked on a four-week guarantee. On opening night the management was stunned to find fewer than 100 people huddled near the stage for her first show. It was her largest crowd. As the end of the initial week approached, management attempted to cancel the engagement. But the canny businesswoman and her troupe showed up for every performance, and she insisted that her contract be honored. The second and third weeks were no improvement. The fourth week, management paid her off and brought in Sammy Davis, Jr., who attracted hordes of people.

At Mae's next booking she again drew her customary standing-room-only crowds. After careful analysis, her agents concluded that the clientele of the Latin Quarter in New York constituted the major portion of the nightclub-going vacationers in Miami Beach. Having just seen Mae's revue, they had no inclination to view it again so soon in Florida.

From the start dancer Joel Friend was delegated to tutor replacements. Accustomed to the camaraderie of Broadway musicals whose casts went out together to unwind after the show, Friend found the nightclub package a bore. Mae and her bodyguard lover Vincent Lopez, who had shown up during rehearsals, disappeared immediately after the last performance. The body builders lived strictly regimented lives, economizing by piling three or four in a room, eating tinned high-protein foods, drinking milk out of cartons and sleeping long hours. When not resting or performing, they pumped iron to inflate their muscles. Worst of all for Friend, when in Las Vegas, Mae made the casinos off limits for the company. "If they wanta see you, let 'em pay," she said.

Friend's salvation proved to be Louise Beavers, fresh from TV acclaim in *Beulah*, who allowed him to share her dressing room, the only permanent one other than Mae's. During long stretches offstage the two became good buddies. Many evenings they went to the house provided for Miss Beavers and her husband in the then strictly segregated gambling resort, where she cooked supper for the men.

246   /

One evening Mae's dresser, Billie, arrived at Miss Beavers's dressing room. "Rather apologetically Billie told Louise and me that Miss West wanted to discourage our friendship because talk might hurt the box-office take," Friend said. "We listened until Billie was through. Then Louise said, 'Look, sister, you go back and tell her anything she has to say about my work I'll listen to and do what she wants. But as far as what I do in my personal life, she can kiss my big black ass.'"

In New York, as weeks passed, it became increasingly clear how circumscribed Mae's life had become. "It was very cloak-and-dagger around the Latin Quarter," according to Friend. "When she was ready to leave the club, she would wait for the limousine to pull up. Then Lopez would go out, look left, look right, look across the street to see that she could make it to the car. I decided that in the 1920's, when she was doing her sex shows, the city was full of gangsters. She'd been friends with some of them and might even have been a target herself, so she developed this paranoia."

Since she couldn't venture out in the daytime without drawing mobs of fans, she and Lopez would saunter along a deserted Fifth Avenue at 2:30 and 3:00 A.M., window-shopping. The most commonplace activity could be an adventurous diversion. Herbert Kenwith, knowing her preoccupation with food, arranged with the manager of a supermarket to conduct her on a tour of the premises after closing hours. Strolling up and down between the shelves filled with exotic cheeses, chocolate-frosted cakes and dozens of other items she relished, Mae mmmmmed and ooooooohed and gasped at the displays—delighted as a child at Disneyland.

She found other diversions, too. Lopez was as fiercely jealous as Timony had been. Like Timony, he insisted upon being put in a room across the hall from Mae, providing an opportunity for just the type of intrigue Mae enjoyed. She once again resorted to a technique she often had used to outwit Timony. Upon arrival at their floor after the show, Lopez would check Mae's quarters. Then she would visit his room. While she kept him occupied, her lover of the evening would quietly let himself into her suite with the key she had provided. After the gratified Lopez was ready to retire, she would cross the hall for a tryst with the man of the hour. This strategy worked perfectly until Lopez happened to open his door early one morning just as her visitor was leaving.

Shortly after, at Mae's request, Lopez returned to South America, but they remained intimate friends on an occasional basis into the 1970's.

Lopez's romantic replacement was one of the musclemen, who, for legal reasons, must be called Number One. Number One was a fair-complexioned twenty-one-year-old all-American-boy type who was as naïve as he was attractive. He was troubled by the relationship and eventually poured out his problems to Joel Friend. "What made it so funny," Friend said, "was that her body builders were so health-conscious. They even rationed their sex lives because at that time many people thought orgasms depleted an athlete's power. And Miss West just couldn't go along with that.

"Because of certain moral reservations, too, Number One was going out of his mind. He complained that Miss West called him over every night. Not only was he worried that he was overindulging sexually, but her two A.M. calls after the last show were depriving him of his scheduled sleeping time. He was becoming a nervous wreck. He obviously had never heard of having the switchboard cut off the phone until he was willing to receive calls. I told him to try it. The next morning I inquired how my scheme had worked. He told me the operator had held the calls, but Miss West sent someone knocking on his door and he had to go over to her. And I mean *had* to go because she insisted on having sex every night. She was very blunt about that."

Friend was even more fascinated by the auditions one of the best-known body builders in the group arranged. Candidates were flown in from various parts of the United States and Canada. "I was curious about what was going on in her suite during tryouts," he admitted, "because it was my duty to teach the routine to those that passed the test. Finally, one guy who was very friendly confided how embarrassing the interview had been. He told me the first thing she said was: 'Take off your pants.' He told her he couldn't because he didn't have any underwear on. And Miss West said, 'That's all right. If you had, I'd ask you to take it off, too.'

"It was a very cut-and-dried proposition. If the guy didn't have what she was looking for, he was shipped back next day," Friend said. "When she found one that excited her, then a place was made for him in the act or he replaced someone who was leaving. It was like a revolving door.

248 /

"But I'll tell you something about Miss West," he went on. "In her own eyes she was a lady no matter what she did or said. No one in the act was ever allowed to call her Mae. It was always 'Miss West' in public. I became so used to it I even call her that today. She demanded respect—and she got it from everybody but one person."

That man was Miklosi "Mickey" Hargitay.

At the end of 1955 Mae finished her first tour and announced she would return with a new act in 1956. There were few changes, including her surprising "Rock Around the Clock" with special lyrics but a true rock sound. And in the spirit of Ringling Brothers and Barnum & Bailey, everything was bigger and better than ever with two leading men instead of one and with Mr. America replaced by Mr. Universe, Budapest-born Mickey Hargitay. He had emigrated from Hungary to avoid serving in the army there, worked in a Brooklyn fruit market and as an upholsterer before forming an adagio act and then winning his body beautiful title. Weighing 230 pounds, standing six feet two inches with a forty-eight-inch chest and a thirty-inch waist, he had brown curly hair and a thick accent.

Mae subsequently claimed that he never appealed to her. If true, Hargitay is a candidate for the *Guinness Book of Records* since she herself maintained that the man she didn't like had not been born. It may have been that Hargitay turned Mae off because she immediately sensed his overweening ambition. Irving Zussman, publicist for the Latin Quarter at that time, claims that Hargitay "was always idling around outside Miss West's dressing room. He was ambitious theatrically, and she could serve as his key to success, you know. But she wouldn't give him a tumble. He had an estranged wife in Indianapolis, and she didn't want to get involved in any messy divorce."

For her part, Mae said she had already become romantically involved with the man who was to become the love of her life and her husband in every way except legally. He was a bulky, square cut, handsome thirty-three-year-old with dark hair, blue eyes and ruggedly cut features. He was a gentle, yet physically powerful man whose natural intelligence helped him adapt easily to difficult situations. He had at various times served in the United States Navy and the Merchant Marine and had operated a gymnasium in New Orleans. Before joining Mae's act, he had had a successful career as a wrestler. His name was Chester Ribonsky, which she changed to Chuck Krauser. He had been smitten with Mae since their first meeting, but he bided his time, gradually moving in until he occupied center stage in her emotions.

Whatever her private feelings about Krauser, Mae was forced to feature Hargitay, the title-holding Mr. Universe, during the second tour. One night Jayne Mansfield, who was appearing as a dumb Hollywood blonde in George Axelrod's Broadway comedy *Will Success Spoil Rock Hunter?*, came to see the act and zeroed in on Hargitay. She returned twice to sit in the upper tiers, fancying him. Finally, she appeared on the arm of songwriter-producer Jule Styne. Zussman joined them, and while Jayne excused herself to go to the powder room, Styne confided to Zussman that she "had a terrific crush on Hargitay." Zussman explained that Mae was protective of all her boys and was sensitive about having them "pandered about."

Jayne persisted, and Styne arranged for someone to summon Hargitay. When it was time for him to go backstage, she gave him a napkin on which she had written in lipstick the number of the Gorham Hotel, where she was staying, and her private number. Mae was so incensed at the spectacle, which she considered demeaning to her image, that she retaliated by dropping her description of Hargitay as "the most perfectly built man in the world" in the next show. That very night Hargitay called Jayne, and their love affair was under way. The following morning he accompanied her to Brooklyn, where she was crowned queen of something and they were photographed nuzzling one another.

Hargitay claimed that when Mae saw newspaper photos of Jayne and him embracing, she offered him a contract doubling his salary in return for giving Jayne up. She asked why he wanted to cheapen himself by running around with a bleached blonde. Hargitay refused her offer, reminding her she also was a bleached blonde. He continued squiring Jayne wherever photographers were likely to be encountered.

Mae fumed and fulminated when she read in the papers that this $250- or $300-a-week featured player had the gall to ask why Hargitay shouldn't prefer a beautiful twenty-two-year-old to a seventy-year-old woman. But each succeeding mention seemed to elate Jayne. Sensing that Mae was reluctant to be drawn into controversy, she bombarded the star with further barbs.

While the act was playing Syracuse, Mae learned that a new Mr. Universe was about to be crowned and announced she was trading Hargitay in for the latest titleholder. "Oh, he can stay around," she conceded, "but he'll have to go back to the line. That's where all last year's models go."

"That's funnee," Hargitay told reporters. "If I'm zee old model, then vat iss she?"

Assuming a mock-understanding stance, Jayne taunted Mae by announcing that she felt sorry for and admired the older actress. She said she had been brought up to respect her elders and had looked up to Mae as a "fabulous entertainer" for as long as she could remember. "If I look that good at sixty-four," she said, revising her previous guess of Mae's age downward, "I'll have no problems."

Mae decided she would not be used further by "publicity seekers," who were attempting to build overnight the reputation she had spent decades achieving. Even though the act was scheduled to break up for the summer after a couple of stands, during the Washington, D.C., engagement at the Camino Real she called a press conference in her dressing room to attempt to counteract the impression that Hargitay had scorned her for Jayne. At her side was her adoring Chuck Krauser. Suddenly Hargitay barged into the room, which was filled with reporters, intent on telling his side of the story. Krauser said that from Hargitay's movements he thought the Hungarian was about to attack him. So he decked Hargitay with a left and a right.

In the confusion Mae accidentally was toppled to the floor. From there she cried, "Yuh can't do this to me. I'm an institution." As they led Hargitay away to take him to a hospital emergency room, she muttered, "They don't make men like they used to!" and then yelled after Hargitay, "If you're Mr. Universe, why didn't you hit back?"

Hargitay claimed that he had suffered a cut on the left temple, a black eye, cuts on his upper and lower lips and a wrenched knee. He complained that Krauser had been jealous because of Mae's affection for him and said he could have handled Krauser but that he hadn't wanted to lose his head. Informed of Hargitay's remarks, Mae scoffed. "He was just an upholsterer 'n' then I glorified him 'n' it went to his head." Describing Krauser as "sort of a boyfriend" who was around all the time, she observed the two weight lifters were well matched, adding, "Only naturally Krauser is the better man."

The brooding Hargitay lodged a complaint charging simple assault at a hearing which was held June 8. Krauser testified he had hit Hargitay in self-defense. George Eiferman, a muscleman with the act who was friendly with Mae, nevertheless testified he had not seen Hargitay make any threatening movement but explained Krauser's protective reaction by saying that he and Mae were "emotionally involved." On September 29 in Municipal Court, Krauser was convicted of the charge.

In confirming the relationship between her and Krauser, Mae must have rejoiced that she had manipulated the situation so that what had begun as a Mansfield-Hargitay publicity coup had ended looking as if two men were battling over her. To underline her point, she scoffed at the idea that she could ever lower herself to feel jealous of the likes of Jayne or, as she snuggled against Krauser's expansive chest, that she could ever have been attracted to Hargitay. "Men have fought over me before," she boasted, "but never in public like this. I prefer doin' such things behind closed doors, know what I mean?"

Caution, however, moved her to secure affidavits from other body builders in the act supporting her contention that she had never shown romantic interest in Hargitay. Years later she suggested a writer friend prepare a story based on these affidavits. When he dismissed the suggestion, saying that Miss Mansfield was dead and Hargitay no longer of sufficient public interest to warrant such a story, Mae sniffed. "That's where you're not thinkin' clear. It's when he gets desperate that he'll try to peddle a story, 'I Was the One Man Mae West Wanted but Couldn't Get.'"

On July 5, in the midst of the Krauser-Hargitay fracas, with only two full days' rehearsal, Mae revived *Come On Up*, which she had retitled *Come On Up—Ring Twice*, at the Capri Theater in Atlantic Beach, Long Island, with Krauser playing a newspaperman. Critics felt that everyone in the cast except Mae needed much more rehearsal and that the play was a ramshackle vehicle at best. But if a playgoer was amused by such wisecracks as "A man in the house is worth two in the street" or (after knocking out a gangster) "This is the first time in my life I don't know what

252 /

to do with a man," Mae provided a pleasant way to while away an evening.

Meanwhile, she signed a contract and began working on her autobiography which she intended to call *Queen of Sex* or *Come Up and See Me Sometime*, but her progress was interrupted by her libel suit against *Confidential* magazine over its allegations about her relationship with Chalky Wright. After the successful court action, she turned her attention to finishing her book, taking time out to appear on the 1958 Academy Awards show, verbally caressing Rock Hudson while they sang "Baby, It's Cold Outside." The audience at the Pantages Theater shouted, stamped, whistled and cheered. The next day's papers carried the good news that Mae was looking more radiant than ever and that she and Hudson injected a much-needed note of saucy informality into the proceedings. Her success stimulated interest in a fifteen-minute five-times-a-week syndicated television show, *Mae West Tells All About Love,* but her proposed advice to the lovelorn proved too flippant for the late 1950's, and negotiations came to nothing.

The next year her friend Hunt Stromberg, Jr., recently appointed head of West Coast programming for CBS-TV, approached her to be interviewed by Charles Collingwood, who was taking over for Edward R. Murrow on *Person to Person*. Mae seized the opportunity to promote her autobiography, now titled *Goodness Had Nothing to Do with It.* When Collingwood sought her opinion on foreign affairs, Mae informed him, "I've always had a weakness for foreign affairs," and as for advice to teenagers: "Ummm! Grow up!" Tepid stuff by today's standards, but the segment was abruptly canceled by producers John Aaron and Jesse Zousmer, who issued a statement saying, "The show speaks for itself and so does Mae West." Collingwood professed to be mystified.

Mae said she was, too. "He mentioned my book. . . . So I took him in the bedroom and told him, I said, 'I do my best writing in bed.' . . . Nobody told me it sounded wrong. Everybody knows I do my best work in the bedroom. It's no secret. It's been in the papers."

Goodness Had Nothing to Do with It received good reviews, and the publishers staged a cocktail party at the Beverly Hilton to celebrate its success. One of the guests, Philip K. Scheurer of the

Los Angeles *Times,* told Mae he had been reading *Groucho and Me.*
"It's full of laughs," he said.

"Read mine. It's full of sex," Mae responded, adding, "I ended
it with 'Watch for Volume II. I love you all.' I did that because I
really wrote 550 pages and they only used half of it. And I don't
want all of my other gentlemen friends to feel neglected."

18

Because of Krauser's patient, unrelenting pursuit and devotion, he assumed an increasingly important position in Mae's life. Eventually, though in a different way, their relationship was to prove as enduring and even more important in sustaining her than the one she had had with Timony during the palmiest years of their association. Both men worshiped her, were stimulated by her glamour and, though intensely masculine, seemed in a deep, somewhat unconscious way to identify with her. Krauser even agreed to change his name legally to Paul Novak, which was to them both more theatrical-sounding and an effective way of stopping people from recalling the Hargitay brouhaha.

Gradually Paul made himself indispensable as a bodyguard and lover. As Mae observed in her autobiography, she began to give him "special consideration." If she represented the Matterhorn of theatrical achievement to him, he personified Rock of Gibraltar security for her. By giving in to her harmless whims and protecting her from her weaknesses, he reached a status never before achieved by any other younger man in her life. Because Paul enjoyed her beach house located at 514 Pacific Coast Highway, about a mile north of the Santa Monica Pier, Mae began using it with greater frequency. On the door and throughout the house NO SMOKING signs were prominently displayed. (Although for characterization she had smoked, without inhaling, in some of her early films, cigarette and cigar fumes gave her headaches.)

But even there she clung to the cocoonlike existence she was leading at the Ravenswood. She kept the curtains drawn in the large downstairs sitting room, preferring subdued illumination to the harsh light reflected by the sand and sea. If that meant sacrificing a view of the water, it was a small price to pay. Throughout the entire house, she duplicated the gold-and-white-and-cream color scheme widely associated with her. Present, too, were the Louis XIV chairs and tables, a white fur rug, numerous favorite paintings and photos of herself and a profusion of mirrors which captured her image with satisfying frequency. There was also a copy of the sculptured nude that graced the piano in her Ravenswood apartment sitting on the baby grand. From the long row of shower stalls, numerous enough to accommodate a football team, to the staircase mural featuring a series of nude gladiators, to her upstairs suite with the inevitable mirrored ceiling and satin-covered bed, the house reflected its owner.

Mae seldom ventured out into the punishing sunlight, not wishing to dry out and coarsen her pink-and-white complexion. She never considered swimming, but sometimes at night she and Paul would go wading.

When she desired his company, he was there, and when she wished to be alone, he withdrew. It seemed that at last she had found a companion whose temperament was suited to the demands and limitations that she had always set on the male-female relationship. Speaking to critic-reporter Frances Herridge around this time, Mae observed: "As long as they [men] serve my purpose, they're fine. But if they take up too much of my time, I eliminate them—see what I mean? I never permit myself to get too absorbed in anything else. I'm not going to stop being Mae West for any man." Those sentiments suited Paul perfectly since Mae's persona—public as well as private—was part of what he loved about her.

After the closing of the nightclub production Mae turned her attention to *Sextette* by Charlotte Francis. First Alexander Ince and now Ince and Lee Shubert thought it a possible Broadway vehicle for Mae. She informed the two producers that a great deal of hard work was involved in shaping it to her character. She began rewriting, and by the summer of 1961 she felt secure enough about the script to advertise "pre-Broadway" engagements. Jack LaRue, Alan Marshall, Marshall's son Kit and Paul were among those who joined the company, which Aaron Frankel directed. Because of Equity rules, rehearsals were limited to one week.

The Chicago opening saw disaster pile upon disaster. Mae, suffering from laryngitis, canceled the first three performances at the Edgewater Beach Playhouse. The premiere finally took place on Friday night, July 7, but the production was in such a rough state that prompting from the wings was audible to the front half of the house. Then, at the first of two scheduled performances on Saturday evening, Alan Marshall suffered a heart attack, causing the second show to be canceled. He died next morning, but his son said Marshall had always believed the show must go on and urged that the engagement continue. That evening producer Henry Guettel walked through the part carrying the script, which, *Variety* said, "made for some improbable love scenes." Tom Conway flew into Chicago to replace Marshall, read the script with mounting disbelief and flew right out again. Francis Bethencourt eventually accepted the role. The Edgewater Beach Playhouse's gross, $13,000 for the week, was the smallest in the theater's history.

Proceeding to Detroit and Warren and Columbus, Ohio, Mae doggedly rewrote and reworked the script. At rehearsals she added surefire shticks from her theatrical past. By the time the show opened in Columbus, a reviewer grudgingly observed: "Without Mae it [the play] could not really exist. For, like it or not, she is an American institution. And the legendary high priestess of sex in the wise-cracking frankly ribald manner did not disappoint paying customers." By mid-August *Sextette* reached the Coconut Grove Playhouse in greater Miami and Mae had accomplished something of a miracle. Helen Muir of the Miami *News* reported the actress had made the most of her opportunities as a playwright and star. Paul Brunn of the Miami Beach *Sun* noted: "Everybody sat glued to his seat and Mae took repeated curtain calls, from about the most enthusiastic audience I have ever seen at this theater."

Through tenacity, ego and long experience, Mae had succeeded in making audiences view her and her play not for what they were but as they existed in her mind's eye. Once more by sheer will this sixty-seven-year-old woman had transformed herself into a slyly humorous cartoon of a sex bomb and the creaking, cliché-ridden play into a speedy, laughter-filled entertainment.

Initially Mae assumed that her relationship with Paul would, like so many others, blaze and burn out. During the first year, when his Merchant Marine seaman's license was about to expire, she encouraged his suggestion that he renew it. "That way," she explained, "if I got tired of him, I figured he'd have someplace to go." But Paul was not about to let her tire of him. He began reorganizing her habits. He encouraged her to consume health food, discouraged her fondness for desserts and other sweets. One summer when the *sri* suddenly reentered her life and became a guest at the beach house, Paul took instruction from him in the preparation of his healthful recipes. Twenty years later he was still making and serving them.

Paul was proud to escort Mae to various functions. Wherever they went he now wore a pistol to protect her against kidnapping or robbery and often carried a generous supply of her postcard-sized publicity photos to accommodate autograph seekers on the spot, while he stood aside and proudly watched over the prize he had captured.

In addition to being Mae's consort, he remained her fan. When she appeared at the Friars' roast of Harry Richman, Paul was on hand to lead the other 500 males in cheering Mae's salute to her long-ago accompanist. Following such comic heavyweights as Bob Hope, George Burns, Jimmy Durante and songwriters Harry Ruby, Jimmy McHugh, Johnny Mercer and Sammy Fain, to name only a few, Mae glided to the platform, surveyed the jam-packed room and purred, "Mmmmmmmm! Just my kind of place—wall-to-wall men!" Then she turned her attention to Richman, reminding him he had begun to make his mark in show business as her accompanist in 1922. "I don't remember, Harry, whether I discovered you or you discovered me," she said, "but I do remember you always had a great touch." She paused, rolling her eyes and grinding her hips as she added, "Even at the piano."

Looking back on the appearance, Mae was gratified that in addition to the laughter and applause she had earned, she had done something else: broken a precedent by becoming the first woman ever to appear at a dinner held in the Los Angeles branch of the Friars Club. She was no prouder of herself than Paul was.

As always when she was in a period of professional inactivity, Mae's interest in the supernatural expanded. This time her companion was open-minded and willing to explore the unexplainable with her. Their shared involvement with spiritualism and ESP, which was to deepen over the years, was another link in the Mae-Paul relationship.

Off and on until her death, Mae worked on a biography entitled *The Amazing Mr. Kelly*. It was filled with accounts of Thomas Jack Kelly's inexplicable psychic demonstrations, such as his childhood prediction, which saved his father's life, of an impending mine explosion. Mae's long friendship with Kelly came under attack after she brought him to the Latin Quarter to demonstrate his powers for the press. The plan backfired when certain reporters wrote that after she had donated $500 to his Spiritualist Church of Life in Buffalo, he had praised her as "a wonderful, spiritual person." The implication was that she had purchased his endorsement. The scandal burgeoned until it was rumored she had given his church $500,000, but their admiration for one another was strong enough to withstand this sniping from the press.

Periodically she and Paul brought Kelly out to California for personal instructions in spiritual development and ESP. Asked how she became interested in ESP in the first place, she replied, "I didn't. The Forces chose me. Most of us have it in some degree if we'd only develop it. It would be a great boon to mankind, ya know."

When Kelly was visiting, she and Paul often invited groups of fifty or more to participate in his demonstrations. Participants were asked to write questions, sign their initials, place their queries in sealed envelopes and return them to the blindfolded Kelly. Then, after running his hands over an envelope to "read" a question, he called out a paraphrase of it and gave his answer.

Mae was enthralled by his gift. Some accepted it all as genuine, but Dan Price, a film collector-historian and amateur magician, took a more jaundiced view. When a magician friend of his offered to show Mae how the reading-of-the-question trick was done, she flatly rejected the proposal. "I thought that was disgusting," Price recalled. "But my friend said, 'Look, the lady has everything. If she has decided that this amuses her, then she's entitled to it.'" Price's private speculation was that by having friends write out these questions, Mae discovered what was on their minds.

A guest at one of Kelly's demonstrations was Arthur Lubin, at the time the producer-director of a successful TV series, *Mr. Ed,* starring a talking horse. He sought out Kelly and, in the ensuing discussion of ESP, made a substantial contribution to Kelly's church. After a decorous period of time he suggested that it would be beneficial to Mae's career if she appeared on *Mr. Ed* since its following consisted of large numbers of children who had never witnessed Mae in action. In fact, Lubin had an idea for the script: word would get out that some horses Mae had imported from France were living amidst posh decor to prevent them from becoming homesick. Ed would hear about it and appear on her doorstep, offering himself for adoption. But he would eventually return to his pal, Alan Young, because Mae would insist on giving him a bubble bath which Ed felt would detract from his virile image.

Kelly enthusiastically endorsed the idea and urged Mae to sign. She agreed, claiming that since her brief appearance on the Academy Awards telecast with Rock Hudson, she had been besieged by fans—predominantly teenagers—to make a series. Because she was playing herself, Mae insisted that the set be dressed with her own furniture to make her comfortable. During the shooting the wardrobe woman noticed her peignoir had fallen open. She interrupted and was about to rearrange it when Mae protested, "No, no, dear. Gotta show 'em the body, see."

That Mae was able to get through the show without bumping into things is a minor miracle, for she was suffering from thickly layered cataracts on both eyes. Shortly after her scenes were completed, Paul checked her into a hospital for surgery which restored her sight. Somehow he managed to keep news of it from the press.

On the evening of the TV showing Hedda Hopper was dining with a couple of friends. When they arrived, Hedda insisted they watch *Mr. Ed* before proceeding to dinner. "Mae West's going to be on," she said, "and I wouldn't miss it for the world."

The friends were intrigued that Mae still aroused Hedda's interest. Mulling the situation over, one of them, a USC alumnus, concluded that curiosity about Mae had never died and realized how infrequently (a Red Skelton TV appearance in 1960 and a brief summer tour of *Sextette* in 1961) she had appeared since closing her nightclub act five years earlier. Subsequently, when the committee on which the alum was serving began organizing the then-novel university-sponsored salutes to film personages for the University of Southern California, it invited Arthur Lubin to one and suggested he bring Mae.

The night of the event, program chairman George Cukor and the honorees—Gloria Swanson, Charles Brackett, Billy Wilder and Jack Lemmon—were on hand. But about an hour before the festivities were to start, Mrs. Frank Seaver, a USC trustee, created a crisis by greeting Cukor, "Oh, by the way, George, Mary's not coming tonight. She asked me to tell you."

Mary was Mary Pickford. Cukor had spent hours preparing her to serve as mistress of ceremonies. He looked wildly about and settled on Miss Swanson to act as emcee in addition to being an honored guest. She rose to the occasion brilliantly, going from table to table during the program, introducing the great stars in attendance. Arriving at Mae's chair, she announced, "I used to think I was something of a sex symbol until Mae West came along." She paused eloquently and shrugged. Mae beamed at her and said, "If there's anything you wanta know, just ask." That remark received the biggest laugh and earned Mae the greatest ovation of the evening.

Lubin subsequently booked Mae for a second appearance on *Mr. Ed* and commissioned the development of a weekly television series in which she was to play a female detective who, naturally, always got her man. She ultimately decided against making the pilot because a series entailed "too much work."

Meanwhile, the USC committee planned another cinema program with Mae as one of the honorees. But in mid-September 1964 she collapsed and was rushed to a hospital, where she attempted to camouflage her identity by registering as her sister. She remained six days, during which time she was diagnosed as a diabetic. Upon returning home, she almost immediately suffered a slight heart attack and had to return to the hospital. Although she was relatively candid about her coronary problem, never once during the rest of her life did she disclose her diabetes. She would not, in fact, even accept it. When Paul began giving her the daily insulin shots, she resisted, asking, "What are you doin' that for?" She always acceded but thought the medication pure nonsense. Diabetes or any incurable disease did not enter into her concept of Mae West.

Paul later said that when he went on errands that required him to be absent for a few hours, he would leave food for her on the kitchen table, but often she forgot to eat it. He would return to find her on the floor semicomatose. He would sweep her up in his arms, carry her to the couch and quickly feed her a couple of tablespoons of honey to bring her blood sugar back to a normal level.

Her health remained precarious during the remainder of the year. She lost weight, grew haggard and went into seclusion, refusing to receive anyone until she had regained her glamorous appearance. Although Paul continued the daily insulin shots, he was unable to persuade her to give up sweets entirely. For being so vigilant about her diet, he was rewarded with the semi-humorous nickname Wicked Stepfather.

Early in 1965 Mae agreed to see society columnist Cobina Wright, who promised to be discreet, and on January 21 Miss Wright wrote of her visit to the Ravenswood, where she found Mae recuperating from a "heart attack. She looks wonderful." Miss Wright ended her column with "I have always felt that Mae only kids sex and is really a very spiritual woman. Let's hope that one of the greatest phenomena in show business history is soon fully recovered and amusing us once more with her wonderful quips."

During Mae's illness Paul, Beverly, secretary Larry Lee, butler-chauffeur Larry Grayson and publicist-turned-publisher Larry Sloan were among the few granted regular access.

At the end of 1965 she felt well enough to record a couple of special material numbers for a small company. They went unnoticed, but by June 1966 she had rallied enough to fight G. P. Putnam's Sons' publication of *The Wit and Wisdom of Mae West,* a collection of photos and wisecracks, threatening an injunction against the book unless the publishers granted her financial participation.

She also took steps to establish herself with the younger generation by recording a rock and roll album, *Way Out West,* which sold approximately 100,000 copies. Included were the Beatles' "Day Tripper" and Bob Dylan's "If You Gotta Go" and "Shakin' All Over." She said she should have seriously been into rock ten years earlier but had realized it only after teenagers, who saw her films on the late show, wrote begging her to do something new. Sales proved sufficiently strong to prompt Tower Records to release a follow-up, *Wild Christmas,* a yuletide salute to hedonism.

By the time *Wild Christmas* appeared on the market, Mae was physically fit enough to grant a long interview. The first went to Kevin Thomas of the Los Angeles *Times,* a longtime fan. It was a memorable occasion for him, both as an assignment and as the beginning of a close friendship. For Thomas's benefit, Mae began their meeting by performing "Doing the Grizzly Bear" and "My Mariooch-a Make-a-Da Hoochy-Ma Cooch" a capella and then explained the connection between rock and ragtime, telling Thomas that the kids had the right idea in wanting something different from conventional pop songs.

Thomas was delighted to find Mae's physical appearance as fresh as her thinking on music:

> She is an ardent advocate of proper diet, rigorous exercise and regular beauty treatments and she has done her long sashay through the spicy life as a non-smoking teetotaler.
>
> But even this intelligence does not quite prepare you for the present Mae West: peaches and cream complexion, fine throat and hands, intense blue eyes and perfect teeth.
>
> The sands of time haven't shifted that hour-glass figure much either.

Nor had they diminished her ambition, although she turned down Ross Hunter's *The Art of Love* because he refused to let her rewrite the part and offered only guest-star billing. "My name always goes above the title," she told Thomas. "What's this guest-star stuff? Why should I pull in a lot of people just to show off these youngsters?" Not that she was averse to moviemaking. She was eager to do a rock version of *Catherine Was Great* and added, "Maybe I oughta do a color version of *Diamond Lil* while I'm still lookin' good."

Gradually, as time passed, she began seeing friends again. Among them was Hunt Stromberg, Jr., who told of going to her beach house and finding her looking only a little more than half her actual age. During his visit he opened a door which he thought led to a bath and was startled to see that the room contained furnishings scaled to the dimensions of a doll's house. "It was a complete set," he says. "I was fascinated and asked Mae about it. She said, 'Hunt, did it ever occur to you there's always one month of the year that nobody sees me?' I admitted it hadn't, and she told me that every year an Oriental shrank her down to twelve inches. And that's how she spent thirty days. Then, when he restored her to normal size, she was as pink and smooth as a newborn babe." Stromberg laughed, then added, "There wasn't a clue that she was putting me on. She told the story totally straight, as if she believed every syllable of it. Did she? Who knows?"

During this time Mae met and became fond of—or at least comfortable with—several women connected with the University of Southern California. Alvista Perkins, a librarian in Special Collections, and USC alumna Heidi Crane were occasionally entertained by her and Paul. Mae enjoyed dining at the home of Masel Stroud and her son, Bill McArthur, where she could always count on rich, sweet desserts. She also grew close to columnists Bonnie and Reba Churchill. But the unlikeliest of friendships developed between the actress and USC trustee Mrs. Frank Seaver. Mrs. Seaver was a rich, conservative, socially prominent woman, whose husband had been an attorney for the Dohenys and the founder of the Hydril Corporation, a huge oil tool company. From these sources the Seavers built an enormous fortune which was used philanthropically both before and after Mr. Seaver's death.

By the time Mae met her Mrs. Seaver was a round little woman with a pretty face made memorable by glinting, severe eyes. Her friends and acquaintances, including then-president of USC John Hubbard and his wife, Lucy, Alfredo de la Vega, Eileen Norris and Anna Bing Arnold, were astonished when Mae began being invited to Mrs. Seaver's dinners and Mrs. Seaver agreed to attend one of the evenings sponsored to promote Dr. Richard Ireland, the psychic who succeeded the Reverend Kelly after his death.

One evening, after a dinner at Mrs. Seaver's, the hostess put on an album of General MacArthur's speeches. Suddenly Mae interrupted, saying, "You know, Blanche, if I'd known you a few years back, your husband would be alive today. That bowel blockage didn't need to have killed him. I'd have sent him to Dr. Walker in Arizona, and he'd have cured him with these colonics."

Mrs. Seaver, who had closed her eyes during MacArthur's

pronouncements, quickly opened them and snapped off the phonograph. Mae continued, unfazed, saying, "I knew this couple of retirement age who wanted to travel, but they weren't feeling well, know what I mean? So I sent 'em to Dr. Walker 'n' he started givin' them colonics. The man responded right away, but his wife still didn't feel too good. So Dr. Walker stepped up the colonics, giving her the higher ones. And all of a sudden she passed a ball of worms as big as your fist."

Mrs. Seaver reportedly almost fainted, managing only to gasp, "Oh! Oh, my stars! My stars!"

Mae said, "But he had to keep givin' the colonics to her because you know, if just two worms was left and they'd start gettin' together—why, then you'd have a whole ball again."

Mrs. Seaver appeared almost done in by the turn of the conversation, but Mae plunged ahead: "I take two colonics every day 'n' I'm careful about what I eat, too. So when I go to the bathroom, there's no odor. Oh, maybe like hot soup—at the very worst, beef stew."

The next day Mrs. Seaver told a friend, "I don't know exactly what I should think about that conversation last night. I never allow even my own sister to speak in such an intimate manner to me. Things of that sort have never been said in this house before." Mrs. Seaver heaved a big sigh and finally concluded, "I think that the way I'm going to view it is that she likes me enough and—well, feels close enough to me—to talk like that, and I'm not going to be offended by it. Besides, all that business about colonics is foolishness. I achieve the same results by eating Roquefort cheese.

19

Mae told USC early in 1968 she was now ready to be honored by the university's cinema fraternity, Delta Kappa Alpha. To share the program with her, the committee selected James Stewart and director Mervyn LeRoy. Co-chairmen of the evening were producers-directors Robert Wise and George Cukor. The standard procedure always had been to seat the participants on stools and let the panel question and reminisce with the guests of honor. Everyone felt this suited Stewart and LeRoy, but that Mae required a unique presentation. Several meetings were held with her, and during one of them Wise asked, "Mae, what about this? Instead of stools, how about a chaise and a fuzzy white rug and a chandelier? Would you go for that?"

"Would I!"

Mae was taken to 20th Century-Fox to go through the property department and pick out whatever appealed to her. Spotting an enormous circular bed, she rolled her eyes and quipped, "I bet I could give some guy a square deal on that round bed."

On Sunday evening, February 10, her appearance on the program of the 30th Anniversary Honorary Award Banquet of Delta Kappa Alpha marked her elevation to a new social plane. It may be true, as one of her friends observed, that acceptance was given to Mae West the character, the survivor, rather than the actress. The friend found that sad, but if it was true, Mae was either unaware or unfazed by it.

Her big black Cadillac limousine drew up to the side entrance of the banquet hall a couple of minutes before the showing of the clips from *Klondike Annie, Every Day's a Holiday* and *Goin' to Town* ended. She was whisked through the darkened banquet hall by her sturdy escorts, who then formed a huddle around her. When the lights went up, All-American football stars O. J. Simpson, Adrian Young, Ron Yary and Tim Rossovich broke their huddle to reveal Mae. Dressed in her jeweled white satin gown, a plethora of diamonds and her silver-blond wig, she perched on the edge of a beige chaise that rested on a white fur rug. A gold candelabrum and a gold-framed mirror completed her personal color scheme. The surprised audience gasped and burst into applause before she uttered a word.

Then, in a voice that was a combination of sauciness and innocence, she announced, "I've been honored many times"—like any seasoned vaudevillian, Mae waited for her laugh—"and for many things." She paused for another laugh, then continued, "Of course, I've been the Sweetheart of Sigma Chi . . ." Her timing was exquisite as she cut into the laughter to build the situation by adding, "I could've been the sweetheart of Sigmund Freud, too . . ." That statement earned such a boffo response Mae wriggled with pleasure. "But I reclined . . . uh—declined." The university audience was no tougher than those in vaudeville, legitimate theaters or nightclubs.

Having insured her reception, she submitted to a series of biographical questions from cochairmen Cukor and Wise, twisting her life history to conceal the seamier aspects of her career and to provide laughter. With the interview completed, Mae threw a pink feather boa around her shoulders and tore into "Doing the Grizzly Bear," which she had first performed in 1910. Then she segued into her *Diamond Lil* soliloquy, which led directly to her rousing rendition of "Frankie and Johnny." She earned a standing ovation and had difficulty quieting the shouting, applauding crowd. As was her custom, she left them laughing by quipping, "I want to thank you for your generous applause—and your very heavy breathing."

Newspaper accounts of the evening read like love letters with

Jim Bacon's paean concluding: "Oh roll me over easy! Roll me over slow! I'm in love with Mae West all over again. . . ."

What followed was one of the most cleverly orchestrated examples of promotion since the disappearance of the old-fashioned circus press agent. Just as those flamboyant gentlemen unblushingly persuaded editors to devote columns to "educational spectacles and death-defying novelties" that existed only in their imaginations, Mae strutted, preened and somehow managed in varying degrees to convince reporters that she was unchanged. "If you didn't know me, you'd think I was twenty-six" made good copy whether reported with a straight face or tongue in cheek. And there was no denying that she looked twenty to thirty years younger than her calendar age.

Columnists Marilyn Beck, Radie Harris, Army Archerd, Hank Grant, Bob Thomas, Bonnie and Reba Churchill, Vernon Scott, Lee Graham, Sheilah Graham and Joyce Haber helped establish her as, in the felicitous words of *Women's Wear Daily*, "everybody's favorite raunchy old lady." Jim Bacon ran almost daily items detailing her flip responses, building a momentum that re-established her as a 1970's celebrity. But his biggest contribution was hinting at some arcane beauty ritual that was responsible for her remarkable physical preservation but that couldn't be explained in a family newspaper.

Jacqueline Susann, Lana Turner and other jet-setters from as far away as Rio, Paris, London and Rome telephoned to try to wring Mae's secret from Bacon. But he realized the depth of interest in the subject only while traveling behind the Iron Curtain. In Belgrade he barely had set foot on Yugoslavian soil when a young reporter inquired through an interpreter, "What is Mae West's beauty secret?"

For her part, Mae always was ready to pull up her wig and show the press that there were no scars from plastic surgery on her pink-and-white baby-soft skin. AP's Bob Thomas, who had originally written, after seeing her at USC, that "despite abundant make-up the face showed her seventy-five years," reversed his judgment in print following a private interview.

After visiting her, George Christy of *The Hollywood Reporter* reported that she washed her face with castile soap. Then she covered her skin with "a little lanolin oil, coco butter rubbed in with water and left in for an hour at a time. 'I don't use a lot of face powder the way other actresses do. I clean off make-up with vegetable oils,' she said. 'Then I steam my face.'"

Eager to scoop Bacon and everyone else on "the secret," Sheilah Graham told her readers Mae had inherited a "double-thyroid"—whatever that is—and drank a strange potion, the formula for which Sheilah begged Mae's doctor. Mae evaded naming the mystery potion but claimed she had inherited her unique thyroid from her three-breasted grandmother and credited this gland for her energy, sex drive and youthful appearance.

It remained for Bacon to reveal that the much-speculated-on "secret" lay in two high colonics each day. (In 1979 Mae confided to columnist Radie Harris that she had reduced the colonic to one each week.) She had begun taking an enema before going to the theater when she worked as a feature player in Shubert productions and did not yet rate her private loo. When skeptics objected that medical experts frowned on such a schedule, Mae smiled knowingly. "Sure," she agreed. "Why wouldn't they? If you never get sick, how are they gonna earn any money?"

Meanwhile, Mae and Rona Barrett discovered their mutual interest in the supernatural, and Miss Rona, with the possible exception of Kevin Thomas, became Mae's closest confidant in the press. A major factor in reviving interest in Mae was Miss Rona's television reports which titillated viewers with news of Mae's dates with Adrian Young (Young: "That's a beautiful ring, Miss West. Let me see it. You can trust me." Mae: "Ooooh, I was hopin' I couldn't."), Chip Oliver (Mae: "You can use my beach house whether I'm there or not. Of course, I'd rather be there.") and other football players.

Paul, secure in his relationship with Mae, stayed discreetly in the background, escorting her to private dinners, sharing her days when nothing much was happening (cooking their meals, supervising her exercise) and then stepping aside for the young football player hype if cameras were present. One evening, when Mae appeared before Arthur Knight's USC cinema class to answer questions about the filming of *Every Day's a Holiday*, Paul gallantly rented a chauffeur's uniform (shades of *Sunset Boulevard*) and drove Mae and Adrian Young to the campus. Nothing was too much to ask of him if it reinforced the image.

Column items were parlayed into newspaper human interest stories and those into magazine pieces, most notably a *New York Times Magazine* story and a *Life* foldout cover with Mae lying on a bed beneath a mirrored ceiling, with Tricky, her furry monkey. The sell line on the cover read: MAE WEST AT 75.

A few contended this was an updated, feminist version of *The Emperor's New Clothes*. Sir Cecil Beaton recorded his impressions of a photographic session:

> . . . the costume of black and white fur . . . [camouflaging] every silhouette except the armour that constricted her waist and contained her bust.
>
> The neck and cheeks and shoulders were hidden beneath a peroxide wig. The muzzle, which was about all one could see of the face, with the pretty capped teeth, was like that of a little ape.

Such attacks only heightened controversy about how she really looked and how old she actually was. (The 1900 census which lists her as six years old had then not been declassified and made available for public use.)

As her publicity burgeoned, requests for her to appear on television talk shows poured in. There were offers from Johnny Carson, Merv Griffin, Mike Douglas, David Frost and Dick Cavett, but she insisted that when she appeared on television, it had to be an event.

This was the approach Robert Wise had in mind when he signed her to an exclusive contract for a television special. Wise found no difficulty in arranging a coproduction deal with Universal. Initially Mae was wary, saying, "I've never liked the idea of television, because people can turn you off." But as verbal commitments from Gregory Peck, Cary Grant and Rock Hudson materialized, Mae's mood changed. Of Wise, who had directed *The Sound of Music,* Mae commented: "Going from Julie Andrews to Mae West—he's certainly versatile." She concluded he understood what she was all about.

Others also rushed in with proposals. Fellini, who had unsuccessfully tried to hire Mae for *Giulietta degli Spiriti,* told the press he and Mae were *molto simpatico* and he wanted to cast her as an "erotic witch," wise in the rituals of ancient bedrooms, in his *Satyricon.* Mae was interested until she learned the witch was a *mother*!

At the same time agent-turned-producer William "Billy"

Belasco and his protégé, Mike Curb; rock agent Todd Shipman; and MGM head James Aubrey produced a Mae West recording, *Great Balls of Fire*. Along with Lloyd Gaines of ABC-TV, this group attempted to package a rival television special based on this album until the Wise-Universal faction took a firm stance with Mae and the volatile Belasco insulted her. (He was no favorite of Mae's after that. When he died following an automobile accident while allegedly high on a combination of cocaine and alcohol, Mae spared no sympathy on him. Using 1920's slang, she sniffed. "I always knew he was a snowbird!")

After initial enthusiasm for the Wise project by various sponsors and networks, interest in the special declined. A network executive summed up the problem: "After we've approached bedding, beer and brassiere sponsors, where are we going to go?" Mae appeared to be in danger of becoming not a working actress but a media event.

It remained for Robert Fryer to capitalize on her renewed celebrity. Fryer, who was producing Gore Vidal's *Myra Breckenridge*, a novel which was specifically about a transsexual and generally about America's hypocrisy and confusion over sexual role playing, offered Mae a starring part. She mistakenly assumed Fryer wanted her for Myra and called the $100,000 compensation offered laughable. Fryer assured her he saw her as the sensuous talent agent Leticia (Mae insisted the spelling be changed from Le*ti*tia, fearing the wrong syllable would be emphasized). She let it be known that she might be interested if the studio gave her a free hand in writing her scenes, top-star billing and $300,000. Twentieth Century-Fox hesitated, and when it finally agreed to the $300,000, Mae told the studio it had dallied too long. Her price was now $350,000. They agreed with alacrity.

One tense moment developed when a journalist, intending to compliment Mae, irritated her by mentioning that she would be given Barbra Streisand's dressing room. Mae responded by launching into a panegyric of self-glorification that peaked as she compared herself to Charlie Chaplin as a writer-composer-star-original personality. "I stand alone," she concluded.

The press conference called to announce Mae's casting seemed to confirm her estimate. It drew one of the largest turnouts in years, and a radiant Mae posed with and exchanged quips with scores of eager reporters.

Darryl Zanuck, 20th's chairman of the board, named Michael Sarne, an Englishman who had made an unpretentious British film, *Joanna,* to direct. Rumor had it Zanuck owed Sarne an important favor. Edith Head, on loan-out from Universal, created Mae's sumptuous gowns, while Theodora Van Runkle designed clothes for Raquel Welch, who was playing the title role, and Farrah Fawcett, the ingenue.

Fryer signed David Giler to make script revisions. Mae and Paul prepared a list of guidelines for the writer to follow in dialogue for or about her. Mae complained she didn't understand the story line. "It's like someone tells you something and just when you get all interested, they say, 'And then I woke up. It was just a dream.' You wanta smack 'em in the face!" When Giler suggested she have more scenes with Raquel Welch, Mae demurred, but once he said she should regard the character of Myra as a drag queen, she became enthusiastic.

Even before the two had met, rumors began to circulate that there was a feud between Mae and Miss Welch. As a gesture of respect Miss Welch visited Mae at the Ravenswood. The ladies were nervous until they discovered both were dissatisfied with their roles and the script. Miss Welch said, "I don't know how to approach my part." Mae responded with feeling, "If I were doing a total rewrite, I'd know how to handle everything." The only mistake Miss Welch made was that she didn't bother to laugh when Mae illustrated a point by saying, "I've been on more laps than a napkin." Miss Welch repaired the damage a few nights later on the Johnny Carson show when she quoted Mae's napkin gag and drew a big laugh.

Although Mae had been announced for the film, no contracts had been signed because the studio, for insurance purposes, was waiting on a report from her physician on the state of her health. She resisted their demand for a complete medical history. A compromise was reached whereby the privileged information went directly from her physician to a doctor at the insurance company. On the day before her examination Paul fed her nothing but salads to lower her blood sugar level, and at the doctor's office he managed to substitute a sample of his own urine for hers. She passed her physical.

At every turn Michael Sarne aroused Mae's natural tendency toward paranoia. She raged that the director had never taken the trouble to view her great hits. She was offended when he sent a spaced-out John Phillips, formerly of The Mamas and The Papas recording group, to her apartment to demonstrate possible numbers for her to sing in the film. After failing to appear at the appointed time, Phillips, barefoot, arrived a half hour late and proceeded to sing his songs. Mae reserved committing herself since, she said, he didn't show proper respect toward her. As Phillips was leaving, Mae singed him with "I hope my white rugs didn't get your feet dirty." He said, "Next time I'll wear shoes." Mollified, she called out, "Okay, but leave your pants off."

After he was gone, Mae complained to Paul about Phillips's behavior but conceded one number, "Hollywood Was Always a Honky Tonk Town," had possibilities. "But Mae West would never say that," she reported, referring to her public image. "Hollywood was always good to her, know what I mean?" Later she came up with a suggestion that the lyric be changed to "Hollywood Was Never a Honky Tonk Town."

Sarne further alienated Mae, who had been looking forward to an Edith Head wardrobe in all shades of the rainbow for this, her first film in color, when he announced his decision that her clothes were to be in black and white to "make her stand out." Mae was even more enraged when she learned that ten of Miss Welch's twenty-six outfits were also in black and white. Edith Head took the brunt of her anger over the clothes. After Mae demanded everything be remade in material that would not wrinkle, Miss Head said to a friend, "There's nothing that won't wrinkle except patent leather. The only reason I'm staying is that she needs every friend she's got for this picture." Mae grew happier with her wardrobe when Robert Fryer vetoed Sarne and allowed Miss Head to order several of Mae's gowns in color.

At the fitting for her first color costume, a pastel pink dress, Mae, looking at herself in the mirror, turned and screamed at Miss Head, "Now you've got me looking like that singer—what's her name?—Kate Smith!" Miss Head picked up the phone and ordered a new girdle for her. Later, as she left the session, Miss Head said, "Gawd, I'm glad I drink."

The day, after hours of preparation, Mae arrived on the set for makeup, hairstyling and wardrobe tests, Sarne offended her by saying, "You look quite pretty." She later seethed, "Did you hear what that amateur son of a bitch said? Not beautiful, not sensational—just pretty!"

She was relieved to find that Miss Welch and Fryer shared her dim view of Sarne. Miss Welch had already begun filming while Mae's segments of the screenplay were still being revised. Fryer and Mae were deep in a script conference at the Ravenswood when Miss Welch urgently called him from the set. Fryer looked dazed when he put down the phone. "My God," he moaned. "Raquel says Sarne is shooting her and John Huston with a waiter going down on a waitress in the background!" Fryer and Mae quickly wound up their conference and he returned to the studio to try to bring the obstreperous director under control.

Sarne, reprimanded by studio head Richard Zanuck, sent conciliatory letters to the principals he had offended. Mae gave hers to Dr. Ireland, who put it to his head and pronounced it was from a man with enormous determination—more of that than talent.

On Mae's first day of shooting, trouble erupted between her and Miss Welch. Mae, in a black-and-white outfit, was startled to find Miss Welch in a black dress which she insisted was blue. Mae refused to shoot, confiding, "Thin as she is, in that black she'll make me look like a house." No one could persuade Miss Welch to change her costume. Finally, Richard Zanuck ordered the dress confiscated, and Miss Welch went home for the day.

Two days later she returned, wearing a light blue outfit and bearing a huge basket of red roses as a peace offering to Mae. While photographers posed the two, Miss Welch set the flowers on the floor. Mae quickly picked them up and held them high enough to block their waistlines. Miss Welch said, "Roses mean affection." Later Mae commented, "Roses also mean a damn good publicity shot. I can read her mind like ABC because my mind is so tricky."

Near the end of shooting Mae's paranoia toward Miss Welch grew boundless. When the sewage receptacle in her portable dressing room began to give off a foul odor, it was discovered it had not been emptied for two weeks. Mae fully believed Miss Welch had bribed the maintenance men to bypass it.

In their last scene together Miss Welch wore a red dress with a snood, causing Mae to ad-lib, "These days you can't tell who's the wolf and who's Little Red Riding Hood." Neither Mae nor Miss Welch attended the wrap party at the end of filming. Sensing a disaster in the making, Mae severely criticized chairman of the board Darryl Zanuck for hiring so inexperienced a director for a multimillion-dollar production. She thought Farrah Fawcett desperate to accept such a pallid role. After approving William Hopper for the judge, she privately talked against him. She respected John Huston, Grady Sutton, Jim Backus, Andy Devine and John Carradine as professionals. She thought Roger Herren was sexy, and handsome Tom Selleck as the Stud drew unqualified praise. She forgave him his height, explaining; "I taught him how to drape himself so he wouldn't be too tall for me—like I did Cary Grant."

She was ambivalent toward Rex Reed. Originally she praised his "sexy eyes," but he drew her ire when he appeared on the *Tonight Show,* criticizing the movie while it was still filming and dismissing her as a good enough comedienne but not much of an actress. "That son of a bitch!" she shouted to a friend. "I oughta get some tough guys to break his legs!" Then she laughed gleefully. "No, I got a better idea. He's a writer. I'll have them break his fingers."

Whatever anyone thought of her acting ability, press reaction left no doubt she was the box-office magnate in the cast. Because of this, in March 1970, she was hurried to Stage Six for an added number, a hard rock version of "Hard to Handle," backed by a chorus of black male dancers attired in white tie and tails. Relatively minor though the role may have been compared to those of her heyday, she was in a position to call the shots. Clearly, exploitational and financial prospects for the film rested on her undulating seventy-six-year-old hips, her singing and wisecracking. She never for a moment doubted the picture would be hers. "I know I've still got a public out there," she told executives. "My last birthday I got over ninety calls from Europe—and at least three hundred fifty altogether. Which ain't bad for one day. Yuh know what I mean?"

Despite her fear of flying ("What goes up must come down—one way or another"), Mae agreed to take a plane to New York for the world premiere of *Myra Breckenridge* at the Criterion Theater. Throughout her stay a *Life* photographer recorded her reactions to Broadway after an absence of twenty years. Among the scheduled appointments was a visit to *Coco,* starring Katharine Hepburn, where a backstage photo was to be taken of the two survivors who had made their screen debuts the same year. On the appointed day Mae suddenly announced she was skipping *Coco* in order to visit her old neighborhood in Brooklyn. Those responsible for setting up the shot urged her to reconsider, but Mae refused. Pressed for a reason, she stunned her listeners by primly announcing, "I never cared much for that party. Yuh know she lived with a married man for years."

Whatever Mae thought of others, everyone seemed beguiled by her. A Mae mania developed that rivaled the one described by Max Beerbohm in his satiric classic *Zuleika Dobson*. On the evening of June 24 Mae again was a full-fledged movie queen setting out with ten escorts—one of whom not so coincidentally was syndicated columnist Earl Wilson—to attend the premiere of *Myra Breckenridge*.

She was preceded at the Criterion by costar Raquel Welch, who received a modest response while Mae's limo was slowly making its way through what one policeman estimated was the largest crowd since the end of World War II. Fans ran alongside, waving, shouting, rapping on the windows and grasping at the doors. Periodically Mae increased the pandemonium by switching on the light inside and waving.

In front of the theater a near riot erupted as Mae's diamond- and ruby-laden hand preceded her platinum hair from the depths of the limo. A roar arose from the crowd while fans waved placards hailing Mae as the Queen of Sex. As she glided toward the entrance flanked by her ten escorts, sixty patrolmen and six mounted policemen struggled to keep the mob from demolishing her white silk gabardine sheath and swansdown-marabou stole. In the melee two officers received injuries, and a grown man was led away, screaming hysterically, "I touched Mae West! I *touched* Mae West!"

Next morning Mae alone emerged unscathed by the debacle on the screen. Her return overshadowed even such an important sociological development as the fact that this X-rated film was the closest thing to a pornographic movie yet released by a major Hollywood studio. Along with its critic's scathing review, *The New York Times* published an interview with Howard Thompson in which Mae violated the code she set for Rex Reed by observing, "I'm not too sure about *Myra Breckenridge* because they didn't use enough of my material. . . ."

That same morning 200 reporters showed up at the Hotel Americana's Royal Box for a press conference. Mae arrived ten minutes late, but clearly most of the newspeople felt she was worth waiting for as she slowly took her stance with a bejeweled hand on her hip and indicated she was ready to work.

What, someone inquired, had she meant by saying that it "was important to keep a firm grip on your essentials"?

Mae smiled provocatively and answered, "Well, if you don't understand what your essentials are, I'll have to tell you some other time."

Her favorite line in the current movie? "Let's forget about the six feet and talk about the seven inches." Runner-up? "All right, boys, take out your résumés."

Women's lib? "I'm all for it. All the way. Gentlemen may prefer blondes. But who says blondes prefer gentlemen?"

Gay lib? "The gay boys? Looks like they're takin' over, doesn't it? They're crazy about me. I'm so flamboyant."

Acting? "I do my best acting on the couch."

As she was about to leave, she paused and said, "I'm gonna give you one more thought—who needs dirty foreign films? We can do so much better ourselves."

Having played her part to the hilt on and off screen, on June 26 she went to the airport to fly back to Los Angeles. Upon arriving at the TWA terminal, her party of five was informed that one of the jumbo jet engines had burned out and another TWA aircraft was not available.

Arrangements were made for Mae's entourage to travel on United. When they reached that terminal, United's public relations man greeted them effusively only to have Mae demand, "Where's my golf cart?" He lamely explained that because of the emergency reservation it had been impossible to find one. "Well, how am I gonna get to the plane? How far is it?" Several hundred yards. "Oh, my God. Ain't there some way besides walkin'?" A wheelchair? "A wheelchair!" she moaned, surveying all the people who would see her being wheeled around. "Well, have you got five of 'em?" United didn't have wheelchairs to accommodate the entire party, and Mae's vanity would not allow her to be the only one in her group looking like a semi-invalid. So, smiling at all the gaping travelers, she maneuvered the distance with her Wedgies cutting into her feet, accepting the pain as part of the price extracted for preserving her glamorous image.

20

The publicity generated by the release of *Myra Breckenridge* brought Mae to the attention of the young. "Mae West is the only sex symbol who has bridged the communications gap between the ages," a USC psychologist explained to columnist Joyce Haber. "Despite what they say, our young people feel much guilt and anxiety about today's permissiveness. That's why Miss West's sexuality, which is implied, rather than flaunted, and laced with humor, is so attractive to the young."

Interest generated in Mae by newspaper and magazine stories caused local television stations throughout the country to run Mae West Festivals. Although pleased by the exposure to youthful audiences who couldn't buy tickets to the X-rated *Myra*, Mae was unhappy with TV's abridged versions of her theatrical films. She complained that if the plot was retained, her musical numbers were cut, and vice versa. Paul regularly wrote station managers to protest the tampering.

Still, nothing caused Mae's smile to flash and her eyes to light up more quickly than a handsome young man's praise for one of her films. When she learned that Lou Zivkovich, the Apple Valley PE instructor who was in trouble with the school district for posing nude for *Playgirl*, was an admirer of her work, she wanted to meet him. Amused by his audacity and attracted by his sexuality, she called her old friend Jules Stein and arranged an audition for Zivkovich at Universal which resulted in his landing a role in the TV series *McMillan and Wife*. Asked by a columnist how Zivkovich got the part, Mae replied, "He came up to see me and read for me. Then I gave him elocution lessons."

Yet in carrying on this flirtation, Mae was only going through the ritual she had developed over the years. She attempted no assignations behind Paul's back as she'd done with other lovers from Timony to Lopez, but she could never resist an opportunity to act like her old self. One evening, after dinner at the Black Forest in Santa Monica, rodeo rider Danny Good and several others stood at the curb with Mae while Paul went to retrieve the Cadillac. As they waited, Good asked how long she and Paul had been together. Casting a speculative glance over the rodeo rider's lanky, well-muscled frame, Mae murmured, "Mebbe too long— lookin' at you."

But perhaps she responded best to a twenty-five-year-old uninhibited grip named Virgil Gauthier, Jr. Gauthier had ingratiated himself at a Christmas party by giving her a "Merry" on the right side of her cleavage and a "Christmas" kiss on the left side after imbibing too freely. The other guests were embarrassed—except for Paul, who was angered. Mae chose to regard the kisses as a compliment. Shortly afterward, at Don the Beachcomber, playwright Aurand Harris, while seated across the table from Mae and beside Gauthier, noticed that the yellow blouse she was wearing seemed to be making her so uncomfortable that she was constantly readjusting it. But a few seconds later he realized she wasn't concerned with the blouse but was fondling her breasts for Gauthier's benefit.

A few weeks later, while Paul and Gauthier were in the men's room at a theater, Mae inquired of a friend of Gauthier's, "How much has Virgil got?" When the friend looked puzzled, Mae pointed between her legs. "I mean, down here." The friend, knowing what she wanted to hear, said that from what he'd seen, a lot. "That's what I thought," Mae said happily. Telling about it later, the man said, "I guess acting out her fantasies had pretty well stopped by this time, but the curiosity was still there."

Stimulated by the response to her return to the screen, Mae's social and professional activities accelerated. Nonetheless, her paranoia made her worry about copyright problems and every-one stealing her ideas.

She fumed that somebody had managed to obtain a copy of *The Drag* and given it to Mart Crowley, who, she believed, had just "changed a few things" and called it *The Boys in the Band*. Someone also had slipped a copy to John Osborne, who incorpo-rated her spectacular drag ball in *A Patriot for Me*. Never mind that she had seen neither play. She had read the reviews and could recognize her material. Similarly she suspected *Pleasure Man* had inspired Warren Beatty's *Shampoo* and Tennessee Williams's *Sweet Bird of Youth*. "Anybody can see Tennessee lifted the castration scene right outa my *Pleasure Man*," she seriously maintained.

In that frame of mind she felt compelled to publish novelized versions of her works to protect her property. One way or another she and Larry Lee turned *Pleasure Man* into a paperback book which came out in 1975. Reviewing it in the October 8 issue of the *Advocate,* Victor Katz described it as "painfully dated and straight laced. . . . I wish I could recommend *Pleasure Man* as a work of art. It isn't; West herself remains her best art work."

Nothing more was heard of the other novelizations, and a screen adaptation by her and Lee of *The Drag* went unoptioned. But in 1973, preparing to put the beach house up for sale, Mae and Paul, in taking an inventory of her possessions, came upon a walk-in closet crammed with elaborate formal gowns from the 1920's and '30's. It struck them that these would make excellent costumes for the drag ball that constituted the third act of *The Drag*. Mae called a producer suggesting a revival with either Herb Kenwith, who had twice directed her in summer stock, or Arthur Lubin to stage it. "I was always ahead of my time, but I think it's caught up with me. The public's ready for *The Drag*," she said. "And as for production costs, you've got half of them right in these dresses." Later, when the producer repeated the con-versation to Bob Wise, Wise remarked, "That's certainly an elevated, artistic approach if I ever heard one."

Around this time composer Dmitri Tiomkin began talking of a plan to produce *Catherine Was Great,* exteriors to be shot in Russia, interiors in England. A meeting between Tiomkin and Mae was set up at Matteo's. The restaurant's press agent saw them and tipped off Rona Barrett, who informed her TV audience that the two had dined together. Mae was greatly upset, moaning, "Oh, my God, now everybody's gonna think I'm runnin' around with old men!" Tiomkin also was dismayed—by Mae. He called one of Mae's representatives to demand, "How old iss Mae Vest? You know; you tell me! She iss eighty, yes?" The representative insisted that he didn't know. "Somebody already tells me," Tiomkin stormed. "If I go to Moscow and say 'Mae Vest,' dey vould laff and say, 'Mae Vest? Mae Vest so old she fall asleep on the toilet!'"

Also in 1973, with censorship now negligible, Mae proposed writing a new book to be called *Sex, Health and ESP*. One writer and his agent went to the Ravenswood to discuss a possible collaboration. Mae made her entrance clutching a sheaf of yellowing pages from Bernarr Macfadden's physical fitness magazines. These, she announced, contained some wonderful health tips. The ESP section would cover the development of her contacts with the Forces under the guidance of the *sri*, Reverend Kelly and Dr. Ireland. At first, she said, there had been only the voice of a tiny elfin creature whispering in her ear. That was replaced by a booming masculine voice which employed "thee," "ye" and "thou." Finally, she claimed to have become so adept at making contact that a deceased pet monkey materialized, rubbing his stomach fretfully to tell her his death had been caused by eating fruit sprayed with pesticide. In the segment devoted to sex, she would teach women how to develop pelvic muscles that would insure against their husbands' straying.

After some discussion the writer mentioned that he would need several weeks to tape her ideas and capture her style. Mae would have none of that, conveying the impression she thought he might have copies of the tapes struck off and make a fortune selling them. Which would have been the only way he could have received a fair share, since she thought a 75-25 percent split in her favor generous. As for credit? "Usually I don't let nobody else have their names on my stuff," she said. The agent reeled off his client's accomplishments. "Mmmmmm, yeah," Mae said. "Well, we'll make it 'By Mae West,' and then below," she said, motioning in the writer's direction with her head, 'Arranged by you.'"

Next day the agent rejected the deal, telling her that no collaborator would accept her conditions, proving that he didn't understand the wizardry of a magical personality. For in 1975 W. H. Allen in London issued *Mae West on Sex, Health & ESP*. Not only had Mae persuaded her ghostwriter to remain anonymous, but she had also charmed him into accepting 10 percent of the royalties, leaving her 90 percent of the take.

A pitch from Dick Cavett's staff for Mae to appear on his interview show was turned down, but her representative countered with the idea of using Mae in a special. Cavett showed enough interest that Mae invited him up to discuss the possibility. Later, on the *Tonight Show*, Cavett told Johnny Carson about his visit—how, after a brush with the law, Mae told the judge, "You can hold me in contempt of court. In fact, you can hold me any way you want to." He said she had also discussed adult films, telling him, "I'm against the sex act in pictures. Only in pictures." When Cavett inquired how it felt to be a living legend, he said Mae replied, "I can't tell you . . . I'm so used to it. It just feels like a natural thing."

If Mae's ego required establishing records, she must have been intrigued by an offer from Larry Flynt, publisher of *Hustler* magazine, who was prepared to pay her $25,000 to pose nude for the magazine's centerfold. After raising the publisher's hopes, she dashed them by suggesting he run the forty-year-old nude painting of her. "Why bother with all the posin'?" she asked. "After all, I haven't changed." One observer of the scene was later unable to make up his mind whether she had seriously considered the proposition or whether she simply enjoyed baiting Flynt.

Her social life flourished. She frequently attended parties given by the Alonzo Bells, Groucho Marx, Mrs. Jerry Wald, Roddy McDowall, Rona Barrett and the Jules Steins, among others. At one of the Steins' cocktail parties Cary Grant marveled at Mae's entrance. The room was filled with celebrities; yet, as if alerted by a fanfare, everybody stopped talking and looked at Mae. To Doris Stein he remarked, "She's such a glorious burst of energy. Always was. Always will be."

Told a dinner invitation from Groucho had been postponed because his attorneys were in town, Mae laughed and asked, "What's he done now?" But occasionally her behavior could be unsettling. For instance, at Rona Barrett's one evening she spotted Lucille Ball. Mae had resented the star since reading an erroneous column item that Jackie Gleason and Lucy were set to play Diamond Jim Brady and Diamond Lil. Even though the columnist corrected Diamond Lil to Lillian Russell a couple of days later, Mae remained suspicious and agitated.

Unaware of Mae's feelings, Lucy's producer-husband, Gary Morton, approached Mae to suggest she appear on his wife's TV show. The mention of the Ball name reawakened Mae's paranoia, and she turned noticeably cool. Not knowing the reason for her reaction, Morton brought over Lucy, who immediately began selling Mae on what a diverting spot could be worked out. "Did you catch the episode with Elizabeth Taylor and Richard Burton?" she asked, mentioning a segment in which the two stars, then at the peak of their popularity, had appeared. "It came off beautifully."

Mae turned her baby blues on Lucy. "Yeah," she said, "I turned it on. I was afraid they'd cheapen themselves by going on TV, but I really enjoyed it."

Lucy mumbled something, excused herself and headed for the bar. Shortly after, when Mae started to leave, Lucy jumped up, threw down her cigarette and stamped it out on the tiled floor, crying, "Kill the cigarettes! Here comes Mae West!"

Mae pretended not to notice, but as she and her escort settled into her limousine, she smiled slyly and said, "I guess I made her mad at me. I didn't mean that the way it sounded. But I thought I'd make it worse if I tried to straighten it out."

In a brief friendship Bette Davis fared only slightly better. After Miss Davis revealed on a television show that Mae was one of two stars she had always wanted to meet, a dinner was set up by Charles Pollock and Glenn Shahan. The first encounter went swimmingly with Miss Davis leaving the room when she felt the compulsion to have a cigarette. At the end of the evening Mae graciously remarked, "Two years ago I met Garbo. Now I've met you. I'm so thrilled, I'm goin' home, rest up a couple of days and then concentrate on meetin' the new quarterback at USC."

At a second meeting soon after, Miss Davis relaxed and had her customary cigarettes. She recounted an evening when she and a friend, in their cups, had bemoaned their mistreatment by men. Suddenly they got the wild idea that lesbianism was the answer. As they were about to climb into bed, they realized they hadn't the slightest inclination for that sort of activity and dissolved with laughter. Miss Davis asked Mae if she had ever experimented with women. "Never had time," Mae said. "I was always too busy with men." Barely out the door, Mae dismissed Miss D, remarking to her escort, "Well, dear, I think we've had the best of her."

Nor was Mae above bringing Beverly Sills up short on the subject of classical singing. At a dinner at Roddy McDowall's, Miss Sills enthusiastically spoke to Mae about the opera scene in *Goin' to Town* and asked, "Who dubbed 'My Heart at Thy Sweet Voice' for you?"

"What do y' mean, who dubbed it? I sang it myself. After all, I've got a trained voice," Mae replied.

"I wasn't aware. How wonderful," said Miss Sills nervously, hoping to end the discussion.

But Mae had more to say. "Do you know that aria?" she asked.

Miss Sills stammered, "Oh, I think I used to. I don't anymore."

"Well, I'll tell you one thing about it," Mae informed her. "It isn't easy."

After an evening at which Mae and Ruth Gordon had been at the same party, Mae's escort pointed out how sweet Miss Gordon had been to her. "Oh, we're not competitive," Mae explained. "She has no sex." She was silent for a moment, then added, "Generally, I like to do the talkin', but I could see she couldn't be stopped."

The restaurants Mae enjoyed ranged from Perino's, a favorite with old Pasadena society, to the drab-looking Man Fook Low, which served excellent Chinese food on San Pedro Street in the heart of the Los Angeles trucking district. One evening the message in her fortune cookie read: "SOMETHING STARTLING IN YOUR FUTURE." Shaking her head in wonder, Mae mused, "Whatever could startle me?"

When the Hollywood Press Club asked her to head a group of stars and executives paying tribute to Kevin Thomas, Mae happily accepted. But as she hung up the phone, it occurred to her that Thomas was only into his thirties. Alarmed, she hurriedly dialed a mutual friend and said, "Kevin seems awfully young to be getting a tribute. There's nothin' wrong with him, is there?"

One of the rare occasions when she invited a man who was neither a current business contact nor a potential lover to come up and see her at the Ravenswood was in 1972, when she asked her former boss at Paramount, ninety-nine-year-old Adolph Zukor, to tea. Aware of Zukor's failing hearing, she also invited his seventy-three-year-old son along to shout her comments and questions in his father's ear. During their reunion she informed Zukor that his loss of hearing was caused by eating too much starch. Then, shortly before the ancient mogul departed, she telephoned a faith healer and had him bless Zukor's ears. That the blessing had no effect did not shake Mae's faith. Later the healer was indicted for conspiracy to commit murder, but not until after she had begun to question his powers and had cut off all contact with him.

President Gerald Ford invited her to attend a White House dinner, honoring Egypt's Anwar Sadat. Using her sister's health as an excuse for not attending, Mae told amused intimates, "That seems like an awful long way to go for just one meal."

Over the years Mae's and Beverly's chief cause of contention was Beverly's alcoholism. At one point, thinking that a change of scene might help, she moved Beverly from the ranch to the beach house—to no avail. Mae never figured out how or through whom, but Beverly managed to obtain more liquor than ever before. As she dangerously deteriorated, Mae had no choice except to commit her to be dried out, at St. John's Hospital in Santa Monica. That accomplished, she returned her to the ranch.

While Beverly's drinking deeply concerned Mae, she could not conceal the pleasure she took in friends' responses when they met her sister. Invariably they would later comment that Beverly looked old enough to be Mae's mother or grandmother. "I know, dear," Mae would agree. "That's what drink has done to her." When one friend inquired what Beverly thought about the situation, Mae replied, "I guess she takes a look at me, then looks in the mirror, then gets herself another drink."

Mae's relationship with her other relatives was uneasy. She was able to cope with—and sometimes enjoy—occasional visits from various cousins, but her dealings with her nephew, John, and his mother, Selma, were troubled. She had never been close to her brother's wife and saw no reason to accept her after his death in 1964. About her nephew, she felt ambivalent. He was a handsome youth, and she helped him land a bit role in *Myra Breckenridge*. However, as they got to know one another better, a series of disagreements developed. Then when a fortune-teller reported John and his mother had supposedly been inquiring how long "Auntie Mae" was going to live, Mae's paranoia was aroused, and she gave orders that John be "watched like a hawk" to see he slipped nothing in the water dispenser.

While she had not, she spread the word that she had rewritten her will, cutting him and his mother off with one dollar each. "That'll discourage 'em if they have any ideas of doin' away with me," she said with satisfaction. Speaking to a friend about this one evening, she said, "You know that's not a bad idea. I'm really going to change my will, making Paul my beneficiary." Another time she told a group at dinner she was already building up her joint bank account with Paul to the point where it would contain half her assets.

When she asked Paul to call in a lawyer to draw up a new document, making him her sole heir with the provision he take care of Beverly for her lifetime, he, aware of her pain at contemplating her own mortality, urged she wait until after Beverly's death. (When Mae's will was finally probated, the press derisively printed that she had bequeathed Paul nothing. In fact, the will she made in 1964 left him $10,000 under his original name, Chester Rybinski, and during their twenty-seven years together she and Paul made some joint investments.)

Meanwhile, Mae continued looking after Beverly. She induced her butler-chauffeur Larry Grayson to move to the ranch. Grayson, upon coming to Hollywood to be a star eleven years earlier, had taken a temporary job with Mae and remained with her as a trusted employee.

At least once a week Mae and Paul would go to the ranch to see Beverly and talk to Grayson. More often than not these trips turned out to be disturbing. "She uses the most terrible language," Mae complained after one visit. "I don't know what to do with her. Grayson couldn't find some keys 'n' Beverly said, 'Maybe they're up Paul's ass.'"

One day Beverly's favorite adjective seemed to be "fucking." Finally, Mae admonished her sister, "We don't use that word!" Beverly mumbled something to Grayson, then screamed with laughter. Later, when Mae asked Grayson what Beverly had said, he reported, "She said you may not use the word, but you've sure done plenty of it."

Beverly grew increasingly hostile toward Mae. She railed against the five crypts Mae had bought for the immediate family at the time of Matilda's death. "She's a hateful, deceitful person," Mae complained. "Beverly pretends to like me, but she told Grayson, 'She's not gonna stick me in that fuckin' crypt in Brooklyn. I've had enough of her while I'm alive. I don't want to be lyin' next to her when I'm dead.'" Mae's listener responded that Beverly sounded as if a demon possessed her when she was drinking. "If that's true," Mae said, "it must be an awful mean demon."

The alcohol began to cause Beverly to hallucinate. She took to her bed and began talking to the pictures on the wall. Imagining that a lesbian was trying to get into bed with her, she attempted to shoot the intruder with Grayson's empty pistol. In the belief that men were coming at her from the mirror on the bedroom door, she called the police. When they arrived and tried to calm her, she accused them of being part of the conspiracy. Finally, the police went along with her delusion and pretended to evict the imaginary men from the premises.

When Grayson reported this to the Ravenswood, Paul advised Mae to call a doctor and again have Beverly committed to be dried out. He also went out to the ranch and with spray paint smoked the bedroom mirror. Beverly peacefully agreed to enter the hospital, causing Mae to observe, "Thank God the doctor was good-lookin'. Blond 'n' blue-eyed. Beverly wouldn't pay attention to any doctor who was ugly!"

While Beverly was away, Paul took steps to protect her against herself. He revoked her credit cards and cautioned neighbors not to allow her to beg or borrow liquor from them. Mae also instructed Grayson to call the Ravenswood if he so much as suspected Beverly had found a way to obtain a bottle.

Upon release from the hospital Beverly predictably resented Paul's efforts in her behalf and responded by calling him Krauser or referring to him as the jerk. Paul reacted mildly, reminding any of Beverly's sympathizers that without the measures Mae and he had taken Beverly was doomed. "One more bout will finish her," he warned.

Ironically Beverly's campaign against Paul strengthened his relationship with Mae, who looked to him for support in controlling her increasingly obstreperous sister.

In early February 1976 Mae agreed to meet with Dick Cavett to discuss the possibility of appearing on his CBS special *Back-Lot,*

USA. She was bright, shrewd and vivacious during the meeting, which went well. Still, she was inclined to let the Cavett offer pass because of her aversion to television. The night after the meeting, during dinner at Man Fook Low, Virgil Gauthier, Jr., became excited about the prospect of seeing her on TV and kept urging her to appear. Finally, she asked facetiously, "Virgil, would you do it with me?"

"Oh, boy! I sure would," he replied.

"Then I guess I'll have to do it," Mae said. The next morning she called her agent, Fred Apollo, and instructed him to accept $25,000 for a fifteen-minute segment consisting of an interview and two songs.

The interview was scheduled to be taped at 2:00 P.M. on Monday, February 23. When Mae learned that Cavett never allowed his subject to look at questions before the taping, she threw a minor tantrum. "I don't work his way," she stormed. "I want to see the questions so I can be prepared. And remember, I been around a lot longer than he has." Nevertheless, the Cavett people remained firm, and Mae showed up for the two-and-one-half-hour taping, from which the program's editors managed to put together a sequence which demonstrated that at least for Cavett, Mae's approach would have been better.

Her working relationship with choreographer Marc Breaux was good, and the two musical numbers were a great improvement over the conversation. "I realized before going to see her she was well over eighty and I would be lucky if she could just walk," Breaux later commented, "but she was a legend, and I treated her as such. In the 'Frankie and Johnny' number she wanted the background entirely quiet with her doing all the movement. I asked whether she could come down steps. She said, 'Of course, I can come down stairs. I can do anything.'"

CBS had hired rehearsal space in the San Fernando Valley. The working areas were roped off, but except for a few tables and chairs and a flight of steps, there was neither scenery nor props. Mae made a stab at rehearsing, pronounced the situation impossible and left.

Breaux, who had great admiration for, and empathy with, the old trouper, advised producer Gary Smith to rehearse the dancers, singers and extras with a stand-in and to rely on Mae's vaudeville technique to get her through. He also suggested that instead of having her attempt to negotiate the stairs in her platform shoes, the camera should discover her at the bottom of the steps. Smith endorsed the choreographer's approach, and along with director-producer Dwight Hemion, they further refined the routine the day they taped.

"She was a little forgetful—as a matter of fact, very forgetful," Breaux said. "I explained what she was to do in the opening segment. Just as the director called action, she said, 'Let's see. This is where I begin to sing "Frankie and—" ' I interrupted, 'No, Miss West, you sweep the room with a glance and say, "This is the kind of room I like—wall-to-wall men." ' " (Mae never believed in throwing good material away. This line had worked in vaudeville and in the recent Friars' tribute. She was confident it would work again.) "Then you begin to move toward the tables, telling the story of 'Frankie and Johnny.' She said, 'Oh, yes,' but we had to tape each shot half a dozen times before she finally did it right.

"After the section with her at the first table, it was 'Cut!' Start again and do eight bars. 'Cut!' Repeat. We did it all that way, and it worked out pretty good. The longest take was when she moved from one room to another all in one. We placed Lou Zivkovich, whom she had wanted on the show, at the table. That made it easier because he was familiar and she seemed to like him very much.

"There was this other guy, Virgil Gauthier. She wanted him used as the croupier at the beginning. That was okay. But when we set up for her move along the bar, he got into that segment, too, and toasted her as she passed.

"After the shot was completed, a cameraman said, 'Miss West, I don't know whether you're aware of it or not, but one of the actors moved in that shot.' Bystanders on the set were startled at how steely-eyed she became. She wanted to know which one. 'That one,' the cameraman said, pointing to Gauthier. Miss West relaxed and smiled. 'Oh, that's Virgil. That's all right.'"

Everyone on the set, including Cavett, was intrigued. "Who the hell is Virgil?" he asked Kevin Thomas, who was covering the taping. "Well, not the young poet," was the reply. "And to explain would require a special in itself."

Mae had no problem with "After You're Gone" as long as she just had to stand by the piano. But at one point Breaux wanted her to go center. She forgot. "It didn't matter as far as we were

/ 289

concerned," he said. "But the cameramen were poised for a move that never came. They just had to accommodate her, which they were glad to do. Because after you'd worked with her, you became very protective. She was more than a legend. She was something else!"

According to Breaux, even Hollywood cynics were impressed with Paul. "I think everybody expected the usual," Breaux said. "Guys who latch on to most stars are opportunists. But he was so wonderful to her, so protective, so genuinely concerned about her welfare, it was touching. One of the first things that impressed me was that she was a little forgetful. Paul would start a thought. Then she'd pick it up and talk until she began to drift a little, at which point he'd come in and finish it for her. Anyone who saw them together couldn't doubt that he must love her deeply. Because that's the only explanation for the attention and affection he showed. You sensed he was not going to let anyone hurt her—ever."

At the conclusion of Mae's second number, "After You're Gone," the other performers and crew spontaneously broke into loud, prolonged applause as Mae headed for her dressing room. Inside, Mae inquired of Kevin Thomas whether he thought her gesture where she caressed herself in a manner that could only be regarded as suggestive would pass the censors. "I think it's time they laid off me," she told him. "After all, I had my clothes on."

The censors laid off, but the TV critics laid it on in the April 5, 1976, editions of their newspapers:

WHAT IS SO RARE AS MAE IN APRIL? headlined the Los Angeles *Times*.

MAE WEST BRINGS SPARK TO CAVETT CATASTROPHE, was the banner over the review in the New York *Daily News*.

And in *The New York Times*: TV: CAVETT'S SPECIAL FLOUN-DERS—UNTIL MAE WEST. Far down in the review, the *Times*'s critic John J. O'Connor went on to describe Mae "peering out from under her blond coiffure again, batting her impossibly long eyelashes before the TV cameras.

"Any reasonable observer might argue that the phenomenon borders on the grotesque. But reason somehow seems puny when confronted with Miss West. She is something—a wonderful, glamorous, talented and marvelously witty something—unto herself."

A promotional stunt for the special that appealed to Mae's ego was proposed: to rent for $250 the Oriental Theater on Sunset Boulevard and display on its marquee CLOSED TONIGHT TO WATCH MAE WEST ON TV. The theater marquee, located on Sunset Boulevard, Hollywood's busiest street, drew comments from dozens of Mae's friends and fans. The commotion was responsible in some measure for arousing interest in the eventual production of *Sextette*. Mae, who had okayed payment for the marquee, got carried away by all the reaction and seriously suggested, "We ought to check and see how many other theaters around the country closed for the night because I was on TV."

21

Every star who has managed to sustain a long career has been forced to behave unconventionally. As the years passed, through revision, omission and a total rejection of anything that reflected negatively on her, Mae maintained her image. She was, like the boxers she admired so greatly, willing to undergo all kinds of sacrifices to remain a contender endlessly training for a championship bout. Her ruthless devotion to sustaining Mae West elevated selfishness into self-worship. Such total dedication won grudging admiration, even from people who had once deplored it. And an occasional dissenter infuriated her. When Las Vegas newsman Ralph Pearl wrote that she was eighty-three and looked every year of it, she fumed, "We've got to stop that guy in a nice way—and if that don't work, have him beat up."

Only rarely was she exposed to the abrasiveness of reality. Paul served as a buffer between her and the outside world, censoring unflattering interviews, screening telephone calls from busybody "friends" who enjoyed bearing bad news, and after the gradual departure of servants, he functioned as lover, confidant, adviser, bodyguard, physical therapist, chauffeur, chef and morale builder.

His attachment to Mae was compounded partly by awe that he had earned the devotion of this living legend, by the pride he took in the stir she created whenever she appeared in public and by his desire to hear her repeat and repeat her repertory of personal triumphs.

His obvious empathy and solicitude were apparent in the tender way he anticipated her desires and needs. No one who spent time with them could question his adoration of her. When they were being privately entertained, he escorted her to the door of the bathroom—partly to guard against her Wedgies' becoming entangled in throw rugs and partly to forestall any attempt to breach her privacy.

Even their closest friends, unaware of Mae's diabetic condition, sometimes gently took Paul to task for his adamant refusal to allow her to indulge in the sweets she obviously craved. He quietly but firmly stood his ground without explanation. One evening when Mae insisted on having a second chocolate parfait, a standoff developed between them. Guests stirred nervously, and actress Natalie Schafer succeeded in diverting Mae's attention by exclaiming over her unblemished hands. Mae beamed, seized the hand of a middle-aged man seated at her left, held it up and said, "Look, his hand looks older than mine!"—which, without question, it did. There were no unsightly spots, veins or blemishes on her hands, arms or neck.

When he knew there would be irresistible desserts at certain homes to which they were invited, Paul, with the approval of Mae's physician, would give her an extra boost of insulin before leaving the Ravenswood. Once he tried a different ploy. He urged her to say, when offered sweets, that she had given them up. She agreed. Then at dinner she accepted two servings of chocolate cream pie. To his reprimand, "I thought you were going to say you had given up sweets," she replied, "I'm not going to lie for you!"

Theirs in many ways was the perfect older woman-younger man relationship. Once, when Mae was not feeling her best, Aurand Harris noted how unobtrusively and sensitively Paul dealt with her needs. As the two men were heading toward the buffet, Harris complimented Paul on his concern for Mae's happiness and well-being. Paul thanked him and said with matter-of-fact sincerity, "I believe I was put on this earth to take care of Miss West."

*   *   *

Paul encouraged Mae to think of herself as ageless and devised a program of exercises to keep her in top form. To preserve her muscle tone, he placed a pair of small dumbbells beneath her bed. Each morning, after studying an attractive photo of herself and setting that image in her consciousness, she would reach for the dumbbells and work out. (Mae frequently astonished new acquaintances by popping the biceps of first one arm and then the other.) When those exercises were completed, Paul would serve the breakfast he had prepared. By the mid-1970's he was fixing all meals. "I plan her menus so she gets what she wants— but in small portions," he explained.

At some point during the day she would ride her stationary bicycle to keep her legs firm and shapely. Until she sold the beach house, Mae, Paul and one of their friends—Herbert Kenwith, film historian David Johnson, memorabilia collector Tim Malachosky or fan club consultant Kent Saxon—would frequently motor to Santa Monica to stroll on the sand at day's end.

In addition to all his other duties, Paul performed simple secretarial tasks, kept track of her photographs, paid bills, screened fan mail, suggested projects and reminded her of special material that might prove useful. When the Masquers' Club designated her the recipient of their annual George Spelvin Award,* they rehearsed Mae's twenty-five-minute act so carefully that it overshadowed the fifty-minute tribute featuring George Raft, Steve Allen, Peter Marshall, Jim Backus, Jack LaRue, Michael Landon, Lloyd Nolan and emcee Hal Kanter. In fact, Mae and Paul spent so much time and energy preparing for the appearance that columnists began speculating that she was revving up for another Las Vegas engagement.

Their mutual need and mutual belief in Mae's perfection strengthened the foundation of Mae's and Paul's relationship. Although she was reluctant to disturb the picture of herself as a love-'em-'n'-leave-'em blonde, she privately acknowledged her deeply felt attachment to Paul. And by 1975 she discussed the matter for publication with George Haddad of *Coronet* magazine, telling him that although she never would "shut herself off from anyone" because she "loved people," she now was essentially

---

*George Spelvin was a fictitious name used in theater programs to disguise the fact one actor was doubling in two roles.

monogamous. "Although I always have and always will continue looking at other men, Paul is all the man I need now. He's from the old school of chivalry. He treats me like a lady, which I expect from any man. When I'm in the mood, he's romantic but he doesn't push himself on me."

Sometime later Paul received a message in a fortune cookie advising him that a new, exciting romantic interest was to enter his life. After reading the message, he put his arm around Mae and announced to their dinner companions, "Miss West is all the woman I'll ever want." It was a rare moment that combined the public respect—"Miss West"—and the private intimacy that they shared. Mae sometimes was less discreet. One evening after having an uncharacteristic glass of beer, she became giddy and insisted upon eating a candied kumquat, a fruit of which she was inordinately fond. Paul attempted to reason with her. "Baby had a beer," he reminded her. "I'm afraid I'm going to have to cut you off on the kumquats." Mae, fully aware of his reticence about any public display, leaned toward him, placed her hand squarely between his legs and announced, "Well, this is one thing you're not going to tell baby she can't have." She got her kumquat.

She and Paul conducted themselves like a conventionally married couple and were regarded as such by friends. But at one point Paul began disappearing for several hours at a time. To Mae that meant only one thing: he was seeing another woman. She privately fussed and fumed and finally hired a detective to have him followed. "If he's two-timing me with another dame, I'll send him back to the Merchant Marine," she threatened. A week later the detective reported that her competition was a small, battered boat that Paul had picked up cheaply at the harbor. He was slipping off when his schedule allowed to put it in shape.

As Mae's sexual adventures waned, she became increasingly preoccupied with the Forces. Materialization became more frequent. One evening, for example, she walked into the living room and saw Reverend Kelly, wearing full evening clothes, sitting on the sofa. Startled, she called to Paul, causing the reverend to dematerialize at once. When she described this incident at Roddy McDowall's house, Ava Gardner inquired why she thought the ghost would have been wearing tails. Mae shrugged. "Just showin' off, I guess."

After the laughter subsided, she said in all seriousness that she had had such experiences many times. She explained that parapsychologists had told her that she had a superabundance of energy upon which spirit souls drew. She also claimed that recently the Forces entered her bedroom through her mind's eye, arriving in the form of startlingly handsome young males. One dark-haired Adonis was particularly forward, almost always trying to approach her bed to touch her. "But I see he keeps his distance," she explained. "How do I know he ain't the Angel of Death?" she asked in one of her rare allusions to her own mortality.

This distrust of even the Forces indicated the ever-deepening paranoia that had overtaken her. It was to surface much more severely after the taping of the Cavett special. She developed an unreasoning fear of fire and applied full makeup before retiring so that she would look attractive should she have to flee the burning apartment house in the middle of the night. When one of her rings disappeared, she brought in a clairvoyant who, among other things, said, "I see the color blue—all shades of blue and chiffons and soft material." Mae at once suspected Beverly of taking the ring.

At one of USC's Friends of Libraries' Functions, Sybil Brand, community leaders in whose honor the women's jail in Los Angeles had been named, was seated next to Paul, and Mae said later she had thought they were "awfully cozy." The next day, Mae experienced some bleeding and claimed she had passed a triangular piece of glass. At first she suspected a student waitress of slipping it in her water goblet, but the more she thought about it, the more convinced she became that Mrs. Brand was the guilty party. "Mebbe Sybil oughta be in the jail they named for her," Mae said, after which she forgot her suspicions and resumed her friendship with her imaginary rival.

In persons of Mae's age, such aberrations sometimes indicate a small blood vessel has ruptured in the brain. If nothing further occurs, the brain repairs itself and the normal personality returns. On the other hand, these ruptures can be precursors of a major stroke.

Whatever the state of Mae's mental keenness in private, the long years of self-discipline protected her in public. With the help of a curled blond shoulder-length wig to hide the hint of a dowager's hump; lifts attached at her temples and connected by a rubber band to smooth out any hint of sagging facial muscles; a light patina of pink-and-white pancake to enhance her color; and a seemingly inexhaustible flow of quotable quotes, she still piqued the curiosity of the public and the press. Job offers continued to arrive. Her triumph on the Cavett special confirmed Mae's belief that unwavering determination and unshakable self-love could persuade the public that she remained unchanged and un-changeable—which led to *Sextette*.

Mae's 1961 summer circuit vehicle had first attracted interest as a screen project from Hunt Stromberg, Jr., and James Aubrey, who, in 1969, commissioned Leonard Spigelgass to convert it into a screenplay. Like so many others before him, Spigelgass tried to parlay a few brief meetings into an implied intimacy. On the Johnny Carson show he said he enjoyed a close friendship with Mae and recounted her asking during a telephone call how he was feeling. When he replied things had been rubbing him the wrong way lately, she responded, "Come on over and I'll rub you the right way."

Mae was indignant. "How does he dare say that!" she fumed. "What'll my public think of Mae West invitin' that dried-out old party over to rub him *any* way! I wouldn't touch him with my gloves on!" Needless to say, after that incident she loathed his screenplay.

To direct the picture, Stromberg and Aubrey had approached both the stylish George Cukor and the boldly theatrical Tom O'Horgan, who had turned the stage version of *Hair* from a flop into a hit. Aubrey grew discouraged and quit. Stromberg per-sisted. Cukor, before returning the script, called him to ask, "Is she really serious about playing that role? . . . She is? . . . Well, let me tell you something. If this script had been offered Marilyn Monroe in her prime, she would have read it and said, 'No, no! I'm too old, too ugly to play this part.'" Eventually Stromberg dropped the option.

Later, after Aubrey became head of production at Metro-Goldwyn-Mayer, Bill Belasco tried unsuccessfully to get the project under way at that studio. Mae was eager to have actor Laurence Harvey as her leading man. "I get the impression he's gay but isn't serious about it," she said. "I just think he does it for the fun of it."

By May 1, 1976, when still another *Sextette* announcement was made, hardly anyone took it seriously. Attorney Harry Weiss had put the package together after meeting neophyte producers Daniel Briggs, twenty-one, and Robert Sullivan, twenty-three. A spellbinder, Weiss soon had the backing of Briggs's mother, Mimi Stauffer, chemical heiress, owner of 51 percent of the Tropicana Hotel in Las Vegas and four other corporations. Warner Toub was engaged as executive producer.

The decision was made to scrap all existing versions of the script and hire television-screenwriter Herbert Baker to create an improved story line. He developed new characters, added the UN Security Council, which was to be meeting at the honeymoon hotel, and tried to clarify the action. Meanwhile, the producers interviewed several directors before settling on Irving Rapper, who had directed Bette Davis in a number of her vintage films.

Toub, Baker and Rapper met with Mae on June 18 for a story conference. Baker outlined his ideas, which Mae appeared to like, but a week later, after no further contact, she groused that he was "bitchin' up" her script. She also complained about some of the proposed casting, objecting to Louis Jourdan as her leading man on the grounds they were trying to turn her English lord into a Frenchman. When Danny Kaye was suggested for the press agent, Mae said, "He's been around an awful long time. I'd look better with someone fresher. How about Gene Kelly?" Finally, after seeing the remake of *Wuthering Heights* at the urging of Rapper, she settled on youthful Timothy Dalton to play her bridegroom, predicting he would score a hit comparable to Cary Grant's. She also responded favorably to the selection of George Hamilton for her gangster ex-spouse.

In his first discussions Rapper had stressed the necessity of producing the film on a budget of around $1 million. Its success, he maintained, would depend upon the hard-core Mae West cult. He voiced doubts that mass audiences would accept the premise that however well preserved Mae appeared, six sexy males would be vying to get into bed with a woman of her age.

Rapper had urged that reliable, inexpensive actors be assembled around her. He also suggested that saturation bookings be arranged to insure return of the investment before the cameras rolled. "Her recent reviews on the Cavett special are the passport to a distribution deal," he said. "What's more, she's promotable, and the studios know it."

Mae's imminent return to the screen prompted numerous stories and columns about her present and past. Both the Los Angeles *Times* and *The New York Times* sent men to interview her. She told Tom Burke of *The New York Times* that in the 1930's William Randolph Hearst, upon reading in the papers that she made more money than he did (actually her earnings were exceeded only by his), telephoned and invited her to San Simeon. "He wanted romance," she bragged. "I coulda married him, but I was busy." She also told Burke that she expected some censorship problems with *Sextette* but assured him the film wouldn't contain anything that would land anyone in court like another recent film whose title she couldn't recall. Burke supplied *Deep Throat* and reminded her that despite its legal troubles, it was still being shown. Mae was curious just what was done in the film that was so shocking, and Burke replied the action was difficult to describe to a lady. He then quoted her as saying, "Oh-h-h all that, huh? I'll get it screened for me. For research. But we're not puttin' any 'a that in *Sextette*. I don't mean I couldn't. I got nothin' against kids doin' it nowadays, but givin' the audience too much was never my style. I didn't *need* to push that stuff; I knew if I did people'd get sick of it, an' they have. They want innuendo again. In one of those *Sextette* scripts they ruined on me, they put me in a steam room fulla naked men. I told 'em, 'Let's face it, the sex organs ain't got no personality.'"

Encouraged by all the coverage, the producers increased the budget to mount a big-league prestige production. For the sixth time Edith Head was hired to design a dazzling Mae West wardrobe; English director Ken Hughes was imported to replace Rapper; Marc Breaux was signed to do the choreography; and Jim Crabbe was engaged as cameraman.

A suggestion that seventy-one-year-old Cesar Romero be cast as one of Mae's ex-husbands was vetoed by her, once again because she considered him "too old." George Raft and Walter Pidgeon were engaged for cameos. Rona Barrett was signed to play herself, and onetime stage-and-screen leading man Morgan Farley was lured out of retirement to utter one line: "Hooray for Hollywood!" Even publisher Hugh Hefner was given a bit— which ended on the cutting-room floor. Harry Weiss reserved a Godfather-type role for himself, which he performed very well.

Mae suggested that Paul be hired as coach of the Olympic

weight lifting team, assuring everyone that he could get himself in shape in three weeks. Paul declined—and for good reason. He knew he would have to concentrate entirely on Mae if she were to get through the film. His greatest concern was the fear she no longer could remember dialogue. Finally, he discussed the potential problem with the producers. After various experiments they decided to place the director in a glass booth from which he could broadcast the lines to Mae, who would have a tiny receiver hidden in her wig.

On December 2, *Daily Variety* carried the head SEXTETTE SHOOTING FINALLY GETS ROLLING. Her first day at the studio, Mae spent trying on her wardrobe. The next, Edith Head labored to find ways of altering it to accommodate what she called Mae's new "early Mary Pickford hairdo."

Mae sat around on December 3 from noon until 8:00 P.M., while the director shot scenes with Dom DeLuise and Dalton. Mae's initial reaction to DeLuise was negative. "He's all wrong for the part," she moaned, "and my God, they're thinking of Ringo Starr for Laslo." Nor was she happy with the producers' idea of using Alice Cooper and Keith Moon, drummer for the Who rock group. Surprisingly, when the ecstatic producers informed her Tony Curtis had agreed to play the Russian delegate ex-husband, Mae came up with her constant reaction: "He's too old. I don't want anybody that old in m' picture." The producers persisted, claiming that the chemistry was right and that Curtis's fans would add box-office clout. Mae was still pouting about what she considered the aspersion that she would need any help from anybody when Curtis, obviously elated at meeting the legendary lady, was brought on the set. His spirits were dampened immediately after their introduction by Mae's first question: "You're goin' to wear a wig to cover the bald spot, aincha?" Curtis, who had done battle with Marilyn Monroe during the filming of *Some Like It Hot,* was quickly taken aside and mollified with the explanation that well preserved though she might be, Mae's responses and behavior were sometimes childlike and at other times downright childish.

Whether true or not, she was shrewd enough to comment when she learned they intended to adhere to the Herbert Baker script, "Well, it's gonna cost them a lot of money because it don't play right for me." Perhaps for this reason, famous Mae West lines—"Is that a gun in your pocket or are you just glad to see me?" or "I'm a girl who works at Paramount all day and Fox all night"—were scattered through the script like raisins in bread pudding.

As shooting progressed, Mae remained enthusiastic about Dalton and Hamilton and distressed about the casting of Cooper and Moon. Once work with Curtis began, she increasingly respected his craftsmanship. And as he observed her receiving her lines by shortwave and moving to marks designated by sandbags because of her nearsightedness, his initial irritation was replaced by compassion for her tenacity and gameness.

Mae's aura continued to bring reams of publicity to the film and everyone involved with it. Speaking of Mae to newsman Guy Flatley, Dom DeLuise (who eventually received good personal notices) said, "I want to tell you not only is she peppy, but she is a sex symbol. I came into her dressing room at eight o'clock one morning with a picture my wife had drawn of her. She looked at it very closely and said, 'I see your wife is very talented.' 'Yeah,' I said, 'but she can't cook.' Mae said, 'I can't cook either. But I can warm you up.'"

Former Beatle Ringo Starr told Flatley, "I thought it would be fantastic to play with Mae, just to see what the legend was really like, but on the first day of shooting I got very uptight. . . . I felt completely left out of things. But by the end of the second day I would have stayed on as long as she wanted me. She's old enough to be my grandmother, so it's sort of embarrassing to say, but she's bloody attractive. And Mae's no Garbo; Mae doesn't want to be alone."

Mae proved she was capable of switching positions to promote a picture. At dinner one evening with columnist Radie Harris she bragged she'd "been smart enough to surround herself with three top rock stars—Ringo Starr, Alice Cooper and Keith Moon—to attract additional young fans." Radie also reported asking Mae about her sex life, and Mae "smiled enigmatically as she looked at Paul. . . . Obviously," Radie concluded, "whatever she's doing, she's doing right!"

As the production fell behind schedule, rumors of problems began to emanate from the set. Ignoring the fact that any star is carefully checked by makeup men and hairdressers, one magazine spread the tale that the inexperienced producers had begun shouting, "Fabulous! Fabulous!" upon Mae's initial appearance for her first big scene—only to have a bystander whisper that she had her wig on backwards and looked as if she had emerged from a barroom brawl.

As various cliques formed, Edith Head, repeating what she had said while *Myra* was in production, declared she was remaining on the picture because Mae needed a friend. The eight-time Oscar winner later remarked that she'd gladly return two of her statuettes *not* to be associated with the film. Peter Simone, the publicist who was replaced by Pickwick Public Relations during filming, told how the shortwave receiver in Mae's wig picked up a signal from a police helicopter, causing the star to place a hand on her hip and flash, "Traffic on the Hollywood Freeway is bogged down near Highland. There is an accident near Echo Park." Cameraman Jim Crabbe called that anecdote apocryphal. "Never happened," agreed Dom DeLuise. "What she did was to repeat Ken Hughes's directions to Crabbe. But to be fair about it, she laughed more than anyone else as soon as she realized what she had done."

Director Hughes admitted to columnist Roderick Mann one scene had required seventy-five takes. "She tries so hard. I adore her. But I wouldn't go through anything like that again. I was there from eight-thirty in the morning in that booth until two the next morning. . . . The really lucky man was Irving Rapper. He got paid off and didn't have to spend twelve weeks in that damned booth."

Sal Grasso, one of the production managers, told Alan Cartnal from *New West,* "I'll never forget the first impression I had of Mae West. She came out in this cuckoo's nest wig and tired old black outfit and I looked at her and thought, 'How pathetic.' She was in full makeup. She was very insecure and she just kept asking, 'Do I look nice?' She really looked like a little old lady just getting through the night. But the minute they hit the lights she became the magic woman that we know."

Patrick Pacheco, the alert managing editor of *After Dark* in 1977, proposed that Mae be chosen as the recipient of the magazine's Seventh Annual Ruby Award. The progression from previous winners Bette Midler and Liza Minnelli to Mae seemed logical to him. On May 12 Mae swiveled into the Beverly Wilshire's celebrity-packed ballroom escorted by an honor guard of seven marines. Before a crowd of 600, editor William Como presented her with a silver loving cup, causing her to quip, "I always say, everything good happens—after dark," and her assembled fans went wild. Pacheco's inspiration generated superb promotion for Mae, *Sextette* and the magazine.

Sextette was sneaked at the Directors Guild Theater in June—receiving, according to columnist Army Archerd, who named his source as one of the producers, an "excellent" rating on 95 percent of the cards. Still, when stories appeared that Briggs and Sullivan were preparing a one-reel promotional teaser to show potential distributors, experienced Hollywood observers concluded that the final cut had turned out to be a disappointment. Shortly there were pink billboards all over greater Los Angeles, proclaiming MAE WEST IS COMING. But as summer passed into fall, there was no distributor for the picture.

Warner Brothers nibbled, renting the United Artists Theater in Westwood for one night to share the bill with the highly acclaimed, small-budgeted *Outrageous,* starring Craig Russell. To Warner's it must have seemed a shrewd move since one of Russell's best imitations was of Mae.

What made it ironic was that at thirteen, Toronto-born Craig Eady had founded a World-Wide Mae West Fan Club and established contact with his idol. In 1965 he boarded a bus bound for Hollywood to meet Mae, and two years later he was living in her beach house. Then an argument occurred—"Something about a couple of old gowns and some of her underthings"—and Craig Eady departed. Not long after, he began making a name as a female impressionist.

As he began to climb, Mae fumed over his parody of her, while Craig Russell, as he now called himself, accentuated the positive. "Once you've worked with Mae West, everybody else becomes a dress extra," he announced. But flattery got him nowhere, and when he attended *After Dark*'s Ruby Party, Mae passed word to Pacheco to keep Russell away from her table. Now her latest struggling release was sharing a theater with his film which had been hailed in New York and for which he had won both "best actor" and "best actress" awards at the Virgin Islands Film Festival.

After the showing, Warners' declined to buy *Sextette*. Universal, 20th Century-Fox and other major distributors followed suit. As 1977 turned into 1978, news stories began mentioning Mae's film as one that might end up on the shelf. But in late February, Briggs and Sullivan signed a lease for the Cinerama Dome near Sunset and Vine, paying $42,000 per week for four weeks on a four-wall basis.

On March 2 Briggs and Sullivan held an old-fashioned Hollywood opening, complete with floodlights, bleachers and an interview platform for arriving celebrities. Emcee Army Archerd whipped up the crowd with the skill of a carnival talker while everyone awaited Mae's arrival.

Two of her leading men, George Hamilton and Alice Cooper, received surprisingly restrained receptions. Hugh Hefner passed almost unnoticed by the crowd. So did George Jessel as well as a number of rock musicians. Incredibly such an important co-worker as Edith Head was not invited. Looking over the crowd, one veteran Hollywood observer asked, "Where did they get this group? Bus them in from Cucamonga?"

Yet as Mae hove into view, leaning on the arm of Paul, who guarded her in his customary, fiercely protective manner, the fans went from apathy to hysteria at the sight of their idol. Inside the auditorium Mae's entrance earned a healthy round of applause and shouts of welcome as she made her way to her seat. For a few moments the sweet smell of success seemed in the air. But the tyro producers blew the excitement, allowing a ten-minute lull before beginning the picture. In the meantime, a transcription of the film's songs was played without sufficient amplification to hold the audience's attention.

Significantly, when the lights dimmed and the names of the producers flashed on the screen, they earned a response exceeded only by Mae's. Reception of the picture ranged from ecstatic to derisive with the audience and the critics. Kevin Thomas in the Los Angeles *Times* diplomatically tipped off readers in the first paragraph just what to expect by saying that *Sextette* "will be cherished by her fans, for whom it was made." Richard Cuskully of the *Herald-Examiner* was also favorable, noting: "We've heard or seen a lot of it before, but the lady seems indestructible as the Statue of Liberty and well worth a visit." Arthur Knight wrote in the *Hollywood Reporter* with tempered respect: "I think there is an odd kind of gallantry in the octogenarian Mae's loyalty to her public. . . . I just happen to prefer the equally octogenarian Mary Pickford form of loyalty:

for the past 40 years she refused to betray her fans by appearing on the screen in roles she knew she could no longer portray."

Paul withheld all unfavorable notices, but such tactics could hardly fool such a shrewd showwoman. Mae was noticeably subdued for six weeks after the film closed its run. The fact that no distributor had come forth to pick it up was not lost on her. She privately complained her script had been "bitched up."

Then one evening she arrived at Man Fook Low, all pink and white and smiling. During dinner she spoke vividly of her experience with the *sri* and behaved once more like the indestructible Mae West. Everyone present was astonished by her high spirits. When she and Paul departed, one of the party inquired what could have wrought this startling transformation. "Beats me," said another guest, "unless one of those high colonics got up there and hit her brain."

Shortly after, the reason for the euphoria became clear. Crown-International, a minor-league but ambitious company, had taken over worldwide release of *Sextette*. Meanwhile, *Time* magazine reviewed the picture in the May 22 issue, heralding it as "one of those movies rarely seen these days, a work so bad, so ferally innocent, that it is good, an instant classic to be treasured by connoisseurs of the genre everywhere. . . . Mae West is her own best invention and no one believes it or enjoys it more than she herself."

Soon after, Crown-International booked *Sextette* into the refurbished, 2,200-seat Warfield Theater in San Francisco for a November 16, 1978, opening. Announcement that Mae would make a personal appearance resulted in an instant sellout. Excitement mounted when the company created a furor among film critics by failing to set up a press screening. Seats were found for daily reviewers, but representatives of such weeklies as *Rolling Stone*, *People*, *US* and *Variety* were given the option of standing or seeing a later screening—without Mae's presence.

Mae, in the meantime, vacillated about whether to appear alone onstage or with one of the male stars in the film. If so, which one? George Raft? "He only has a bit, dear." Timothy Dalton? "Who, dear?" Timothy Dalton. She shot a stricken glance at Paul. "Your leading man, Miss West," Paul explained. Mae beamed and began worrying about what to wear. Something from the picture? Or from her own wardrobe? She was also undecided about which hotel had the proper cachet. She finally settled on the $350-per-day Royal Suite at the Mark Hopkins. She and her entourage of twelve made reservations for Thursday, November 17. Then Dr. Ireland warned that Thursday was a bad day for travel. So Mae insisted on leaving on the sixteenth.

After driving Interstate 5 north, Paul, Mae and Kevin Thomas arrived in the Bay City near midnight, throwing the Mark Hopkins into minor chaos since the current occupants of the Royal Suite had to be persuaded to move and the rooms made ready for Mae. A confirmed night person, she was not in the least disturbed by the late hours and seemed to enjoy the frenzied preparations that had the hotel staff in an uproar. Reporting the incident, columnist Herb Caen began by announcing that Mae, who was "anywhere from 87 to 92," depending upon which source book was consulted, had been driven to San Francisco because of a fear of flying and concluded, "I can't imagine anybody being afraid of flying at 92 so she must be 87."

Despite the advance hullabaloo, the department in charge of crowd control seriously underestimated the number of policemen needed to handle the swarming mass of humanity that had been unable to obtain seats but was determined to get a glimpse of Mae. The 2,200 ticket holders had difficulty wedging their way into the theater. Word that Mae was on her way sent the more dedicated shinnying up lampposts and climbing grilles on storefronts. A tap dancer appeared wearing a World War I naval uniform, waving an American flag in one hand and a WELCOME MAE WEST sign in the other. Efforts to clear a path on Market Street resulted in a near riot. In the interest of her safety, police slipped Mae through the stage door.

The audience—a conglomeration of well-dressed elderly fans, a sprinkling of long-haired, jean-clad kids, sailors, Orientals, blacks, leather freaks, musclemen and at least two dozen drag queens in Mae West garb—went wild when promoter Phil Sinclair announced: "Ladies and gentlemen—the living legend." Ten titleholding musclemen formed a backdrop as Paul and Mae slowly made their way center stage. The tumultuous reception ran on like a delegate demonstration at a political convention until at last it wore itself out. Then Mae swiveled to the microphone to thank her idolators and announce, "I hope you'll enjoy my little demonstration of progressive education," after which she and Paul moved with stately grace toward the wings.

Judy Stone of the *Chronicle* found the proceedings embarrassing, but conceded, "Well, each to her own old age; she [Mae] obviously adored the adulation, and wept tears of pleasure through globs of mascara." In the *Examiner* Stanley Eichelbaum paid homage to Mae for her past achievements and concluded, "What we are confronted with is West as a geriatric sex symbol." Edward Gutman in the *Sentinel* noted, "The lighting on West is such that she seems to be swimming in some gauzy halo, even when the other actors in the frame appear in focus." In spite of the reviews, business was good the first week, but took a severe dip the second and plummeted during the third.

Finally, in June 1979, the picture opened at the Eighth Street Playhouse, the New Yorker, Gemini and the Victoria in Manhattan plus theaters in Levittown, Valley Stream, Manhasset, Yonkers and East Hampton. The multiple booking worked against the film—and reviews made previous attacks seem benign. Vincent Canby of the *Times* denounced *Sextette* as "a disorienting freak show" and compared Mae to "a plump sheep that's been stood on its hind legs, dressed in a drag-queen's idea of chic, bewigged and then smeared with pink plaster."

Sextette inspired Rex Reed to rise to his vituperative best:

> They've dusted off Mae West and trotted her out before the cameras for yet another round of mock-scandalous double-entendres. Only now the hip-grinding is arthritic and the voice that used to purr now sounds a bit like an old cat having a bad dream. . . . It will probably be shown decades hence as a monument of ghoulish camp, but that's no excuse. . . . Most pathetic is seeing her enter in full bridal regalia, the groom at her side. He looks 25, she looks like something they found in the basement of a pyramid. "How do you like it here in London?" a reporter asks. "Oh, I like it anywhere," she drools, her left eye involuntarily taking a look at her right eye. . . . Then the music starts and Mae has to clear out of the way, maneuvering with the agility of an ocean liner in a fish pond as the lobby bursts into "Hollywood" and ranks of bellhops holding yellow chrysanthemum centerpieces tap-dance down a carpeted stairway. . . . Even those who enjoy Mae West films from the vaults are going to find this one hard to take.

After *Sextette,* Mae talked less about new plans, although occasionally she spoke hopefully of reports that the picture was becoming a cult film similar to *The Rocky Horror Show.* Devotees, she claimed, were seeing it over and over and could recite the dialogue along with her. If this was wishful thinking, those who knew and were fond of her went along with the fantasy.

More realistically on her part, during the disco craze, she toyed with an offer to give some of her famous numbers disco treatment but shrewdly decided against doing an album, sensing that the fad had already peaked. Paul suggested an album of western songs instead, but nothing came of the idea.

On a day-to-day basis, her lucidity varied. Much of the time she was normal, but occasionally she would slip into fantasy. Once she suddenly turned to Paul and asked him to take her to her mother. On several occasions she temporarily failed to recognize him. Yet at parties where several handsome young studs happened to be present, they would gravitate to her and she would play Kitty Fascination, flirting and wisecracking and eliciting bursts of loud laughter. Often, however, she was content to sit quietly beside Paul, holding his hand and letting others carry the conversation.

After an extended period when she had grown increasingly quiet, Andrew Barclay, a young New Zealander who resembled Errol Flynn, stirred her interest at dinner one evening. When someone mentioned *Pleasure Man,* Mae took her cue to launch into a long poem about her trials and tribulations with the play for Andrew's amusement. (She said she'd written the humorous doggerel for a Walter Winchell benefit in the 1920's.) When her dinner companions received her efforts with laughter and applause, she launched into the *Diamond Lil* soliloquy, sang "Frankie and Johnny" a capella and concluded with a chair dance that astonished everyone present. It was a brilliant flash of the seemingly indestructible Mae West, and at that moment it seemed entirely possible that her psychic adviser Dr. Ireland might be correct in predicting that she was going to live to be a hundred and fifteen without changing.

A few weeks later she suffered an attack of nausea and a short period of disorientation. Paul called her physician, Dr. John Masson, asking him to come to the apartment. Dr. Masson suggested she be hospitalized but deferred to Mae after examining her and finding her vital signs normal.

And so the days passed, some better than others. Then on August 10, a week before Mae was to celebrate her eighty-seventh birthday, she fell out of bed. Paul helped her into the sitting room and served her tea and toast. As he placed it before her, she attempted to speak but uttered only gibberish. She began to weep. He comforted her, and when she stopped crying, he gently asked her to write her name. She scrawled illegibly on the paper. Suddenly she arose from the chair and started toward the front door, intending to leave in her negligee. Paul carried her into the bedroom and hurriedly called Dr. Masson.

After giving Mae a careful examination, the doctor wavered between the opinion that she had suffered a slight stroke or that she had received a concussion when she fell out of bed. On his second visit that day he advised hospitalizing her. Twenty-four hours later, indulging in the intrigue she had always enjoyed so much, Paul signed Mae and himself into rooms 673 and 674 at Good Samaritan Hospital under the aliases Gloria and Paul Drake.

Aliases or not, Mae was not able to escape into anonymity. To forestall gossip, Paul maintained that Mae had fallen out of bed and suffered a concussion during a dream. He reported that when asked whether it was a bad one, she responded, "No, a good one. How bad can a dream about Burt Reynolds be?"

Dolly Dempsey, longtime president of the original Mae West fan club, formed after the release of *She Done Him Wrong,* immediately came to the hospital from her home in the San Diego area, and throughout Mae's illness Mrs. Dempsey made frequent trips to her bedside.

Test results revealed that Mae had suffered a mild stroke which had paralyzed her tongue. Unable to swallow, she received a liquid formula by means of a tube inserted through her right nostril into her stomach. Although she failed to regain use of her tongue, she began showing daily improvement. By August 23 Paul was able to take her on a thirty-foot walk, and during the entire next day she sat in a chair when she wasn't making increasingly longer forays into the hall.

To entertain her, Paul played cassettes of her *Fabulous Mae West* and *Wild Christmas* recordings. He was so pleased to see her nodding her head to the beat that he brought in a movie projector and 16 mm prints of her favorite Mae West films.

On August 27 she suffered a setback, sleeping almost the entire day. Tests revealed that the formula she was receiving contained too much sugar for her diabetic condition. This was corrected, and she again rallied. Paul's spirits rose as she became increasingly suspicious of the nurses, a sign that her reactions were returning to her normal pattern.

About a month before entering the hospital, Mae, rationalizing that her diet consisted mostly of fruit, discontinued the high colonics she had taken for years, but on August 29 Paul gave her one, and she became noticeably more relaxed. The visiting therapist, however, had difficulty in provoking any response. But later in the day, when the doctor arrived, she shook his hand and flashed what Paul always called her million-dollar smile.

As August turned into September, she was able to walk along the hospital corridors with Paul, peering into other patients' rooms. Although still unable to speak, she grew more and more curious about her surroundings. By September 8 Paul, alarmed at her failure to respond to conventional treatment, brought in a psychic, who advised setting up purple-and-pink lights which he claimed would regenerate damaged brain cells. Determined to give Mae every chance, Paul dutifully had the lights installed. He also investigated a hospital in San Clemente that specialized in rehabilitation of stroke victims. The specialists studied Dr. Masson's reports and concluded she was beyond help.

Undiscouraged, with a nurse in attendance, Paul took Mae for a drive to the beach on September 11 and on September 12 arranged a meeting at Kevin Thomas's in hopes that such a close friend would bestir her memory. But at 5:00 P.M. he called Thomas to say Mae had fallen asleep in the chair while he was making her up. The visit would have to be postponed.

A second stroke on September 18 paralyzed Mae's right arm and leg. She was placed in intensive care, suffering kidney failure, very low blood pressure and weak heart function. During the next eleven days she remained there. Each morning Paul arrived at the hospital to spend five minutes out of each hour with her until visiting hours ended. Nine days after her second seizure, Mae was running a fever of 101 degrees. A pinkish fluid showed up in a spinal tap, and edema had set in in her right arm and leg. Her lungs had to be vacuumed every hour to clear them of fluid. Friends expected to hear at any moment that she had slipped away. Dolly Dempsey refused to give up. She persuaded Paul and hospital authorities to allow her to remain overnight. Except for the five minutes each hour she was allowed with Mae, she spent her time in the chapel, offering prayers for her idol's survival. Incredibly, on the eleventh day Mae rallied enough to be moved out of intensive care into private room 65.

During the first week in October, USC librarian Alvista Perkins and Kevin Thomas dined at a restaurant with Paul, who gave them Mae's private number at the hospital and invited them to visit her. He informed them that she was sitting up six hours a day to avoid contracting pneumonia and seemed diverted when looking at photos he had brought in to entertain her. He had discharged one of the three nurses and was sleeping on a cot, taking the night shift himself.

Approaching Mae's room at the Good Samaritan on October 19, a friend heard unearthly sounds emanating from it. When he entered, the only light came from two candles, and the sounds were being made by five Filipino faith healers, who were talking in tongues. Mae appeared unaware of what was going on, and Paul reported she had shown no interest in the six dozen roses and get-well message sent by Elizabeth Taylor.

Even though Mae failed to respond to any treatments beyond standard medical practice, Paul vowed to leave no stone unturned in attempting to restore the health of this woman with whom he had shared the past twenty-seven years without a single serious disagreement. A few days later he toyed with the plan of placing her in the Motion Picture and Television Country House Hospital for therapy but abandoned the idea when the hospital's therapist, after conferring with Dr. Masson, said they could do nothing.

Instead, Paul decided to replace the fabled canopy bed at the Ravenswood with a hospital bed, hire three nurses and make Mae as comfortable as possible among familiar surroundings. Grim as the picture appeared, he refused to abandon hope that some miracle—whether wrought by faith healers or traditional medical men—would restore her health. The final week in October, television and newspaper reports had Mae back at the Ravenswood, although actually she was not discharged until November 3.

During her illness Paul privately worried what would happen to Mae should he by some trick of fate be taken before she was. But whenever he was asked about her progress, he optimistically would report the tiniest of changes as if they provided hope for full recovery. He seemed determined to will her return to health.

But at 7:30 A.M., Saturday, November 22, the nurse on duty

advised Paul that Mae had developed chills. By the time he reached her bedside she was dampened by a cold sweat, and her complexion had taken on an alarming grayish tint. He hurriedly summoned Dr. Masson, who gently informed him that all that could be done had been done.

Paul rushed to the telephone to call the Hollywood Presbyterian Church but was unable to contact a minister. In his anxiety that Mae receive religious rites, he phoned a nearby Catholic church. Within minutes a priest arrived to say a prayer and offer his blessing. The priest's ministrations seemed to bestow a comforting sense of well-being on Mae, and ten minutes after he left, she slipped away. Paul kissed her farewell and drew a sheet over her body.

Numbed by her death, he went into the living room. As he passed the telephone, he remembered their friend Sybil Brand was sending over a turkey dinner for Thanksgiving. He suddenly picked up the phone, called Mrs. Brand and told her to cancel her plans, saying, "Miss West just left us."

The next friend he reached was Herbert Kenwith, whom he asked to join him and Dolly Dempsey, who, sensing a change in Mae's condition, had stayed the night.

He then phoned Jerry Martin, Mae's last representative at the William Morris Agency, and suggested organizing the largest funeral Hollywood had ever seen. Martin tried to discourage the plan, but for the moment Paul seemed committed to it as a last act of devotion.

For all his telephoning, he was reluctant to contact a mortuary, explaining that he wanted his beloved companion's soul to rest peacefully before removing her from familiar surroundings. Finally, Martin took it upon himself to call Forest Lawn, Hollywood Hills. When the attendants arrived to pick up Mae's body, Paul resisted authorizing embalming and changed his mind only when he discovered it was legally impossible to move her to the family mausoleum at Cypress Hills Abbey in Brooklyn until this had been done.

That evening Paul continued to lean toward a public service, but others pointed out that Mae had broken many records in life and there was nothing to be gained by staging a circus after her death. They urged that the service be kept low-key, small and dignified. After mulling over the suggestion, Paul agreed. Next morning he and friends went to Forest Lawn to plan the ceremonies which were to be held at 3:00 P.M., Tuesday, November 25.

The day after her death the Kevin Thomas-Ted Thackery obituary in the Los Angeles *Times* paid loving tribute to Mae. "She was painted by Dali," they wrote, "admired by George Bernard Shaw, photographed by Avedon and Scavullo, praised by the critics, damned by the censors, loved by audiences and pursued by the ambitious. . . ."

The same day *The New York Times* printed:

> Mae West stood as the epitome of playfully vulgar sex in the United States, portraying the role of a woman who made men slaver when she crossed a room in her sinuous walk.
>
> Dressing in skin-tight gowns, bedecking herself in jewels, maintaining an impeccable blondness and offering innuendos in a sultry voice, Miss West posed as a small-town Lothario's dream of sexual abandonment in Sodom and Gomorrah.

There were many misty eyes when Paul gazed down into Mae's face and unobtrusively placed his hand over hers in a gesture that was familiar to most of the 100 close friends in and out of show business who were attending the memorial service.

The assumption had been that the casket would be closed. But when Paul saw Mae after she had been made up, he complimented the cosmetician by saying, "Miss West is pleased," and decided on the spot to have an open coffin. Among those who had come to pay tribute to Mae, there was general agreement that the eighty-seven-year-old actress looked less than half her age.

A medley of unfunereal songs associated with Mae—"After You're Gone," "Frankie and Johnny," "Easy Rider," "My Old Flame," among others—greeted mourners entering the Old North Church at Forest Lawn. As the guests sat listening to the organ music, a gentle breeze wafted through an open window, and light, as the sun emerged from behind clouds, shimmered from Mae's sequined neckline, creating an eerie illusion that she was breathing and might at any moment rise and go into one of her numbers.

Dr. Lloyd Ogilvie, pastor of the Hollywood Presbyterian Church, noted: "We are all here by invitation. Millions of others would have liked to be here too." He went on to praise Mae as a good woman who went beyond caricature to character, adding, "What more need we say than 'Goodness had everything to do with it.'"

Film producer Ross Hunter then delivered the eulogy, written by Kevin Thomas. Hunter, who added his own touches, reported that only a few months before Mae's stroke, as she was emerging from her long low-slung black limousine in front of Man Fook Low, a burly truck driver had caught sight of the beaming octogenarian blonde and shouted, "Hey, Mae! You're still looking good!"

Hunter observed that one could dine with Mae three times in a single week and realize she remained essentially an enigma to all but a handful of people. "She had an absorption that seemed to border on the total," he said. "Yet the more she concentrated on Mae West, the more she gave to others." Citing her importance in helping redefine attitudes of both women and men toward female sexuality, he emphasized her wit. When named "Woman of the Century" by UCLA, the apolitical actress was asked about the Black Panthers, who were then hot news. She replied in a voice filled with the familiar innuendo: "Depends on what angle you're lookin' at 'em from."

Penetrating beyond the façade of Mae's much vaunted need for multiple men, Hunter touched Mae and Paul's friends when he alluded to "a singularly tender love story in which she had been caught up for more than a quarter of a century." He reminisced that when her lover was absent, Mae often said, "Paul's the greatest."

Besides Paul, the immediate mourners included Mae's nephew and some cousins. Beverly sat alone in a limousine outside the church. She had planned to wait until the services were concluded before going in to say her private good-bye. But with all her resentments and hostilities toward Mae obliterated by death, Beverly was too benumbed by grief to leave the car.

That same evening Paul and Mrs. Dempsey accompanied Mae's body back to Brooklyn. Shortly after seven the next morning two priests and a bishop blessed the interment. At the abbey where Mae's mother, father and brother lay, Mrs. Dempsey placed a small bouquet on the casket before it was put in the top berth. The piece of marble used to seal the crypt reads: MAE WEST,

AUGUST 17, 1893–NOVEMBER 22, 1980. Everything had been handled as Mae would have wished. In the words of the eulogy, "The Mae West character never wanted anybody to feel sorry for her and she wouldn't want them to start now."

And so with her flattering coiffure, firm chin line and beautiful complexion, Mae perpetuated the illusion of eternal youth beyond her final day on earth. In her devotion to "playfully vulgar sex," she had made the world love her. Her impact on American life was so great that her obituary appeared on front pages of newspapers around the world, including the London *Times* and the Sunday edition of *The New York Times*, whose editors gave her a photo and the story of her demise precedence over the death of former Speaker of the House of Representatives John W. McCormack.

She again had proved the wisdom of her remark "It's not what I do but how I do it. It ain't what I say, but how I say it, and how I look when I do it and say it." The image of this zestful, lusty, self-reliant woman of the world is preserved in twelve films and will prevail as long as they are shown and as long as people quote such as witticisms as:

"When I'm good, I'm very good, but when I'm bad, I'm better."

"I used to be Snow White, but I drifted."

"Too much of a good thing can be wonderful."

"It's better to be looked over than overlooked."

"Keep cool and collect."

"I'm no angel, but I've spread my wings a bit."

"Between two evils, I always pick the one I never tried before."

"Give a man a free hand and he'll try to put it all over you."

"I always say, keep a diary and someday it'll keep you."

"The score never interested me, only the game."

"I believe in the single standard—for men and women."

"Come up and see me sometime. Come up Wednesday. That's amateur night."

These are but a few of the lines that made her perhaps the most quoted woman in history.

In the end what Mae stood for went beyond legend and myth, and she was well aware of it. Summing herself up, she wrote: "I became a star in the third person, even to myself. It didn't frighten me. I got fun out of being a legend and an institution."

Mae West in Performance

PLAYS

A LA BROADWAY
(Shown in conjunction with HELLO, PARIS*)*

Folies Bergere Theater. Opened September 22, 1911. 8 performances.
Book: William LeBaron. Music: Harold Orlob. Lyrics: William LeBaron
and M. H. Hollins. Produced by Henry B. Harris and Jesse L. Lasky.

CAST:

James Bradbury
James Cook
Margaret Taylor
Ida Harris
Octavia Broske
Emily Monte
Pat Neaves
Gladys Turner

Will Phillips
John Lorenz
Wallace Nedringhaus
Glenn Eastman
MAE WEST
Virginia Gunther
Miriam Sanford
Florence Warner

Agostino Vaci
Ted Westus
Ernest Collins
Kitty Kyle
Harriet Leidy
Betty Scott
Martha Edmonds

Vera Violetta

Winter Garden. Opened November 20, 1911. 112 performances. Book: Leonard Liebling and Harold Atteridge (from the German of Leo Stein). Songs by various writers. Winter Garden Producing Company.

CAST:

Edward Cutler	Lew Quinn	Mel Ryder
Van Rensselaer	Al Jolson	Doris Cameron
Wheeler	James B. Carson	MAE WEST
Barney Bernard	Billie Taylor	Florence Douglas
Jose Collins	Melville Ellis	Gaby Deslys
Estelle Mayhew	The Gordon Brothers	Harry Fisher
Clarence Harvey	Maidie Berker	Jane Lawrence

(Mae, according to the press, was out of the cast until after the premiere with "pneumonia." Broadway gossip blamed Al Jolson. Purportedly, he was so jealous he shut his dressing-room door and covered his ears whenever a performer received a big hand. Mae's enthusiastic reception moved him to persuade the producers to remove her from the show temporarily.)

A Winsome Widow

Moulin Rouge. Opened April 11, 1912. 172 performances. Three-act comedy with music. Adapted from Charles H. Hoyt's *A Trip to Chinatown*. Music: Raymond Hubbell. Produced by Florenz Ziegfeld, Jr.

CAST:

Mrs. Gadder	Fawn Conway
Mrs. Noyes	Katherine Smythe
Mrs. Howell	Lottie Vernon
Mrs. Flippant	Marie Baxter
Flirt	Ethel Kelley
Slavin	Harry Kelly
Rashleigh Gay	Charles J. King
Wilder Daly	Charles King
Ben Gay	Leon Errol
Tony	Ida Adams
Isabel	Elizabeth Brice

Mrs. Duer	Natalie Dagwell
Mrs. Guyer	Emmy Wehlen
Willie Grow	Kathleen Clifford
Welland Strong	Harry Conor
Noah	Frank Tinney
Bryton Early.................	Sidney Jarvis
Rosie and Jenny	The Dolly Twins
La Petite Daffy	MAE WEST
Mons. McGinnis	Jack Clifford
Mlle. Bridgite................	Irene Weston
Proprietor of Cliff House	Charles Mitchell

SOMETIME

Shubert Theater. Opened October 4, 1918. 283 performances. Book and lyrics: Rida Johnson Young. Music: Rudolf Friml. Director: Oscar Eagle. Dances: Allan Foster. Producer: Arthur Hammerstein.

CAST:

Mayme Dean	MAE WEST
Phyllis	Beatrice Summers
Henry Vaughan	Harrison Brockbank
Loney Bright	Ed Wynn
Enid Vaughn	Francine Larrimore
Dressing room girls	Betty Stivers and Virginia Lee
Joe Allegretti	Charles De Haven
Mike Mazetti	Fred Nice
Richard Carter...............	John Merkyl
Sylvia de Forrest	Frances Cameron
Argentine dancer	Mildred Le Gue
Argentine singer.............	William Dorian
Apthorp	Albert Sackett
George Gray.................	Harold Williams
Roof Garden manager........	Francis Murphy
Mr. Jones	George Gaston

THE MIMIC WORLD OF 1921

Century Promenade. Opened August 15, 1932. 32 performances. Sketches and lyrics: Harold Atteridge, James Hussey, Owen Murphy.

Music: Jean Schwartz, Lew Pollack, Owen Murphy. Director: Allan K. Foster. Producer: The Shuberts.

Times Square at Midnight, Act one, Scene two
Cliff . . . . Cliff Edwards
Officer . . . . Eddie Hickey
Blind man . . . . Frank Masters
Anti Volstead . . . . Lou Edwards
Yonson . . . . El Brendel
Evelyn . . . . Evelyn Martin
James Bradstreet . . . . Albert Wiser
Card shark . . . . William Moran
Gunman . . . . Lou Edwards
Shifty Liz . . . . MAE WEST
Salvation Army officer . . . . Frank Masters

Café de Paris, Act one, Scene five
Phil . . . . William Moran
Louis . . . . Albert Wiser
Entertainer . . . . Frank Masters
Miss Promenade . . . . Gladys James
Madelon . . . . MAE WEST

Shakespeare's Garden of Love, Act one, Scene ten
Page . . . . Ann Toddings
Shakespeare . . . . Frank Hurst
Hamlet . . . . Lou Edwards
Ophelia . . . . Helen Neidova
Romeo . . . . C. L. Henderson
Juliet . . . . Madeline Smith
Othello . . . . Cliff Edwards
Desdemona . . . . Marjorie Carville
Portia . . . . Flo Burt
Bassanio . . . . Eddie Hickey
Antony . . . . Albert Wiser
Cleopatra . . . . MAE WEST
Petruchio . . . . Frank Masters
Katherine . . . . Elizabeth Morgan
Richard II . . . . Clarence Harvey
Queen Anne . . . . Gladys James
Henry VIII . . . . William Moran

An Interlude with Mae West, Act two, Scene seven

SEX

Daly's Theater. Opened April 26, 1926. 375 performances. Comedy drama in three acts by Jane Mast (pesudonym for MAE WEST). Director: Edward Elsner. Nominal producer: C. William Morganstern.

CAST:

Margie LaMont	MAE WEST
Lieutenant Gregg	Barry O'Neill
Rocky Waldron	Warren Sterling
Agnes Scott	Ann Reader
Clara Smith	Edda Von Beulow
Jimmy Stanton	Lyons Wickland
Robert Stanton	Pacie Ripple
Dawson	Gordon Burby
Jones	D. J. Hamilton
Curley	Al Regalia
Marie	Constance Morganstern
Jenkins	Frank Howard
Captain Carter	George Rogers
Walter	Gordon Earle
Red	Mary Morrisey
Condez	Conde Brewer
Spanish dancer	Michael Markham
Fleet band	The Syncopators

THE DRAG

First performance Poli's Park Theater, Bridgeport, Connecticut, January 31, 1927. Closed out of town. Homosexual comedy in three acts by Jane Mast (pseudonym for MAE WEST). Director: Edward Elsner. Nominal producer: C. William Morganstern. Sixteen principals and forty supers.

THE WICKED AGE

Daly's Theater. Opened November 4, 1927. 19 performances. Satirical comedy in three acts by MAE WEST. Director: Edward Elsner. Producer: Anton F. Scibilia.

CAST:

Aunt Elizabeth	Emily Francis
Ruth Carson	Doris Haslett
Peggy McShane	Peggy Doran
Willie Weller	Hassell Brooks
Gloria Carson	Ruth Hunter
Robert Carson	Hal Clarendon
John Ferguson	Francis Reynolds
Warren Hathaway	Carroll Daly
The Count	Robert Bentley
Mrs. Martha Carson	Marjorie Main
Evelyn "Babe" Carson	MAE WEST
Bob Miles	David Newell
Al Smalley	Hub White
Tom Hathaway	William Langdon
Jack Stratford	Raymond Jarno
Ray Dempster	Harry W. Williams
George Smith	Harold Leonard
Lou Ginsberg	Harry W. Carter
Gladys Blake	Louise Kirtland
Nell Brown	Ethel Maynard
Norma Faire	Wilva Davis
Dolly Acker	Phoebe Otis
Annie Lawrence	Billy Le Seur
Mack Hadden	Hal Findlay
Bert Astor	Arthur Boran
Stephanie Joy	Veritza Winter
Chauffeur	Pete Segreto
Jazzbo Williams	Mike Jackson
Henry Lee	Thomas Morris
Jeanette	Georgia Clark
Dick Adams	Harry W. Williams
Henry Arthur	Harold Leonard

DIAMOND LIL

Royale Theater. Opened April 9, 1928. 176 performances. A drama in three acts by MAE WEST; periods and locales suggested by Mark Linder. Scenery: Vimera Studios. Director: Ira Hards. Producer: Mark Linder.

CAST:

Diamond Lil................. MAE WEST
Captain Cummings........... Curtis Cooksey
Chick Clark .... Herbert Duffy
Gus Jordan.................. J. Merrill Holmes
Dan Flynn................... Ernest Anderson
Rita Christinia .... Rafaela Ottiano
Jim .... Mark Linder
Spider Kane................. Jack Cheatham
Pablo Juarez................ Jack LaRue
Sally .... Lois Jesson*
Jacobson .... Louis Nusbaum
Jimmy Biff .... Frank Wallace
McGary .... Jo-Jo
Frances .... Marion Day
Ragtime Kelly .... Pat Whalen
Kitty....................... Mary Martin
Flo .... Helen Vincent
Mary Ryan .... Thelma Lawrence
Mike....................... Joseph A. Barrett
Pete, the Duke.............. Ronald Savery
Waiter Bill .... Jack Howard
Steve, the porter .... George O'Donnell
Bessie...................... Marion Johns
Violet...................... Mildred Ryder
Polly....................... Annabell Jaenette
Gloria...................... Debora Kaye
Frank Kelly................. David Hughes
Maggie Murphy............. Patsy Klein

Members of slumming party: Lloyd Peddrick, Richard K. Keith, Adah Sherman, Elaine Jones, Agnes Neilson, Elizabeth Pendleton, George O'Donnell, Josephine Wehn, Evelyn Ortega, Elizabeth Lowe.

PLEASURE MAN

Biltmore Theater. Opened October 1, 1928. 2 performances. A comedy drama in three acts by MAE WEST. Scenery: Livingston Platt. Costume designer: Dolly Tree. Director: nominally, Charles Edward Davenport; actually, MAE WEST. Producer: Carl Reed.

*Replaced by Beverly Osborne (Beverly West)

CAST:

Stanley Smith	Stan Stanley
Rodney Terrill	Alan Brooks
Tom Randall	Jay Holly
Steve McAllister	William Augustin
Dolores	Camelia Campbell
Ted Arnold	Edgar Barrier
Mary Ann	Elaine Evans
The Bird of Paradise	Leo Howe
Lester Queen	Lester Sheehan
Edgar "It" Morton	Wally James
Nell Morton	Martha Vaughn
Toto	Ed Hearn
Fritz Otto	William Selig
Herman Otto	Herman Lenzen
Flo	Julie Childrey
Bobby	Margaret Bragaw
Jewel	Anna Keller
Jane	Jane Rich
Bill	Frank Leslie
Bradley	William Cavanaugh
Peaches	Charles Ordway
Chuck	Chuck Connors II
Joe	Fred Dickens
Mother Goddam	Harry Armand
The Cobra	Sylvan Repetti
Bunny	Gene Drew
Rene	Albert Dorando
Ray	Lew Lorraine
Billie	Jo Huddleston
Sonny	Walter MacDonald
Ripley Hetherington	James F. Ayres
Mrs. Hetherington	Augusta E. Boylston
The Male Jeritza	Gene Pearson
The Varsity Kid	Howard Chandler
Lizzie	Marguerite Leo
Maggie	Kate Julianne
Tillie	May Davis
Bridget	Mae Russell
Burbank, Chief of Police	Edward F. Roseman
Officer	Joe Delaney
Pork Chops	Herman Linsterino
Sugarfoot	Robert Cooksey
The Leader	Harry Ford

THE CONSTANT SINNER

Royale Theater. Opened September 14, 1931. 64 performances. A comedy by MAE WEST, adapted from her novel. Scenery: Rollo Wayne. Star's gowns: Jenkins. Director: Lawrence Marsden. Producer: Constant Productions.

CAST:

Cokey Jenny.................	Adele Gilbert
Harry......................	Donald Kirke
Lou........................	Jack McKee
Joe Malone.................	Walter Glass
Bearcat Delaney	Russell Hardie
Buck.......................	Ralph Sanford
Babe Gordon	MAE WEST
Charlie Yates	Arthur R. Vinton
Bellhop	James Dunmore
Man-in-the-booth	Bernard Thornton
Mr. Gay....................	Rudolph Toombs
Liverlips	Robert Rains
Money Johnson	George Givot
Headwaiter.................	Lorenzo Tucker
Waiter	Hubert Brown
Wayne Baldwin	Walter Petrie
Leonard Colton..............	Paul Huber
Barry Washburn	William Daly
African strutter	Paul Meers
Detective sergeant............	Joseph Holicky
Annette	Leona Love
Clara	Ollie Burgoyne
Liza.......................	Trixie Smith
Defense attorney.............	Paul Huber

Dave Nelson's "Hot Shots" Band

Policemen, Harlem fight fans, hotel loungers, nightclub habitués and others	Billy Rapp, Adele Gilbert, Marie Remsen, Grey Patrick, Florence Lee, Christine Wagner, Allen Cohen, Cora Olsen, George Williams, George Bush, Harry Howard, Henry Matthews, George Bloom, Harry Owens, Billy Kohut

Shubert Theater. Opened August 2, 1944. 191 performances. A three-act comedy with prologue by MAE WEST. Scenery: Howard Bay. Costumes: Mary Percy Schenck and Ernest Schrapps. Director: Roy Hargrave. Choreography: Margaret Sande. Producer: Mike Todd.

CAST:

Prologue

Jim	Hubert Long
Mike	Robert Strauss
Greg	Philip Huston
Roy	Mischa Tonken
Corporal Joe	Joel Ashley
Soldiers	Milton Gordon, Carl Bensen, Jack Burke, John Colby, Boyd de Brossard, Anthony Fortune, Eddy Grove, William Skelton, Carl Specht

Play

Count Nikolai Mirovich	Coburn Goodwin
Captain Dronsky	Philip Cary Jones
English ambassador	Henry Vincent
Ambassador Choiseul	Owen Coll
Ambassador Murad Pasha	Don de Leo
Captain Danilov	Don Gibson
Alexis Orloff	Hubert Long
Count Panin	Charles Gerrard
Chief Chamberlain	John Stephen
Gregory Orloff	Philip Huston
Catherine II	MAE WEST
Prince Potemkin	Joel Ashley
Varvara	Elinor Counts
Florian	Ray Bourbon
Lieutenant Bunin	Gene Barry
Marshal Suvorov	John Parrish
Ivan VI	Michael Bey
Pugacheff	Bernard Hoffman
Innkeeper	Harry Bodin
Maurice	Leon Hamilton
Admiral Semechkin	William Malone
Semyonev	Victor Finney

Vanya...................	Frank Baxter
Chimneysweep............	Lester "Red" Town
Chechkovski.............	Dayton Lummis
Pageboys................	Buddy and Dickie Millard
Ladies-in-waiting.......	Edna Eckert, Michael Mauree, Mila Niemi (Vampira), Gloria Pierre, Mary Reid, Gerry Brent
Councillors.............	William C. Tubbs, Frank Stevens, Albert Bayne, Joseph Mann, Charles Hart, Robert Morse
Chamberlains............	Michael Spreder, Victor Finney
Ushers.................	Dick Ellis, Reginald Allen
Guards.................	George Anderson, Eden Burrows, Jerry Lucas, Richard Spohr, Raymond Stenzi, John Frederick

Diamond Lil, London

Prince of Wales Theatre. Opened January 24, 1948. Performed twice nightly. Closed May 8. Directed by William Mollison. Presented by Val Parnell in association with Tom Arnold.

Cast:

Prologue................	Alan Bailey
O'Donnell...............	Ken Buckle
Al.....................	Rufus Cruikshank
Hank...................	Steve Donohue
Olsen..................	John Wadham
Charlie................	Ben Valentine
Kitty..................	Honorine Catto
Frances Donovan	Mai Bacon
Flo	Pamela Bevan
Beef	Robert Tranter
Steak	Tony Hulley
Bill, the barman	Barry O'Neill
Pat Whalen..............	Bert Weller
Jim	Mark Bakerian
Iceman.................	Jack Beaumont
Beerman................	Arthur Jago
Woman	Elsie Senior

Girl on tandem	Joyce Paton
Dan Flynn	Francis de Wolff
Kane	Danny Green
Gus Jordan	David Davies
Sally	Margaret Stallard
Rita Christinia	Noele Gordon
Pablo Juarez	Bruno Barnabe
Mike	Victor Hagen
Polly	Beryl Ostlere
Violet	Gina Cachia
Gloria	Barbara Todd
Diamond Lil	MAE WEST
Captain Cummings	Richard Bailey
Pete, the dope	Jack D'Ormonde
P. C. Doheney	George Pughe
Jack Jacobson	Daniel Green
Chick Clark	Hal Gould

DIAMOND LIL, New York 1949 revival

Coronet Theater. Opened February 5, 1949. 181 performances. Scenery: Ben Edwards and William DeForest. Costumes: Paul Dupont. Director: Charles K. Freeman. Producers: Albert H. Rosen, Herbert J. Freezer.

CAST:

Jim	Billy Van
Bill	Jack Howard
Porter	James Quinn
Ragtime	Dick Arnold
Spike	George Warren
Jerry	Harry Warren
Card players	Fred Catania, Patsy Perroni
Kitty	Harriet Nelson
Frances	Sheila Trent
Flo	Sylvia Syms
Maggie	Louise Jenkins
Flynn	Charles G. Martin
Kane	Mike Keene
Gus Jordan	Walter Petrie
Sally	Frances Arons
Rita	Miriam Goldina

Juarez	Steve Cochran
Mike	James Fallon
Diamond Lil	MAE WEST
Charlie	Peter Chan
Bessie	Buddy Millette
Violet	Margaret Magennis
Barbara	Marilyn Lowe
Captain Cummings	Richard Coogan
Pete the Duke	Lester Laurence
Doheney	Ralph Chambers
Jacobson	Louis Nussbaum
Chick Clark	Jeff Morrow
Sailor	Jerry Tobias
Cop	F. Ben Miller
Singer	Michael Edwards
Miss West's accompanist	David Lapin
Bowery pianist	Arnold New

Cyclists, customers, Bowery characters, policemen, society women, society men: John Quigg, Robert Behr, Frederic Meyer, James Wiler, Robert Allender, William H. Miller, Hiram Breckenridge, Harry Miller, Curtis Karpe, Hyacinth Melon, Ethel Curtis, Lawrence Holmes, Marjorie Dalton, Lucille Perroni, Joli Coleman, Lillian Martin

DIAMOND LIL, New York popular-priced revival

Broadway Theater. Opened September 14, 1951. 67 performances. Producer: George Brandt.

CAST:

Jim	Richard King
Bill	Jack Howard
Ragtime	Arnold New
Spike	George Warren
Jerry	Harry Warren
Card players	Jerry Ford, Les Colodny
Kitty	Linda King
Frances	Sally Lewis
Flo	Helen Waters

Flynn	Charles G. Martin
Kane.	Patsy Perroni
Gus Jordan	Walter Petrie
Sally	Alice Martin
Rita.	Zoya Talma
Juarez	James Courtney
Mike.	James Fallon
Diamond Lil.	MAE WEST
Charlie.	Charles Brown
Bessie.	Lois Harmon
Barbara	Marion Gates
Captain Cummings.	Dan Matthews
Pete the Duke	Lester Laurence
Jacobson	Louis Nussbaum
Chick Clark	Val Gould
Sailor	Bert Remsen
Dan Darcy.	Sid Lawson
Doheny	Harry Kadison
Lefty.	Fred Ardath
Miss West's accompanist	David Lapin
Bowery musicians	Roy Johnson, Willie Creager, Adrian Tei, Bernie Friedland

FILMS

NIGHT AFTER NIGHT (1932)

Paramount production and release. Producer: William Le Baron. Director: Archie Mayo. Adapted by Vincent Lawrence; based on Louis Bromfield's *Single Night*. Continuity: Kathryn Scola. Additional dialogue: MAE WEST. Costumes: Travis Banton. Photography: Ernest Haller. Running time: 76 minutes.

CAST:

Joe Anton	George Raft
Miss Healy	Constance Cummings
Iris Dawn	Wynne Gibson

Maudie Triplett...............	MAE WEST
Mrs. Jellyman.................	Alison Skipworth
Leo..........................	Roscoe Karns
Blainey......................	Al Hill
Dick Bolton	Louis Calhern
Jerky	Harry Wallace
Patsy........................	Dink Templeton
Frankie Guard...............	Bradley Page
Malloy	Marty Martyn

SHE DONE HIM WRONG (1933)

Paramount production and release. Producer: William Le Baron. Director: Lowell Sherman. Adapted by John Bright and Harvey Thew; based on *Diamond Lil*. Music and lyrics: Ralph Rainger. Costumes: Edith Head. Dance director: Harold Hecht. Photography: Charles Lang. Running time: 75 minutes.

CAST:

Lady Lou	MAE WEST
Captain Cummings...........	Cary Grant
Serge Stanieff	Gilbert Roland
Gus Jordan.................	Noah Beery, Sr.
Russian Rita	Rafaela Ottiano
Dan Flynn..................	David Landau
Sally	Rochelle Hudson
Chick Clark	Owen Moore
Ragtime Kelly	Fuzzy Knight
Chuck Connors	Tammany Young
Spider Kane................	Dewey Robinson
Frances	Grace La Rue
Steak McGarry..............	Harry Wallace
Pete	James C. Eagle
Doheny	Robert E. Homans
Big Bill	Tom Kennedy
Barfly......................	Arthur Houseman
Pal	Wade Boteler
Mrs. Flaherty	Aggie Herring
Pearl.......................	Louise Beavers
Jacobson	Lee Kohlmar
Mike.......................	Tom McGuire
Second barfly	Al Hill

Paramount production and release. Producer: William Le Baron. Director: Wesley Ruggles. Story, screenplay and all dialogue: MAE WEST. Story suggestions: Lowell Brentano. Continuity: Harlan Thompson. Music: Harvey Brooks. Lyrics: Gladys Du Bois, Ben Ellison. Costumes: Travis Banton. Photography: Leo Tover. Running time: 80 minutes.

CAST:

Tira	MAE WEST
Jack Clayton	Cary Grant
Benny Pinkowitz	Gregory Ratoff
Big Bill Barton	Edward Arnold
Slick Wiley	Ralf Harolde
Kirk Lawrence	Kent Taylor
Alicia Hatton	Gertrude Michael
Flea, the barker	Russell Hopton
Thelma	Dorothy Peterson
The Chump	William B. Davidson
Beulah	Gertrude Howard
Maids	Libby Taylor, Hattie McDaniel
Aerialist	Nat Pendleton
Rajah	Nigel de Brulier
Attorney	Irving Pichel
Judge	Walter Walker
Sailors	Monte Collins, Ray Cooke
Chauffeur	Morrie Cohen
Reporter	Dennis O'Keefe
Courtroom spectator	Ed Hearn
Second aerialist	Harry Schultz

BELLE OF THE NINETIES (1934)

Paramount production and release. Producer: William Le Baron. Director: Leo McCarey. Screenplay: MAE WEST; based on her original story. Music: Arthur Johnson. Lyrics: Sam Coslow. Photography: Karl Struss. Costumes: Travis Banton. Art direction: Hans Drier, Bernard Herzbrun. Running time: 73 minutes.

CAST:

Ruby Carter	MAE WEST
Tiger Kid	Roger Pryor

Brooks Claybourne	John Mack Brown
Ace Lamont	John Miljan
Molly Brant	Katherine DeMille
Kirby	James Donlan
Dirk	Stuart Holmes
Slade	Harry Woods
Stogie	Edward Gargan
Jasmine	Libby Taylor
St. Louis fighter	Warren Hymer
Blackie	Benny Baker
Butch	Morrie Cohen
Comedian	Tyler Brooke
Brother Eben	Sam McDaniel
Gilbert	Tom Herbert
Colonel Claybourne	Fred Burton
Mrs. Claybourne	Augusta Anderson
Editor	Wade Boteler
Leading man	George Walsh
Comedians	Fuzzy Knight, Eddie Borden
Chorus girl	Kay Deslys
Fire chief	Sam Flint
Best man	Frank Rice
Crooner	Gene Austin
Extras	Mike Mazurki, Walter Walker, Edward Hearn, James Pierce

Duke Ellington and His Orchestra

GOIN' TO TOWN (1935)

Paramount release; from Major Pictures production unit. Producer: William Le Baron. Director: Alexander Hall. Story: Marion Morgan, George B. Dowell. Screenplay: MAE WEST. Music: Sammy Fain. Lyrics: Irving Kahal. Costumes: Travis Banton. Art direction: Hans Drier, Robert Usher. Photography: Karl Struss. Running time: 74 minutes.

CAST:

Cleo Borden	MAE WEST
Edward Carrington	Paul Cavanagh
Ivan Valadov	Ivan Lebedeff
Mrs. Crane Brittony	Marjorie Gateson
Taho	Tito Coral
Buck Gonzales	Fred Kohler, Sr.

Fletcher Colton	Monroe Owsley
Winslow	Gilbert Emery
Young fellow	Grant Withers
Annette	Adrienne D'Ambricourt
Signor Vitola	Luis Alberni
Senor Ricardo Lopez	Lucio Villegas
Dolores Lopez	Mona Rico
Donovan	Paul Harvey
Sheriff	Francis Ford
Ranch foreman	Wade Boteler
Engineer	Stanley Andrews
Senor Alvarez	Rafael Storm
Lt. Mendoza	Robert Beckoff
Toby, bartender	Dewey Robinson
Bet taker	Julian Rivero
Laughing Eagle, Cleo's jockey	Joe Frye
Cecil, interior decorator	Leonid Kinsky
President, Racing Association	Andres de Seganola
Deputy	Robert Dudley
Workman	Ivar McFadden
Head steward	Albert Conti
Bartender	Gino Corrado
Cleo's butler	Carlos Villar
Captain Dupont	George Renault
Mrs. Brittony's jockey	Frank Mundin
Cowboys	Bert Roach, Joe Twerp, J. P. McGowan, Jules Cowles, Jack Pennick, Sammy Stein, James Pierce, Tom London, Sid Saylor, Irving Bacon
Girl	Pearl Eaton
Attendant	Stanley Price
Conceited-looking man	Bert Morehouse
Colton servants	George Guhl, Lew Kelly, Harold Entwhistle, Howard Mowbray
Miss Plunkett	Virginia Hammond
Society women	Laura Treadwell, Nell Craig
J. Henry Brash	Morgan Wallace
Stage manager	Cyril Ring
Man outside saloon	Jack Kennedy
Tango dancers	Ramon Ros, Dolores Duran
Men at bar	William Beggs, Ronald Rondell
French maids	Myra Royl, Paulette Paquette

English butler	Tom Monk
French butler	O. M. Steiger
Swedish butler	Max Lucke
Eligible bachelor	Tom Ricketts
Homely polo player	Sheldon Jett
Rand	Frank Mayo
The Match King	Henry Roquemore
Indian seller	Tom Ricketts
Policemen	Ted Oliver, Charles McMurphy
French officer	Eugene Borden
Italian officer	Frank Corsaro
French servant	Germain De Neel

KLONDIKE ANNIE (1936)

Paramount release; from Major Pictures production unit. Producer: William Le Baron. Director: Raoul Walsh. Screenplay: MAE WEST; based on a play by MAE WEST and a story by Marion Morgan and George B. Dowell. Additional material: Frank Mitchell Dazey. Music and lyrics: Gene Austin, Jimmie Johnson. Costumes: Travis Banton and Edith Head. Art direction: Hans Dreier, Bernard Herzgrup. Photography: George Clemens. Running time: 77 minutes.

CAST:

The Frisco Doll	MAE WEST
Bull Brackett	Victor McLaglen
Chan Lo	Harold Huber
Jack Forrest	Phillip Reed
Fah Wong	Soo Young
Big Tess	Lucille Webster Gleason
Annie Alden	Helen Jerome Eddy
Lun Fang	Tetsu Komai
Brother Bowser	Harry Beresford
Vance Palmer	Conway Tearle
Grigsby	Ted Oliver
Fanny	Esther Howard
Buddie	John Rogers
Quartermaster	George Walsh
Organist	Gene Austin
Marinoff	Vladimir Bykoff
Sir Gilbert	Lawrence Grant
Bartender	James Burke
Ship's cook	Chester Gan

GO WEST, YOUNG MAN (1936)

Paramount release; Emanuel Cohen's Major Pictures. Producer: Emanuel Cohen. Director: Henry Hathaway. Screenplay: MAE WEST; based on Lawrence Riley's *Personal Appearance*. Music: Arthur Johnston. Lyrics: John Burke. Gowns: Irene. Art direction: Wiard Ihnen. Photography: Karl Struss. Running time: 80 minutes.

CAST:

Mavis Arden	MAE WEST
Morgan	Warren William
Bud	Randolph Scott
Harrigan	Lyle Talbot
Mrs. Struthers	Alice Brady
Gladys	Isabel Jewell
Aunt Kate	Elizabeth Patterson
Joyce	Margaret Perry
Professor Rigby	Etienne Girardot
Clyde	Maynard Holmes
French maid	Alice Ardell
Nicodemus	Nicodemus (aka Nick Stuart)
Chauffeur	John Indrisano
Emcee	Charles Irwin
Andy	Walter Walker
Officers	Lee Shumway, Jack Perrin

Characters in *Drifting Lady* film

Rico	Jack LaRue
Philip	G. P. Huntley, Jr.
Officer	Robert Baikoff
Xavier Cugat	Xavier Cugat
Bumpkin	Si Jenks
Reporter	Dick Elliott

EVERY DAY'S A HOLIDAY (1938)

Paramount release; Major Pictures production. Producer: Emanuel Cohen. Director: A. Edward Sutherland. Story and screenplay: MAE WEST. Songs: Sam Coslow, Coslow and Trivers, Hoagy Carmichael and Stanley Adams. Dance director: LeRoy Prinz. Gowns: Schiaparelli.

Art direction: Wiard Ihnen. Photography: Karl Struss. Running time: 80 minutes.

CAST:

Peaches O'Day/Mademoiselle Fifi	MAE WEST
Captain McCarey	Edmund Lowe
Graves	Charles Butterworth
Nifty Baily	Walter Catlett
Van Reighle Van Peltor Van Doon	Charles Winninger
Honest John McQuade	Lloyd Nolan
Bandleader	Louis Armstrong
George Rector	George Rector
Fritz Krausmeyer	Herman Bing
Trigger Mike	Roger Imhof
Cabby	Chester Conklin
Danny the Dip	Lucian Prival
Assistant police commissioner	Adrian Morris
Henchmen	John Indrisano, Francis McDonald
Quartet	Irving Bacon, Allan Rogers, Otto Fries, John "Skins" Miller
Bar patron	Dick Elliott
Bartender	James C. Morton
Cop at store window	Edgar Dearing

MY LITTLE CHICKADEE (1940)

Universal Pictures release and production. Producer: Lester Cowan. Director: Edward Cline. Screenplay: MAE WEST, W. C. Fields. Lyrics: Milton Drake. Music: Ben Oakland. Musical Score: Frank Skinner. Gowns: Vera West. Photography: Joseph Valentine. Running time: 83 minutes.

CAST:

Flower Belle Lee	MAE WEST
Cuthbert J. Twillie	W. C. Fields
Jeff Badger/Masked bandit	Joseph Calleia
Wayne Carter	Dick Foran

/ 337

Mrs. Gideon . . . . Margaret Hamilton
Clarence . . . . George Moran
Old man . . . . Si Jenks
Bartender . . . . James Conlon
Gene Austin . . . . Gene Austin
Candy . . . . Russell Hall
Coco . . . . Otto Heimel
Henchmen . . . . Eddie Butler, Bing Conley
Cousin Zeb . . . . Fuzzy Knight
Miss Foster . . . . Anne Nagel
Aunt Lou . . . . Ruth Donnelly
Uncle John . . . . Willard Robertson
Budge . . . . Donald Meek
Sheriff . . . . William B. Davidson
Judge . . . . Addison Richards
Clerk . . . . Harlan Briggs
Printer . . . . Otto Hoffman
Boy . . . . Jackie Searle
Chinaman . . . . Chester Gan
Sheriff . . . . George Melford
Indian woman . . . . Lita Chevret
Porters . . . . Bud Harris, Lane Chandler
Bowlegged man . . . . Slim Gaut
Townsman . . . . Mark Anthony
Bit players . . . . Fay Adler, Jan Duggan,
Morgan Wallace, Wade Boteler,
Jeff Conlon, John Kelly, Walter
McGrail, Billy Benedict, Delmar
Watson, George Billings, Bob
McKenzie, James Morton, Joe
Whithead, Lloyd Ingraham,
Ben Hall, Charles McMurphy,
Dick Rush, Hank Bell, Buster
Slaven, Danny Jackson, Charles
Hart, Jack Roper, Alan Bridge,
Ed Hearn

THE HEAT'S ON (1943)

Columbia production and release. Producer: Gregory Ratoff. Director:
Gregory Ratoff. Original story: Boris Ingster, Lou Breslow. Screenplay:
Fitzroy Davis, George S. George, Fred Schiller. Music and lyrics: Jay
Gorney, Edward Eliscu, Henry Myers, Jule Styne, Sammy Cahn.

Costumes: Walter Plunkett. Photography: Franz F. Planer. Choreography: David Lichine. Running time: 80 minutes.

CAST:

Fay Lawrence .... MAE WEST
Tony Ferris .... William Gaxton
Hubert Bainbridge .... Victor Moore
Mouse Beller .... Lester Allen
Janey Bainbridge .... Mary Roche
Hannah Bainbridge .... Almira Sessions
Forrest Stanton .... Alan Dinehart
Andy Walker .... Lloyd Bridges
Frank .... Sam Ash
Hazel Scott .... Hazel Scott
Lina Romay .... Lina Romay
Bit players .... Leonard Sues, Zina Torchina,
                            Jack Owen, Joan Thorsen, Roy
                            Engel, Harry Tyler, Harry
                            Shannon, John Sheehan, Leon
                            Belasco, Edward Earle, Harry
                            Harvey, Kernan Cripps
            Xavier Cugat and His Orchestra

MYRA BRECKENRIDGE (1970)

Twentieth Century-Fox production and release. Producer: Robert Fryer. Director: Michael Sarne. Screenplay: Michael Sarne, David Giler; from Gore Vidal's novel *Myra Breckenridge*. Music and lyrics: John Phillips. Conductor and supervisor: Lionel Newman. Miss West's costumes: Edith Head. Other costumes: Theodora Van Runkle. Choreography: Ralph Beaumont. Photography: Richard Moore. Running time: 95 minutes.

CAST:

Leticia .... MAE WEST
Buck Loner .... John Huston
Myra .... Raquel Welch
Young man Myron .... Rex Reed
Mary Ann .... Farrah Fawcett

Dr. Montag	Roger C. Carmel
Rusty	Roger Herren
Charles Flager, Jr.	George Furth
Irving Amadeus	Calvin Lockhart
Doctor	Jim Backus
Surgeon	John Carradine
Coyote Bill	Andy Devine
Kid Barlow	Grady Sutton
Charles Flager, Sr.	Robert Lieb
Chance	Skip Ward
Bobby Dean Loner	Kathleen Freeman
Tex	B. S. Pully
Jeff	Buck Kartalian
Vince	Monty Landis
Stud	Tom Selleck
Student	Nelson Sardelli
Judge	William Hopper
Woman in dentist's chair	Genevieve Waite
Man in posture class	Michael Sarne
Secretaries	Ray Foster, Cal Bartlett

SEXTETTE (1978)

Crown International Pictures release; Briggs and Sullivan production. Producers: Daniel Briggs, Robert Sullivan. Executive producer: Warner G. Toub. Associate producer: Harry Weiss. Director: Ken Hughes. Screenplay: Herbert Baker; based on MAE WEST's play. Music: Artie Butler. Choreographer: Marc Breaux. Miss West's costumes: Edith Head. Photography: Jim Crabbe. Running time: 91 minutes.

CAST:

Marlo Manners	MAE WEST
Sir Michael Barrington	Timothy Dalton
Dan Turner	Dom DeLuise
Alexei Karansky	Tony Curtis
Laslo Karolny	Ringo Starr
Vance	George Hamilton
Waiter	Alice Cooper
Waiter (Alexei's suite)	Keith Allison
Rona Barrett	Rona Barrett

Delegate .... Van McCoy
Dress designer .... Keith Moon
Regis Philbin .... Regis Philbin
The Chairman .... Walter Pidgeon
The Don .... Harry Weiss

Index

McDowall, Roddy, 12
McGivney, Owen, 38
McKee, Joseph B. "Holy Joe," 70
McLaglen, Victor, 153
McVeigh, Blake, 122
Madden, Owney, 76–77
Mae West on Sex, Health & ESP, 282
Malachosky, Tim, 294
Mander, Miles, 221
Mann, Roderick, 302
Mansfield, Jayne, 250–52
Marakenko, Dan, 123
Marshall, Alan, 257
Marshall, Kit, 257
Martin, Charles G., 220, 227, 230
Martin, Dean, 242
Martin, Jerry, 312
Marx, Groucho, 282
Masson, John, 308, 309, 312
Mayer, Arthur, 117
Mayer, Louis B., 202
Mayo, Archie, 106
Mazurki, Mike, 141–43
Meers, Paul, 100
"Memphis Blues," 138
Mendl, Lady, 190
Menken, Helen, 70, 211
Merling, Howard, 98
Michaels, Gertrude, 124
Michaux Pictures Corporation, 121
Miljan, John, 137
Miller, Bill, 242–44
Milner, Victor, 152
Mimic World of 1921, The, 48–50
Mr. Ed, 260
Molnar, Ferenc, 195
Monroe, Marilyn, 12, 244, 245
Moon, Keith, 300, 301
Moore, Owen, 113
Moore, Victor, 199, 200
Moral Producing Company, 60, 63, 64, 71, 72
Moral Rearmament Movement, 193
Moreno, Kid, 153
Morgan, Marion, 143, 151
Morganstern, Clarence W., 34, 60, 65, 67, 70–73
Morton, Gary, 283

Muir, Helen, 257
My Little Chickadee, 193–98, 209
"My Old Flame," 138
Myra Breckenridge, 271–78

Nathan, George Jean, 138, 147–48, 231
Nation, 127, 218–19
NBC, 185
Newman, Lionel, 187–90
New York *American*, 149
New York *Daily Mirror*, 64, 93
New York *Daily News*, 219, 290
New Yorker, 79, 231
New Yorker profile (1928), 21, 26
New York *Evening Post*, 50, 75
New York *Evening Telegram*, 79
New York *Graphic*, 64
New York *Herald Tribune*, 149
New York *Journal-American*, 94
New York Times, The, 44, 62, 75, 78, 149–50, 193, 200, 233, 270, 276, 290, 299, 313, 315
New York *Tribune*, 75
New York *World*, 75, 78–79
New York *World-Telegram*, 118, 191
Night After Night (previously *Number 55*), 104–8
Nizer, Louis, 157
Nolan, Lloyd, 166
Novak, Paul (previously Chester Ribonsky, Chuck Krauser), 249–52, 255–56, 258–62, 269, 272, 278–80, 286, 287, 290, 292–96, 299–300, 304–6, 308–14
Number 55 (later *Night After Night*), 104–8

Oberon, Merle, 12
O'Brien, Edwin K., 221
O'Connor, John J., 290
O'Curran, Charlie, 42, 242–44
Ogilvie, Lloyd, 313–14
O'Horgan, Tom, 297
Old Gold cigarettes, 114
Oliver, Chip, 269
O'Neill, Barry, 72
O'Neill, Bobby, 34

Sinclair, Phil, 306
Sinnott, James B., 67
Sitosky, George, 190
Skinner, Joe, 80
Skipworth, Alison, 104, 106–7
Sloan, Larry, 15, 262
Smith, Gary, 288, 289
Smith, Kate, 108, 117
Smith, Queenie, 191
Smith, Trixie, 100
Society of Prevention of Vice, 67
Sometime, 45–47
Spigelgass, Leonard, 297
Sporting Widow, 29
Stanley, Stan, 82
Stark, Mabel, 124
Starr, Jimmy, 134
Starr, Ringo, 300, 301
Stauffen, Mimi, 298
Stein, Doris, 168
Stein, Jules, 19, 282
Sterling, Robert, 81
Stevens, Ashton, 220
Stewart, James, 266
Stone, Christopher, 84
Stone, Judy, 307
Streisand, Barbra, 13
Stromberg, Hunt, 130
Stromberg, Hunt, Jr., 130, 253,
    263–64, 297
Stromberg, Kitty, 130
Stroud, Masel, 264
Struss, Karl, 138, 139, 152, 160
Stuart, Norman, 228–29
Styne, Jule, 250
Sukul, Sri Deva Ram, 88–91,
    211–12, 258
Sullivan, Robert, 298, 303, 304
Sumner, John S., 67
Sunday, Billy, 115
Sutherland, Eddie, 163–65, 221
Swaffer, Hannen, 224
Swanson, Gloria, 261
Syms, Sylvia, 229, 230, 235, 237–38
Szatkus, Frank. *See* Wallace, Frank.
Szatkus, Mrs. Anthony, 155

Talbot, Lyle, 96, 161–63

Tanguay, Eva, 34–36
Taylor, Elizabeth, 12, 311
Taylor, Kent, 124–27
Taylor, Libby, 123
Tetzlaff, Teddy, 152
Thackery, Ted, 313
Thew, Harvey, 111
Thomas, Bill, 108–9, 113–16,
    121–22, 132, 133, 136–37
Thomas, Bob, 268
Thomas, Kevin, 107, 263, 284, 289,
    290, 304, 306, 313, 314
Thompson, Harlan, 121, 122
Thompson, Howard, 276
Thompson, Marion Spitzer, 101–2
Time (magazine), 200, 207, 305
Timony, James, 55–61, 63–69,
    71–74, 76, 77, 80, 81, 90, 91, 96,
    100, 104, 105, 114, 115, 122, 132,
    133, 139–46, 153, 154, 188–91,
    211, 212, 221, 241
Tinney, Frank, 47
Tintel, Laura, 76
Tiomkin, Dmitri, 280–81
Todd, Mike, 212–17, 219
Toddings, Ann, 50
Toombs, Rudolph, 100
Toub, Warner, 298
Towne, Lester, 213, 218
Tracy, John, 67
Trent, Sheila, 229
Tropicana, 198–99
"Troubled Waters," 138
Troy, William, 127–28
Tucker, Lorenzo, 100, 101
Tucker, Sophie, 34
Turner, Lana, 12
Tuska, Jon, 129
Twentieth Century-Fox, 271

Universal Pictures, 192, 195
University of Southern California,
    261, 266
Uraneff, Vadim, 221

Vallee, Rudy, 167
Van, Billy, 227
Van Dyke, Woody, 131